D1617386

DAUGHTERS
AT RISK:
A Personal DES History

DAUGHTERS
AT RISK:
A Personal DES History

by
STEPHEN FENICHELL
and
LAWRENCE S. CHARFOOS

DOUBLEDAY & CO., INC.
Garden City, New York
1981

Direct quotations in chapter 2 attributed to Sir Edward Charles Dodds are from his book *Biochemical Contributions to Endocrinology,* Stanford University Press, 1957. The quote on p. 15 and the concluding citation are from "Stilbestrol and After," *The Scientific Basis of Medicine Annual Reviews,* Athlone Press, London, 1965.

Direct quotations in chapter 4 attributed to Dr. Don Carlos Hines are from a stenographic transcription of a deposition taken on March 1–4, 1976, in Oakland, California. Direct quotes from Dr. Theodore G. Klumpp and certain letters and facts associated with his activities at FDA during his tenure there are from a stenographic record of a videotaped deposition taken on October 20, 1974, in Detroit.

Direct quotations by Dr. W. J. Dieckmann and associates are excerpted with permission from *American Journal of Obstetrics and Gynecology* 66: No. 5, 1062–81, 1953; copyrighted by The C. V. Mosby Company, St. Louis, Missouri.

ISBN: 0-385-17154-4
Library of Congress Catalog Card Number 80-2854

To Anne and Mary

Acknowledgments

The authors would like to thank our editor at Doubleday, Adrian Zackheim; we would also like to thank Roberta Pryor and Amy Handelsman at International Creative Management. We are grateful to the following people, all of whom were generous with their advice and time: Peter Alson, Allan Arffa, Sally Brim, Anne Hochschild, Deborah Pines, Michael Pollan, Sterett Pope, Mary Reilly, James Schwartz, Tony Schwartz, Forrest Stone, Thomas Teicholz, Jeffrey Tuchman.

Stephen Fenichell would also like to thank the members of his family for their support, encouragement, and detailed editorial advice.

PART I

1

It was a warm Sunday late in February. Anne and John had been sitting around John's parents' house, and they wanted to take a drive. It was John's father's birthday, and John wanted to get a birthday card to give to him that evening. He borrowed his dad's big Buick—it drove better than John's old Impala—and they headed for the Newman Pharmacy on Blackhawk Road, where his mother worked behind the counter.

It was sunny in the afternoon, but still early enough in the season to be chilly. John put the heater on. Anne lit a cigarette and stared blankly out at the little houses lining Blackhawk Road. Park Forest is a fairly new planned community about thirty miles south of Chicago. They passed the house on Gold Street where Anne had lived in fifth grade. Except for the small addition her folks had added, it was exactly like the house to its right and to its left.

Anne wore a pair of faded jeans and a dark red velour shirt. Her fair hair fell loosely around her shoulders. She leaned back in the warm seat, feeling the sun on her face and in her eyes. She turned lazily in her seat to look at John, who really loved to drive. He loved machines and cars and motorcycles. Last summer he'd spent most of his time on his dirt bike, and sometimes Anne had gone with him. Her mom had had a typical mother's fear something was going to happen, but of course nothing ever did. Anne's mother had been afraid of John at first, because he had long hair and a moustache. John was tall, almost six feet, and pretty thin.

They'd been going together since senior year of high school, almost three years.

John pulled neatly into the little parking lot right by the little conservatory where Anne used to take ballet. The Newman Pharmacy and the Needham Pharmacy were the two main drugstores in Park Forest. The Needham was owned by Anne's dad. The Newman, where John's mother worked, had a big card section in the back, past the face creams and the magazines. Anne was looking forward to picking out the card. She had always been crazy about cards.

John got out first and came around to her side. She took his arm for a second as they walked across the lot. John smiled at her and gave her a little squeeze. Anne had been feeling delicate lately —nothing the matter, just delicate. She'd always been delicate, self-assured, but delicate. Anne let go of John's arm as they headed through the glass doors. John's mom was right there, right behind the counter. Anne left John there to talk with her and headed straight to the cards in the back.

At first it felt like a stomach cramp. Then it got really bad. When it came, the pain was sharp and sudden, like a blade in the abdomen. For a couple of seconds it doubled her up. She called John's name. He was heading toward her. Now he was with her. She tried to stand up, she reached out to grab him, to say something: "I'm heading out to the car."

She winced then, she became unsteady, holding her stomach, doubled over. She gasped, "My stomach hurts." That was it; she blacked out. John carried her out to the car.

When Anne was little, Anne's mom and Meagan's mom used to put the girls in the front windows, facing each other. Anne and Meagan were next-door neighbors, and they used to sit for hours in the windows and watch each other. Anne's house and Meagan's house were the same, but Anne's was green and Meagan's was red. That was just after Anne moved to Rich Road. They lived in Park Forest. Anne was two.

The twins came home from the hospital when Anne was three. Pammy was fine, but Patrick didn't come home from the hospital for a long time. Patrick had really bad heart trouble, and the doctors were afraid they couldn't keep him going. One of the nuns at the hospital used to sit with him all night and hold him, and before Patrick came home the nun told Anne's mom, "Don't ever put this baby down." So Anne's mom would prop Anne up in a chair, and Anne would hold Patrick while Mom vacuumed.

Anne's dad worked all the time. He was usually home in the morning when they went to school, but they mostly didn't see him at night because he didn't close the store until nine or ten. Anne's dad started out in a store that was like a little closet, in the Medical Building, which was really just an old house with a couple of doctors' offices in it. But then he moved to a building across the street and knocked out a wall. He opened up a bigger pharmacy.

Anne would go there on Sunday morning and make green rivers at the soda fountain. A green river is really sweet, just green syrup and soda water mixed. Anne would sit up on the candy counter, she could ring up the candy. They sold gallons and gallons of Gold Medal Ice Cream. Anne would be back there behind the fountain, doing dishes and trying to help, but she was too little to do anything.

When Anne came to, she was stretched out on the cold seat, with her back flat against the door. She opened her eyes and could just make out the spindly blue legs of the town water tank, which stands high above the parking lot with giant block letters: PARK FOREST. From that angle, and the way she was lying, it looked like something from Mars.

The pain came and went, but it never went away for more than a few seconds. It was strange because it would suddenly get bad, then just subside rapidly. She looked up at John. "You all right?" he asked. She couldn't say anything. She just nodded and tried to breathe deeply.

She had felt nothing in the car on the way over, nothing that morning, nothing before that. The pain was concentrated right in her gut, not on the right side, like appendicitis. She knew it wasn't a cramp, or gas, or a virus. It had to be something else.

They went straight to John's so she could lie down for a while. She didn't want to go home right away; she just wanted to lie down and forget about it. She didn't call the doctor, she figured it could wait until tomorrow. She lay on John's couch, thinking, "I'll go see Dr. Warren tomorrow." She thought it was some sort of yeast infection, something she could handle quietly, by herself.

Anne felt a bit better after a few minutes, and she asked John to give her a ride home. When he asked her a few times if she felt any better, each time she said simply, "Yes." But, really, the pain came back every few minutes, and though it wasn't quite so severe it was still very much there. She got out of his car in her driveway and assured him everything was all right. When she went inside she didn't mention it to anybody. The twins, Pammy and Patty, were home, and so was her little sister Mary, who was ten. But she didn't want to frighten anyone, so she didn't tell them what had happened. When her mother came home, she just acted normal and helped her get dinner. She went to bed early that night. But she didn't fall quickly to sleep.

The first trouble had been a problem with her skin. Around Christmas, she'd developed a rash on her upper body and under her arms. Her face had been breaking out quite a bit. She assumed the body rash was from her deodorant, but she couldn't imagine what was causing the problems with her face. After a while she went to see a dermatologist. He couldn't tell her anything, but he suggested she see her gynecologist. Skin rashes, he said, can be caused by yeast infections. That was in the early part of January.

Dr. Warren had been on vacation then, and his secretary gave her an appointment for five weeks off. He was all booked up. Anne had been having a discharge lately that was pretty unpleasant, and she wanted to see him about that. The discharge had come and gone, but like the skin rash and the face problem, it had never really disappeared. She lay in bed that Sunday night, and the pain was still there. She had noticed some bleeding, some hemorrhaging, immediately after coming home. She decided to call Dr. Warren the next morning, Monday, February 25, 1974.

In first grade, Anne started Catholic school. She didn't like the uniform. It was a gray scratchy jumper-type thing with a U-neck and an emblem on the pocket. The boys had to wear ties and navy blue pants. There was a second grade teacher Anne was afraid of. She was afraid to get in her class. Anne thought she was so mean. She had blond hair and a limp. One leg was shorter than the other.

Anne would sit in the rocking chair and rock the twins. Her mom just had to give her a little push, and she'd rock and rock. It was fun when the twins got old enough to go into rocking chairs, because there'd always be food flying. After Mary, the youngest, was born, all the kids got together and had a vote. They went to Mom and said they thought she should have another baby in the house. They were worried there wouldn't be any more. Actually, Mom had had a hysterectomy by then, but they didn't know that. They had a real close family, and they just didn't want to see it end.

One of the best things about going to school was this great big field, full of wild flowers in the springtime. There'd be tulips everywhere and huge tufts of grass. The boys would get behind those tufts of grass and try to scare the girls. There was a creek too, where all the kids would hang around, but Anne and her brothers and sisters couldn't go down there much because Mom didn't like it. Later on, they put a big Phone Center in there, and a True-Value, and a Jewel, and a restaurant, and a parking lot. They'd been used to cutting through that wild flower field coming home from school.

Anne graduated from high school in the summer of 1971, and in the fall she'd gone up to nursing school at the College of Saint Teresa in Winona, Minnesota. At Saint Teresa's, the courses were tough, and the girls were informed that only about half the entering class would eventually graduate. Anne had terrible trouble with anatomy. She would study and do the drill, but she'd blank out completely when it came to tests. During exams, it was as if the human body had become a foreign object, a total stranger.

It was tough for Anne to decide to leave Saint Teresa's, but she figured if she wasn't going to be able to do the work anyway, she might as well get out and not waste any more of her parents' money. There wasn't really enough money around anyway; Anne's little brother Nicky had been having problems reading and had to be taken out of public school and sent to private school. She also knew her parents were having marital difficulties, and she was aware that by going home she'd be stepping right back into them.

Her mother was very upset when Anne came back home in March of '72, at the start of her second semester. She walked through the door with her suitcases, and Mom walked up to her and said, "Where did I go wrong?" She turned right on her heel and stomped away. Anne's brother was right there saying, "Don't worry, Annie, she'll get over it." But she never really did.

Anne knew it kind of burned her mom that she was coming home without a profession. Her mother had gone to pharmacy college for a while, before she met Anne's dad, got married, and dropped out. Her dad went on to get his degree, but Anne's mom never had a chance to go back. Instead, she went on to have seven children. Anne knew her mom thought she was just throwing in the towel, but Anne really intended to go back to school once she figured things out.

Now two years later she was still figuring things out. She'd come home in March of '72, and by May she'd gone and gotten herself a job at the Applewood Manor Nursing Home right down Route 30. Anne was a nurse's aide, which meant she changed linens and bedpans. The pay was $1.75, full-time, night-shift: eleven at night to seven in the morning.

The nursing home was quite an education. A lot of people died. There would be spurts when three or four would die, then no one would go for a while. But there was one little old lady, Mrs. Gilbert; Anne got really close to her. She started getting sick, and Anne started getting mad. She didn't think the doctors were giving that old lady the right kind of care. Mrs. Gilbert ended up dying, and of all the deaths, Anne really noticed that one.

Because she worked nights at the nursing home, Anne's days were free. She took a day job at Marshall Field's, in Park Forest. She was working there a few days a week and taking classes in nursing over at Prairie State. She'd work nights at the nursing home, go home and change, then go to her eight o'clock class.

She was usually home by eleven o'clock, and she'd sit down and have something to eat, then go to sleep for a while. Sometimes she wouldn't get to sleep until late in the afternoon; at that time she could get by on four or five hours. She'd get so worn out by it all, once a week she'd sleep for twelve hours straight. John wasn't real happy about it. Lots of times she'd be over at his parents' house and she'd fall asleep in front of the TV. He must have thought she was a real dud.

Anne was certainly in love with John but they didn't think seriously about getting married. Neither of them was very sure about the future, and getting married seemed like it would just double up their problems. They had a couple of friends who had gone ahead and done it. John and Anne used to go over to their house, and they were struggling. After seeing that, Anne and John were very conscious of how easy it was for it not to work out. Besides, both of them were used to living in nice houses and had no desire to be poor.

When Anne thought about the future, she thought she'd fall in love, get married, have babies. She was sure she'd still be going into nursing. She thought of nursing because of the family. After all, her father was in the medical field, and her mother had studied pharmacy. She didn't think of pharmacy because she thought to herself, "Oh my God, it's such a tough field"; nursing seemed more apropos for her. Anne's folks knew a lot of doctors, and there was a good deal of respect for the science of medicine in the house. Anne sometimes thought her dad really should have been a doctor.

Anne got herself a little Falcon. It cost practically nothing, and it ran like a top. John and Anne would spend a good many evenings at her house. Her mother would usually offer them a drink in the evening, because she would rather have Anne and her friends drink at home than cruise around in cars. Still there was a fair amount of aimless driving around, because there was nothing to do in Park Forest. The kids around town had got to calling it "Dark Forest." When you drive into town on Route 30, a sign tells you the whole story: "Park Forest: The All-American City." You had to be twenty-one to drink, and Anne wouldn't be until July of '74. The bars all carded pretty heavily, and there weren't any coffee shops or places to go in town. Most of the time Anne spent with John was at her or his parents' house, watching TV. She quit her night job at the nursing home. During the days she worked at Marshall Field's. Anne worked downstairs in "Young Chicago"; her mom worked upstairs, in luggage.

Anne wasn't exactly clear on what to do with her life, but she was getting along, figuring things out. She was going to classes at Prairie State, working at a department store, trying to save money; she had a good relationship with a boy she loved. When she was young, she'd been good at ballet and good in school, and in junior high she'd been good at the harp. She'd written poetry late at night, and she used to practice water colors. Now she didn't read very much, or keep up with her other interests, but she was working and hadn't much time. She'd grown up and was settling down, with hopes to get married and eventually have children.

All through the winter of '73, Anne had been getting very pale. She felt low and mopey and kind of morose, and she felt like things weren't going well at home, at work, in her life. Her energy started flagging, and her moods would shift suddenly into irritation and despair. During her breaks at Marshall Field's, she'd stand by the mirror, brushing her hair. No matter how much blush she'd put on her cheeks, she just couldn't get any color. She'd put a dab on one cheek, then on the other, and she'd look at herself again, and think, "God, I could use some more." It was like the color was washing right through her skin.

2

Sir Edward Charles Dodds was Courtauld professor of biochemistry at the University of London, and director of the Courtauld Institute of Biochemistry at the Middlesex Hospital. He was an international authority on food, poisons, and contaminants, holder of sixteen separate university lectureships, and the author of a book on bread. In 1938 Sir Edward made a remarkable announcement which would bring him numerous honors, not the least of which would be the British Cancer Campaign Medal for "distinguished contributions to the fight against cancer." In the February issue of the prestigious British scientific journal *Nature,* a brief note appeared reporting simply that Dr. Dodds and colleagues had created the first synthetic estrogen.

Estrogens are one of a group of substances known as hormones. These chemicals are released from certain glands in the body and circulated through the bloodstream. Hormones control a wide variety of processes, from the changes of pregnancy to the slow processes of growth. Estrogen is one of the female hormones, controlling the development of female sexual characteristics. During pregnancy it is secreted by the ovaries. It regulates the growth of the uterus and prepares the breasts for milk production.

The study of hormones is known as endocrinology, as the hormones are secreted by the endocrine glands. These glands, among which are the thyroid, the thymus, the pancreas, the ovaries, and the testes, confused anatomists for centuries. Most glands in the body release their secretions through visible ducts, but these glands apparently had no ducts, which left physicians bewildered as to their purpose. In the 1800s, Claude Bernard of the Collège de France conceived the notion of an "internal secretion," suggesting that these ductless glands nevertheless added some vital ingredient to the blood.

Bernard's successor at the Collège de France, Brown-Séquard, performed the first modern attempt at hormonal therapy in 1885, when at the age of seventy-two he injected himself with an extract of dogs' testes in a confessed attempt at self-rejuvenation. In a series of articles which aroused the interest of the scientific world, he vividly and intimately described the miraculous effects he claimed as the results of this unusual treatment. Interest in harnessing the fabulous properties of hormones was stimulated by this promise of a virtual "fountain of youth," and into the twentieth century scientists were powerfully impelled by the possibility of uncovering marvelous secrets of prolonging, sustaining, and enhancing life in the search for new hormones and new uses for them.

As the importance of hormones as messengers in the blood began to be more clearly understood, a great deal of excitement began to infect the endocrine field. This aura of discovery, even revelation, was enhanced by the successful experiments in 1924 of the Canadian researchers Banting and Best, who were able to crystallize the hormone insulin from extracts of the pancreatic tissue of dogs. With the aid of the American pharmaceutical company Eli Lilly and Company, which developed a method of mass production for insulin, the field of endocrinology was able to claim its first major clinical breakthrough: the mass production of insulin provided a means of saving the lives of millions of diabetics.

In clinical terms, physicians had long been performing, without any real awareness of the scientific basis of their actions, various operations which tended to mitigate the more troublesome effects of the sex hormones. John Hunter, a British surgeon of the 1700s, learned that castration was a severe but effective remedy for advanced cancer of the prostate. In 1886, George Beatson began to perform removal of the ovaries for cancer of the breast in women. In both cases, it was suspected that the cause of the cancers lay in the effects of these sex-determining glands. But until a proper understanding of the nature of the sex hormones had been achieved, it was impossible to account for the remarkable results accomplished by these intuitive methods.

As clinicians began to learn more about the endocrine system they began to perceive the sex hormones as being at once the cause of and the solution to numerous medical problems. It was found that the productions of the ovaries were overseen by the pituitary gland at the base of the skull, which at certain profound changes of life, such as puberty and menopause, stimulated the ovaries to produce varying amounts of estrogen and its sister hormone, progesterone.

A primary focus of scientific attention became the medical problems associated with the onset of menopause in women. Medical science in the first quarter of the twentieth century had been remarkably successful in conquering a wide range of infectious diseases. But the intention of doctors in using hormones to alleviate certain troublesome menopausal symptoms was radically different: rather than hoping to cure a few virulent, contagious, and epidemic diseases such as syphilis, strep, malaria, and sleeping sickness, clinicians began to dream of enhancing the natural processes of life, not merely sustaining them. Disease was a term now endowed with a broader meaning. Menopause, by the 1920s, became not just part of a natural and inevitable cycle of life, but a malady which demanded a cure.

Unlike the gruesome and usually highly visible effects of the infectious diseases, the symptoms of menopausal women are considerably more impressionistic. Of the many women who go through menopause in any single year, a large proportion never suffer sufficient symptoms to warrant medical attention. But approximately one quarter of the female population may be prone to suffer from a cluster of complaints which clinicians term "menopausal syndrome." The most common and noticeable part of this syndrome is what is commonly termed the hot flash, a fleeting period of discomfort which brings alternating sensations of extreme warmth and cold.

By the early 1900s it was understood that menopause, just like puberty, is brought on by changes in the natural hormonal balance. In most menopausal women, the level of estrogen in the bloodstream is observed to precipitously decline. But not all menopausal women suffer a debilitating estrogen depletion, and only a relatively small number of women suffer genuine atrophy, or extreme loss of estrogen. In all women going through menopause, some symptoms are likely to occur at times, but doctors began to treat and consider many natural effects of menopause as evidence that the body was sick, not simply changing.

The processes by which scientists first began to produce small amounts of estrogen were so complex and time-consuming that the clinical use of estrogen became the exclusive province of the wealthy. By the late '20s, estrogen preparations, most of them crystallizations from animal urine, were coming onto the market. But these natural extracts were extremely expensive and in exceedingly short supply. The therapeutic uses of these remedies were limited by their cost, their complexity, and their low relative strength. Therapeutic doses of natural estrogen were so cumbersome, a tremendous impetus was created to produce one in the laboratory.

For Edward Charles Dodds, as an endocrinologist and biochemist, it was natural to think in terms of breakthroughs in scientific research leading to specific medical solutions. "Today scientific research is constantly scrutinized with a view to its application in therapy," Dodds announced in a lecture before the Royal Society of Arts in 1939, "but this is a very modern trend. . . . From 1910 onwards, the eyes of therapists were firmly fixed on the laboratory. . . ." For enlightened researchers like Dodds, the stated goal of such research was to help people. But the more immediate beneficiary was usually a drug company. The vanishing gap between research and medicine was bridged by private enterprise: biochemical research in the twentieth century had gradually evolved into a genteel product development division of the pharmaceutical industry. In proclaiming that useful preparations would be the goal of science, science had selected the human population at large as the final test-subjects of its ambitious experiments.

In the case of the estrogenic preparations, the clinical experience had been established before Dodds's work began. As early as the late 1920s when the first costly hormone extracts were coming onto the market, women were encouraged to undergo prolonged estrogen replacement therapy to assist in an easy and painless transition through the change of life. The feeling was that estrogen depletion was primarily responsible for menopausal syndrome. As the most ambiguous but difficult symptoms observed were vaguely psychiatric, such as nervous conditions, forgetfulness, and general irritability, estrogen replacement therapy was enthusiastically adopted by impressionable clinicians and their patients as a panacea for many of the complaints of feminine old age. Hormone treatments were popularly considered the latest scientific method of restoring lost powers, of achieving both physical and mental rejuvenation. For millions of women who might have been considered overly irritable, nervous, or simply troublesome, the estrogenic preparations held out the hope of convenient, painless relief.

The Courtauld Institute of Biochemistry was part of London's prestigious Middlesex Hospital. As director of the Institute, Dodds had the resources and the knowledge to attempt the creation of a synthetic estrogen. What struck Dodds as he first began to examine the natural estrogens was the remarkable fact that at least three different natural estrogens occurred in the urine of pregnant women. All three have similar effects on the body, but each is different in its chemical structure. He deduced that estrogenic activity was not necessarily limited to compounds of the same chemical structure. Dodds was aware that all the female hormones share a common nucleus, called a "steroid" nucleus. All these "steroid" hormones possessed this nucleus, but each type had a different arrangement of atoms bound to it at different points.

Dodds later recalled in a memoir entitled "Stilbestrol and After," "In 1933, it occurred to my colleagues and myself that it might be interesting to try to see whether one could depart from the structure of the naturally occurring hormones, and still obtain estrogenic activity." Dodds took the steroid nucleus at his starting point and began to synthesize various molecules, all containing this nucleus. He took each compound synthesized and tested it for the development of secondary sexual characteristics in rats. In January of 1933 *Nature* published a paper by Dodds outlining the direction of his research. He reported the synthesis of a steroid molecule, which had definite, but very feeble estrogenic activity.

"The result is of some importance," he modestly noted, "for this is the first [artificial] compound . . . to have definite [estrogenic] . . . activity. . . ." Right at the outset of his researches Dodds had been able to synthesize an estrogen, but it was so feeble it took a hundred milligrams to produce feminine characteristics in a rat. His compound, Dodds recalled, "did not attract much attention at the time. . . . Still, it was a rather miraculous discovery. . . ."

In this first report to *Nature,* Dodds included an intriguing disclaimer:

> The observation that estrogenic properties of a low order are possessed by suitable extracts of peat, brown coal, coal tar, and petroleum, is of much interest. But in view of the fact that many such materials are known to contain carcinogenic constituents, the clinical use of such extracts without very stringent refinement is scarcely to be entertained. . . .

Dodds was aware that estrogens and some powerful carcinogens are structurally related. In a report to *Nature* in February 1933, entitled, "Sex Hormones and Cancer-Producing Compounds," Dodds mentioned that he and his colleagues had been struck by the similarity of some of the cell changes produced by estrogens and the early stages of malignant growth. Because estrogen is a growth hormone, which stimulates growth in sexual tissue such as the breasts and the uterus, and because cancer is a malignant growth which can be caused by overstimulation of tissues, it was natural for Dodds to attempt an investigation of an interrelationship. He took a number of known, potent carcinogens such as those previously mentioned and injected them into ovariectomized rats. Dodds reported, "We have found estrus-exciting [estrogenic] activity in the most potent carcinogenic substances known to man. . . . We confess this last result was entirely unexpected; it is very striking that both types of biological activity should be shown by one and the same compound."

As striking as the connection may have been, Dodds at no point alluded to any misgivings concerning the widespread administration of large amounts of estrogens to women. Nor did he question the fact that the goal of his research was to make such therapy more widespread, by making it cheaper and more convenient. Dodds was in quest of a synthetic estrogen that would be far more powerful than the natural estrogens. Though he drew the obvious connection between estrogenesis and carcinogenesis, in that both are processes of cellular growth in affected tissues, Dodds had set on a path to achieve acclaim by the production of a synthetic estrogen. Entertaining doubts about the future purposes of his invention would do little to further that mission.

Instead, Dodds made the imaginative leap which finally brought him results. He resolved to diverge radically from nature in order to mimic it.

He began exploring the properties of a substance which had a similar chemical construction to the natural estrogen, but with a crucial difference: It hadn't the steroid nucleus present in all natural estrogens, though it did have feeble but definite estrogenic activity. The compound had no therapeutic value, but the point had been established to Dodds's satisfaction that he could remove the steroid nucleus and continue the search for a powerful estrogen. Eventually, he found one: a nonsteroid compound known as anol was highly estrogenic. Dodds hastily published his results in *Nature,* June 1936: "It has been found that the [steroid nucleus] structure is not necessary for estrogenic activity. . . ."

This quick publication proved to be quite an embarrassment. After the announcement of this simple solution, scientists around the world attempted to duplicate Dodds's experiment. They dutifully mixed their batches of anol, following Dodds's precise recipe, but while some of the chemical cocktails they mixed were quite powerful, others were totally ineffective. "We found ourselves in perhaps the most maddening position of the research worker," Dodds wrote later on, "knowing [estrogenic] activity was present, but that it is not due to what we originally claimed."

A degree of anxiety was entirely warranted. By prematurely publishing incomplete results, Dodds had placed half a decade of research in serious jeopardy. He had planted a critical signpost for other researchers to follow, but he had not achieved the final solution which would make the discovery his alone. "Since the production of such a substance could have very great clinical and therefore commercial possibilities," Dodds reasoned, "it was obvious that all those who had interest in this group of therapeutic agents would commence work to try to produce the active substance, and then try to protect it with patents."

In order to outflank the opposition, in the spring of 1937 Dodds decided to enlist the aid of one of his foremost academic competitors, Sir Robert Robinson of the Dyson Perrins Laboratories at Oxford. Robinson had for many years been trying to synthesize a steroid molecule. Robinson had been working with several derivatives of anol, the compound Dodds had found so promising. Dodds's people at the Courtauld Institute joined forces with Robinson's at Oxford in a crash program to be the first to synthesize an estrogen.

With Robinson's help, Dodds managed to isolate a white crystalline substance with roughly three times the effect of natural estrogen. The substance was a derivative of stilbene. "We had obtained a substance of astonishing potency," Dodds proudly recalled. In February of 1938, Dodds and Robinson formally announced in *Nature* the invention of their new synthetic: "In view of the fact that it is the mother substance of a series of estrogenic agents, we suggest it may be termed *stilbestrol.*" Later, it would be called simply DES.

Dodds was not content to allow his simulated estrogen to remain in the isolation of the lab. To a scientist of his inclinations, the most important triumph would be outside, in the world of practical therapy. As far back as 1934, Dodds had been handing out batches of an earlier, more feeble estrogenic compound to "an extremely skeptical clinician, who had very encouraging results in the treatment of menopause. . . ." Now that he had the final compound firmly in hand, he was understandably eager to release his new drug into the world.

Stilbestrol had its earliest, most dramatic and prolonged success in the treatment of prostatic cancer. In Middlesex Hospital, Dodds began testing his invention clinically for this purpose. "Ever since John Hunter in the 1700's, castration had been one rather severe treatment for tumor of the prostate," Dodds later wrote. Ingesting large doses of synthetic female hormone produced the same effects as castration nonsurgically. "It may be said," Dodds concluded with understandable pride, "that stilbestrol is the first substance ever administered by mouth having an effect on one form of cancer. . . ."

As research on this promising new drug continued in Great Britain, manufacturers around the world became extremely interested in this simple and powerful compound. Production in England began immediately after the release of the necessary data, with one rather ominous occurrence marring stilbestrol's otherwise splendid track record.

"In the early days of manufacture of Stilbestrol in Great

Britain," Dodds later recalled, "adequate precautions were not taken to protect the workers, and a number of cases of marked gynomastia [the growth of breasts and other female character- istics] occurred in males working on the production of Stilbestrol . . . tablets. . . . The gynomastia was very marked indeed, and was accompanied by complete impotence."

This rather bizarre occupational hazard became the first cause for alarm in dealing with this potent chemical. But the man- ufacturers handled the problem most expeditiously. "The main danger," Dodds ascertained, "lay in inhalation of Stilbestrol dust. The substance itself is highly electric, and flies about quite eas- ily. . . . In most factories, women were employed in the manu- facture of Stilbestrol, and precautions such as extractor fans, air- line masks, etc., were taken. . . ." With this negligible hazard neatly disposed of, the route was opened up for the mass produc- tion of diethylstilbestrol around the world.

Within a few months of the first publication of the synthe- sis of stilbestrol the substance was being marketed. . . . No long-term toxicity tests on animals such as dogs were ever done with stilbestrol, and I suppose we have to be very thankful that it did prove to be such a non-toxic substance. . . .

Sir E. C. Dodds
"Stilbestrol and After"
London, 1965

3

The first time Anne ever went for a pelvic examination, she had no idea what they were going to do. She was about thirteen. Her mom just said, "Go see this doctor," and Anne didn't know what was going on. When it actually happened, she was a little surprised; but she trusted Dr. Warren, and she wasn't afraid. She kept seeing Dr. Warren regularly; the only time she saw another gynecologist was when she was eighteen and went down to Carbondale, where her sister was living, to get birth control pills. She was afraid to go to Dr. Warren because he was so close to her parents. The funny thing was, she went down and saw the man and never did anything about getting the pills. Because John's mom worked at Newman's and her dad ran Needham's, there was no place in Park Forest where she could fill the prescription.

When Anne was a freshman in high school, she went to Dr. Warren because her periods hadn't been regular. He put her on birth control pills, though she didn't know it at the time. The pill box wasn't identified: it was just a long oval kit, and you took one pill a day for twenty-one days, then you were off for seven. Her father filled that prescription without comment. She wasn't getting them for birth control, and she didn't know they were birth control pills until she was a senior. Dr. Warren put her back on the pill for three or four months, and at that time he told her what they were.

On Monday morning, Anne drove to Dr. Warren's office in the Park Forest Shopping Center. He had a typical doctor's office with a typical doctor's waiting room, with green Naugahyde furniture and forgettable prints on the walls. She was scared; she knew something was terribly wrong. From the time she had gone to see the skin doctor the discharge had been getting steadily worse.

A pregnant lady was sitting there. She was huge, her feet spread wide on the floor, and they looked at each other for just a second, enough for their eyes to meet. Anne sat reading a magazine. The nurse came out from behind her desk and led her back to the doctor's room. He didn't have a changing room, he would just give his patients a couple of minutes alone in the examining room to get undressed, then he would come right in.

Dr. Warren came in with kind of a surprised look on his face. He said, "What can I do for you?" Anne was a little hesitant. He asked, "Is there something wrong?" She said, "Yeah, well, I've got a couple of problems." It was all somewhat lackadaisical at that point. He was standing there, and the nurse by then had checked her pulse and had already taken the blood pressure. Anne was sitting there, he was thumping on her back, generally checking things out, listening to her heart, and he asked, "What's the problem?" She said, "I've got this discharge that's driving me crazy. It's heavy, and I'm uncomfortable with it, and it's so bad I'm wearing pads." He was checking along as usual; he always just moves down the body and starts checking the breasts. He was nodding and saying, "Well it could be this," and "It's probably nothing," being just generally soothing. He got ready to start the internal. Anne was lying there in the stirrups, and she said, "Plus, Dr. Warren, I kind of hemorrhaged yesterday, and I've had some really severe pains."

He went on with the internal and at one point his hands literally jumped. "Oh my God," he said, "I've never seen anything like this before." He stood up from the table and ran across the room to a little counter, where he stood rapidly glancing through her charts. Anne immediately thought to herself, "He's checking to see the last time I was in here." Something seemed to break in her head at that point. He came back, obviously agitated, took a second look, and ran quickly to the door. He called his nurse in and snapped at her, "I've never seen anything like this." He was acting very erratic.

Anne was lying on the table. She was calm, she was in control, but she couldn't help thinking, *"What is going on?"* There he had been telling her nothing was wrong, and she knew something was wrong, and now it was worse because suddenly all her fears had been verified. The worst part of it was when he kept repeating, "I've never seen anything like this before." Anne kept thinking, "My God, my God, what *is* it?" By this time they were whispering together, he and his nurse, and they were taking turns looking inside her. Anne was just lying there with this lady looking up, and Dr. Warren's next statement was: "You're going to the hospital, *right now.*"

Anne said, "I can't go to the hospital." First of all, she couldn't imagine just walking out of his office and going to the hospital, just like that. It seemed insane. Second of all, she didn't have any insurance. Third of all, she had no idea what was going on. She said, "I can't go, I can't go, I've got this job." She was trying to think of any kind of excuse under the sun. It was impossible to accept, it was as if he was about to call an ambulance immediately. She thought, "I walked into this office, I can walk right out."

Dr. Warren frowned for a moment, and shrugged deliberately. "All right," he said, "well this will be faster anyway. We'll take the biopsy right here." Anne knew what biopsy meant. She was lying there thinking, "Oh my God . . ." Dr. Warren then said something that didn't quite register. He looked at Anne and asked, rather sternly, "*Whom* have you been with?" She stared right back, not yet realizing he must have thought it looked like a canker or something, like syphilis. Anne said, "John, that's all. You know about John." She didn't understand what he meant by it at first. She knew it couldn't have been that. He took the biopsy right away. He told her, "This is probably going to hurt a little." She only felt a little smarting. She was only slightly tuned in to what was going on, her eyes were closed and she was kind of off somewhere. Dr. Warren gave her the biopsy sample, in a paper bag. Anne ran right out and jumped into her maroon Galaxy 500. The Falcon had finally died. She took Route 30 down past the McDonalds and the Burger King, the Robo Wash and the Handy Shoppe, the new mall and the old mall, down a jumble of shifting stop signs and stop lights with lots of traffic. The paper bag sat right on the seat. She didn't touch it or look at it once all the way to St. James Hospital.

She parked in front of the hospital, a big square warehouse-like building with a statue of the Virgin Mary out front. Dr. Warren had told her, "Second Floor, Pathology." She ran up the stairs and found a lady behind a window. She said, "I'm supposed to bring you this." The lady said nothing but took the bag, and Anne just stood there waiting, expecting some sort of receipt or response. But the woman just turned and went back to her business. Anne asked, "Is that all?" The lady snapped, "We'll let the doctor know in about five days." Anne stood there thinking, *"Five days."*

She didn't want to go home. She thought of Diane Davis, Randy Davis' sister. The Davises were some of her oldest friends, they'd been neighbors and gone to school together, and Anne had gone out with Randy for a while in junior high. Anne wanted to talk to somebody. She drove straight to the Davises' house.

Anne walked right in and sat down, saying, "Diane, they found something. Something's wrong." Diane just closed her eyes. She finally said, "What happened?" Anne started telling her about the hospital and Dr. Warren and the biopsy and all, but Diane didn't know what to do with her. At the end of the story she sighed and said, "Want some tea?"

Anne thought it was really serious at that point, but Diane kept saying, "No, don't worry about it." She told Anne about a friend of theirs, a girl her brother had gone out with, who had been told she could never get pregnant. She'd had trouble with tumors of some kind, close to her tubes, and Diane said, "Look at her now, she's pregnant." Diane was trying to say not to worry until she found out for sure. But Anne just sat there at Diane's for a long time, not wanting to go home.

Paramount in her mind was not wanting to go home and have to run into her little brothers and sisters coming home from school. They wouldn't understand. John was at work at Sears. She didn't think first about telling him, she wanted to figure it out for herself. Diane sat there drinking tea and trying to change the subject, but Anne was still really frightened because every fifteen minutes or so she'd look down and sigh, "I don't know, Diane, I'm scared." Diane kept trying to keep Anne thinking about something else, but it wasn't easy. She knew Anne was upset, and she was upset too. But neither of them knew how serious it was, and why get worked up until you know for sure?

By the time she got home, her mom was home. For her mom it had been a very strange day. She was all upset and on the phone already because Dottie Hughes, her immediate superior at the store, had had a heart attack that morning. She was in the kitchen upset about that and finally Anne went in and looked at her and said, "Mom, I got some bad news today." They were right by the stove.

Mary Needham said, "Anne, I've got bad news too." She went on to tell all about Dottie and the heart attack. Anne just stood there and listened and didn't say anything. Finally, during a lull, Anne leaned forward against her mom and said, "Mom, Dr. Warren found something today." But Mrs. Needham was occupied with Dottie and right in the middle of getting dinner, and it didn't seem to sink in. She had come home expecting dinner to be ready and it wasn't. Anne usually had dinner all set by then.

After dinner, Anne and her mom were cleaning up. Anne told her the details. They didn't mention anything to the kids because they didn't know what it was, and it would be hard for them to understand. The next morning Anne went to work, even though Dr. Warren had told her not to. "What do you mean I can't work anymore," had been her response at the time. She knew he didn't want her fainting and hemorrhaging again in the store, but she didn't know what she was supposed to do with herself. When she went in to work she was glad she did, because she would have gone stir crazy sitting around the house, especially with no one to talk to. She was working full time, by Marshall Field's standards, about thirty-seven and a half hours a week, and she kept thinking how if she'd worked two more months she would have qualified for the health plan.

That was about the time she went into another world. Everything was going on around her, and she was just somewhere else. She couldn't believe any of this was happening to her to begin with; she'd always led such a normal life. Now everything was completely up in the air with regards to what was going on between herself and her body. At times she felt apart from her body, like: "That isn't really me." At other times she felt her body was somehow attacking her. But most of the time she didn't know how she felt.

She had no contact with Dr. Warren. They'd find out on Friday. She went through five days of not knowing anything, just knowing something was really wrong. She was even numb to dying. She decided that whatever fate had been bestowed on her, it was going to happen whatever she did. It was out of her hands completely.

On a Friday night, Anne ordinarily would have gone out. But she went home and waited for the call. She was home, her mom was home; the kids were out, and her dad wasn't home. Anne just kept roaming around from room to room, but then she ended up sitting in the den, staring at the TV. Her mom was wandering through the house picking up stuff, like she usually did on Friday nights, because she had the night off.

The phone rang at nine o'clock. Anne answered it in the kitchen, and she recognized Dr. Warren's voice. He said: "Anne, would you put your mother on?" She paused, wanting to say something, but then she just said, "Okay." She went off to get her mother. Then she walked into the living room and stood there waiting for the worst. She didn't try to listen to her mother's voice, too many things were going on in her mind. The major concern was how far it had gone, and what they were going to do. She also kept wondering if they'd be able to do anything at all. She was pretty sure she knew what it was. She stood in the living room for at least two minutes with the TV set on.

When Dr. Warren had said, "Put your mother on," her first response was to go and get her. But then she thought, "This is ridiculous, this is *about* me." She went into the girls' room and got on the phone. She told them she was getting on. She told them, "I think I should be involved in this." She didn't want them to keep anything from her.

Dr. Warren wouldn't say too much to Anne. He just kept saying, "Don't worry, we'll take care of it." Anne kept saying, "Is it malignant?" and he kept saying, "Don't worry, we'll take care of it." For Anne, the "it" stuck right in her mind; she kept wondering, "What is *it?*" He wouldn't even answer. He found it very difficult to say, "It's cancer." He couldn't use the word. He couldn't even say "malignancy." Anne was aware it was hard for him to picture her as an adult: Dr. Warren had delivered her. But she was twenty years old, and she kept thinking, "It's *my* body he's talking about, not Mom's."

Since Dr. Warren wouldn't answer her, Anne just went back into her own world again. She was there on the phone, and she was listening but nothing was being registered. They did talk about arrangements to be made, about a specialist who would get back to them at around ten o'clock, but Anne found it hard to pay attention. The whole situation seemed to draw away from her, because they wouldn't let her in on it.

Anne hung up, and sat for a while on the bed. One lamp was on, by the phone. What made her sit there for so long was when Dr. Warren had said, "radiologist." She didn't want anything to do with radiology. At the nursing home, she'd seen patients under radiation therapy. Once Anne had turned an old woman over in bed; her hair had fallen out all over the pillow.

When the phone rang at ten o'clock, Anne let her mother answer. She knew it was the radiologist, but she made no request to talk to him. Her mom came in later and put her arms around her, and she was very upset. The radiologist had wanted them to come to some lecture in about two weeks: "Come sit at this lecture, and see what you think, whether this might work for you." It seemed like such an odd idea, to go to some lecture in two weeks; Anne didn't even want to hear about it.

Saturday morning Anne was alone in the house. Everyone else was out and about. Anne was upset and she really didn't want to be by herself. She got into her car and went to see Denny Rauen. John was working at Sears. She wanted to see Denny because he was such an old friend, because she knew where he was, and he was the only person she could get hold of.

In junior high, Anne had wanted to go steady with Denny. At that time, everyone was going steady, and since Anne and Denny knew each other it seemed natural. They couldn't go steady because their parents wouldn't allow it. But even if they couldn't, they knew they were. They knew they were in love with each other.

Anne had met Denny in first grade. They were both the smallest kids in the class. They used to line the kids up by height, so Anne and Denny were always next to each other. Anne and Denny would hang out in Canteen, and on Friday nights there'd be dancing. Denny and Anne stayed together through seventh grade. They were going steady but they weren't really. Going steady meant you got to wear the guy's ring, and everyone knew you were. But by eighth grade they'd kind of realized it had been just a seventh grade fling. They broke it up, though they stayed friends forever.

She pulled up at Denny's house, and she heard rock and roll coming out the windows. She thought, "Oh, he's with his band." She knew he often practiced with his band on Saturday mornings, but for some reason it hadn't occurred to her. She walked right in and there were all these musicians sitting around with their instruments, but she wasn't upset to see them. Actually she was glad to be around people. All the same, she really wanted to talk to Dennis.

They were still setting up. Anne went into the kitchen for a while, then she went back into the living room. They were just about to practice, and Denny was roaming around hooking up wires. Anne started getting upset, and when Denny walked into the kitchen, she walked in too. There were three or four people standing around the table. She finally said, "Dennis," and it was almost like she was trying to grab him and shake him. "Dennis, I've got cancer." Denny just looked at Anne, and his mouth dropped open, and he looked at her again and no words came out. There was another guy standing there, and all of a sudden it was awfully quiet. Denny said finally, in a strange voice, "I thought something was wrong." Denny just grabbed her by the arm and said, "Let's go."

They drove up to Saumanac Park, a big park with lots of swings and picnic tables. They drove over there and sat in the car. They got out and sat on the swings. Later, they sat for a while at a picnic table. Then they got back in the car. Most of the time they didn't talk. They sat for a while on the ground. Anne kept pulling at the dead grass, tearing it apart, throwing it around. She had a few cigarettes; she loved smoking. It was the first real warm spring day.

4

The Food and Drug Administration (FDA) was not established until 1931, but other agencies began the task of ensuring the safety of food and drugs in 1906, with the passage of the Pure Food and Drugs Act. After years of popular outcry over contaminated food, the publication of Upton Sinclair's landmark exposé of the meat-packing industry, *The Jungle,* finally forced Congress to act. But the placing of "Food" before "Drug" in the title of the new act reflected what would become an entrenched emphasis: Harvey Wiley, chief chemist of the Department of Agriculture, and the foremost activist in the passage of the needed reforms, was in general agreement with the popular consensus that the well-publicized dangers of food contamination posed a more pervasive and immediate evil than any problems caused by impurities in legitimate medicine.

Enlightened medical experts at the turn of the century thought of drugs as useless concoctions. The endless varieties of questionable cures circulating in the country tended to discredit all drugs. The number of compounds of recognized merit had dwindled by the early 1900s to a mere handful of agents, compared to the vast quantities in popular use both before and after that period:

> In 1903 Frank Billings, President of the AMA, expressed
> what probably a large part of the profession believed when
> he told the House of Delegates [of the AMA] that with the

exception of quinine for malaria and mercury for syphilis, drugs were "valueless as cures."

But a revolution in drug therapy was still to come. In the next half century the number of remedies introduced into general practice would dramatically increase. As drugs became more and more potent and complex, the 1906 law which merely required that drugs be "pure" came to appear like a legacy from another century. For thirty years after the passage of the Pure Food and Drugs Act, drugs did not even have to be proved safe, let alone effective.

In 1937, disaster struck. A number of tall dark bottles labeled "Elixir of Sulfanilamide" were accidentally filled by a chemist of the S. E. Massingill Company with a deadly chemical solvent used to make antifreeze. One hundred and seven people, mostly children, were killed. Again it was time for reform. Stringent legislation that had been roundly defeated through intensive lobbying by the drug industry in 1933 passed quickly through Congress four years later.

The new amendment required that companies seeking to market "new" drugs submit extensive applications with multiple studies in both humans and animals to the FDA for approval. The FDA for its part was mandated to review these test results scrupulously before allowing the drug into the marketplace. For these extensive monitoring duties Congress in fiscal year 1940 appropriated the impressive sum of $103,000. The new amendment initially confused both industry and government, because no one could be sure exactly what a "new" drug was. For the first three years under the law, applications for new drugs flooded the agency at a rate of over a hundred a month.

In January of 1940, Dr. Don Carlos Hines was settling into a new office at Eli Lilly Headquarters in Indianapolis. Two years before, Dr. Hines had left the private practice of internal medicine in Palo Alto, California, to become a staff physician at Lilly, a job which he felt would allow him to stay at the cutting edge of medicine. The recently stiffened FDA barrier to drug marketing made it essential that large drug companies recruit talented people for their growing drug research departments. Hines was not a drug researcher by training, but a promising internist: as a recent graduate of Stanford Medical School, he was something of an expert in the latest trends in internal medicine. In January of 1940, Dr. Hines was made medical monitor of the new drug stilbestrol. As medical monitor, Hines was responsible for keeping abreast of all the latest research on this new and exciting remedy.

DES certainly seemed to be the perfect low-cost substitute for the troublesome natural estrogens used in hormone replacement therapy. The use of natural estrogen was both difficult and expensive, because the extracts had to be suspended in oil and administered by injection. Injections were usually in the buttocks and were often painful, as an abscess would commonly develop at the site. DES seemed remarkably superior to these costly preparations not only because it could be cheaply synthesized, but because it could be administered orally and taken on a regular and convenient basis at home.

Hines was required by law not merely to monitor published results, but to conduct research of his own. The FDA refused to allow foreign data to be submitted; United States companies were required to perform independent research, often only duplicating work already published abroad. According to Hines, "You did experiments on animals first." But this animal testing, in Hines's opinion, did not precisely lead to an awareness of the drug's effects on human beings: "Now, with animal testing, you try to find a model for human beings. You try to get some leads without subjecting people to experiments. . . . Rats are closer to people than frogs, but they just aren't really close, because their hormonal systems are different. . . . These animal tests were interesting," Hines later insisted, "but they didn't have anything to do with human beings."

Not all researchers or clinicians would have been quite so sanguine in 1940 about the growing body of animal data indicating that estrogens could cause cancer in humans. Numerous researchers, whose scientific experience persuaded them that animal data did have something to do with human beings, were busily testing estrogens for carcinogenic properties. A review of recent work in the field by Dr. Edgar Allen, one of the original team to isolate estrogens in the urine of pregnant animals, was published in the *Journal of the American Medical Association* in May of 1940. It would presumably have been one of the major sources of information on these compounds available to Hines at Lilly.

"Even in these first experiments," Dr. Allen wrote, "it was clear that the outstanding effect of [estrogen] was to produce growth in the female genital organs. . . ." And even in those early days, it was realized that cancer was literally malignant growth: "The beginning of my point of view on experimental cancer was an appreciation of the estrogenic hormone as a stimulator of growth of female genital tissues, and the vague recognition that a definition of cancer must include the matter of growth—excessive and atypical growth."

In 1932, the French investigator Antoine Lacassagne began conducting a famous series of experiments on the influence of sex hormones on cancer. Lacassagne was able to induce mammary cancer in male mice of a strain in which only the female mice were genetically susceptible, thereby proving that estrogen was a potent carcinogen, at least in mice. At Yale, Dr. Allen went on to confirm Lacassagne's conclusions. Allen and his colleagues used estrogens to produce all kinds of tumors, in male and female mice, in rabbits, in monkeys, and in rats.

"I realize," Dr. Allen continued, "it's a long way from cancer in mice to cancer in women. I realize that results obtained experimentally in mice may require years for confirmation in women. But surely these experiments in mice have some application clinically!" In Allen's opinion, "After the demonstration that estrogenic activity, long continued and at high levels, is followed by abnormal growths of the female genital organs, including fibroid tumors of the uterus, cervical carcinoma, and mammary cancer, the following question may be asked: 'Is the clinician justified in prescribing enormous doses of concentrated estrogenic preparation for aging women?' "

In spite of Dr. Allen's words of caution, the results of animal work done at Lilly seemed to reinforce the general opinion that DES faithfully mimicked the action of its more expensive natural counterparts. The only exception, Hines said later on, came with "some very odd results in some very odd animals." Hines immediately proceeded logically and legally to his next step, to try the drug out on humans. "The first consideration was safety," Hines later recalled. "You did all you could with animals, and then you went to human volunteers. . . . You only gave a new drug to patients who had not responded to standard treatment: This is basically an ethical consideration. You don't experiment gratuitously with people. . . ."

In April of 1940, the editors of the *Journal of the American Medical Association* had pointed out that clinicians had been remarkably eager to experiment gratuitously with estrogens, and with people. Under the headline "Contraindications to Estrogen Therapy," the editors had sternly admonished practitioners all over the world for ignoring a growing body of laboratory evidence:

> The Council on Pharmacy and Chemistry, and the Journal have repeatedly warned against the indiscriminate and prolonged use of estrogens and have emphasized the possible occurrence of mammary carcinoma in patients . . . It would be unwise to consider that there is safety in using small doses of estrogen if they are maintained over a long period.

> Reports which have appeared are quite appropriate at the present time, as new potent estrogens, easily administered, are being prepared for therapeutic purposes. The new synthetic estrogen, diethylstilbestrol is far more active than the natural estrogens in the production of uterine and extra-uterine fibroids in guinea pigs. . . . It is hoped that it will not be necessary for the appearance of numerous reports of estrogen induced cancer to convince physicians that they should be exceedingly cautious in the administration of estrogens.

After the appearance of this and other warnings, Lilly and other manufacturers proceeded with the next step toward final FDA approval: clinical trials. "You first give the drug to recognized experts in the field," Hines later recalled. "You give them all your information, you tell them what you think the drug is good for; you study it carefully, and you keep in touch with the experts."

In the final months of 1940, the FDA received more than ten applications to market stilbestrol primarily for postmenopausal syndrome. Since Dodds had gallantly denied himself the financial proceeds of his research, companies were permitted to test the drug independently, and market it without the protection of patents. The FDA's problem was first to assure that the various stilbestrols circulated by different companies met established standards of purity and performance, and then to determine whether stilbestrol was safe.

Theodore G. Klumpp, Chief Medical Officer of the FDA, had been coaxed down to Washington in 1938 from a faculty post at Yale University to aid the newly reorganized bureau in enforcing the new mandate for drug safety. Dr. Klumpp was faced with the task of evaluating a large number of separate new drug applications to market a single drug. In order to expedite matters in dealing with this group of drug companies, Klumpp consulted first with a man named Carson Frailey, executive director of the American Drug Manufacturers' Association, the drug industry's major lobbying presence in Washington. Frailey became an indispensable conduit of information between the FDA and the drug companies in the matter of stilbestrol.

Klumpp had a meeting with Frailey, during which he asked Frailey to tell the drug companies that the data submitted by them to market stilbestrol were, when evaluated individually, insufficient for approval. He suggested that the most efficient way to rectify the situation would be for the various companies to combine their clinical data. The objective was to obtain a single "Master File" by which the FDA could evaluate stilbestrol as a generic drug. He suggested a meeting on December 30, 1940, of all would-be DES manufacturers. Five days after Christmas, representatives from companies all over the country gathered at the FDA to talk about DES.

The meeting of December 30, 1940, was held not in Klumpp's office, but in that of Dr. Durrett, his colleague as head of the New Drug Division. Klumpp was unable to attend, but Durrett succinctly outlined the FDA's position on stilbestrol: they were concerned about some recent reports of toxicity in the medical journals. The clinical data included in each one of the applications submitted was individually inadequate and incomplete. But if the data could be combined and submitted jointly, as a single "Master File," it might be possible for all the companies to gain approval at once. The manufacturers responded by withdrawing their pending New Drug Application. They left Durrett's office and took a suite at the Hotel Washington, where in Hines's words, "We began to organize."

The manufacturers formed a study group. As their head, they elected Don Carlos Hines, of Lilly. Lilly was the largest of the DES manufacturers and Hines had gathered the most extensive clinical information to date, so the choice was a logical one. Hines at Lilly was joined by Dr. Gifford Upjohn of Upjohn and representatives from Squibb and Winthrop. The other seven manufacturers agreed to abide by the decisions of the committee. It was agreed that they would standardize the drug along the Lilly model, adopt Lilly literature, labeling, and composition. By creating a uniform generic product and agreeing to begin combining data, they were essentially following Klumpp's request. It was not a very large committee, four men only; they called it the "Small Committee."

Hines spent the next few months traveling across the country, assembling data, interviewing clinicians and experts, and generally coordinating the group effort. Meanwhile, Klumpp was doing his own traveling, talking to many of the same experts, in an attempt to achieve an independent view of the drug's successes and shortcomings. This represented the most extensive premarketing trial for any drug up to that time. The drug companies had selected fifty doctors who were judged expert in the field of hormonal therapy. Many of these men were selected precisely because they had experience with the nonsynthetic hormones, and so were somewhat favorably disposed to the use of hormone products.

Of all the experts, only four doctors in New York were steadfast in their opposition to the approval of stilbestrol; they had observed numerous instances of acute nausea and vomiting in patients given DES, findings which they had released to medical journals. Only this fragile barrier of suspected toxicity stood in the way of the drug's approval in the eyes of the majority of clinicians. Symptoms such as nausea and vomiting could indicate liver damage. Hines and Klumpp both interviewed these four steadfast hold-outs, who came to be known as the "New York Group."

March 1941 was the crucial month for DES. On the fifth, Klumpp circulated a memo through the FDA: "Dr. Hines states that they have received replies from a majority of clinicians. The only responses in the negative were all from the New York area, and Dr. Hines stated that they were at a loss to understand the apparent antagonism of the N.Y. Group." On the same date, Hines was writing to Gifford Upjohn of Upjohn: "Reports have now begun to come in and we are anxious to know how many we can count on in the next week or so . . . it seems to me we are justified in pushing Stilbestrol before the FDA, but of course it will be much easier if the New York Group is willing to soften its opinions. . . . We know that one of the group is at least willing to be open minded. . . ."

Klumpp went to New York to talk to the New York Group, to examine their reported findings of nausea and vomiting. Hines did the same, and both did a close check of their dosage schedules. They both compared this data with that of other clinicians, and insisted that the dosages the New York doctors were using were higher than the average. Klumpp and Hines independently reached the same conclusion: there was a "threshold dosage" for DES below which nausea and vomiting were thought not to occur.

That was the turning point for DES. On the twenty-fifth of March, Hines was able to write optimistically to his superiors at Lilly, after a meeting in Washington, "This meeting was marked by an entirely different attitude on the part of Dr. Klumpp and his assistants than was shown by Dr. Durrett at the previous meeting on December 30th. Dr. Klumpp was much more willing to discuss DES pro and con and appeared to be much more frank and responsive than Dr. Durrett. . . . Dr. Klumpp stated that the Administration was anxious to approve Stilbestrol as soon as evidence could be advanced as to its safety."

By May 1941, the DES manufacturers heard what they had been waiting for. On the twelfth, Dr. Hines received a letter from Carson Frailey, suggesting somewhat mysteriously, "The time now seems propitious that you refile the new drug application for Stilbestrol. I am making no commitments that the Application will be permitted to become effective, but the suggestion has official background. . . ."

Frailey's official background at the FDA was entirely correct. The mood was indeed propitious. All through the spring of 1941, as case after case poured in, an overwhelming consensus developed at the FDA in favor of stilbestrol. "We were impressed by the quantity of the data submitted," Klumpp later recalled. "More than for any previous drug application." By May, the Small Committee had flooded the agency with over 5,300 different reports of safe and successful DES treatment. How two doctors and their assistants at the New Drug Division were able to wade through that mountain of data in forty-five days remains a bureaucratic mystery, but by mid-June, Klumpp recalls he was "convinced."

On Friday, September 12, 1941, the FDA notified the drug companies that their applications had "become effective." The Small Committee was dissolved by Hines. Six months later, Klumpp resigned from the FDA to serve on the staff of the Council on Pharmacy and Chemistry of the American Medical Association, considered by many to be a far more rigorous examining body for new drugs than the overworked FDA. At the time Klumpp served on the council, DES was granted the coveted Seal of Approval, the nation's most prestigious hallmark for new prescription drugs. A year after leaving the FDA, Klumpp resigned from the AMA to become President of the Winthrop Chemical Company, one of the original eleven manufacturers of DES.

5

Kate and Felix Holland wanted babies. After a while, they knew they were going to have one. What befell was as unexpected as it was pathetic. And Felix, if possible, was more grieved than his wife.

"Never mind dearest," she comforted him with conviction. "Dr. Ashton says it's better so. He says it can happen to anyone, and there's no reason to think everything won't be all right next time."

Well, the next time was not all right. Kate lost a second baby. Felix was frightened. "I can't have her going through all this if there's no hope. You mustn't deceive us. It's cruel," he said to the doctor.

"I'm not discouraged," the physician soothed him. "The cause for this mishap was different from the other. I'm quite sure you'll have children." . . . Dr. Ashton realized that a law of nature is that the species shall be strong . . .

M. Davis
"Most Women Can Have Babies"
Good Housekeeping
September 1940

George and Olive Smith met at Harvard in the 1920s. He was a fellow in gynecology at the medical school, she was a graduate student in biochemistry. By 1930 they were married and just beginning what would be a lifelong mutual exploration of the mysteries of the female hormones. George became head of the Gynecology Department at Harvard, Olive joined the Fearing Institute in Brookline, Massachusetts, as a staff researcher. In the mid-1930s, they began publishing a series of papers on the behavior of hormones in the female reproductive system.

While Sir Edward Charles Dodds was avidly pursuing the synthesis of a female hormone in the laboratory, George and Olive Smith were interested in how hormones worked in the body. In the early days of endocrine research, estrogen had been isolated in the urine of pregnant women. The Smiths began their investigation by comparing the levels of estrogen in the urine of pregnant and nonpregnant women. For one of their early papers, published in the *New England Journal of Medicine* in 1936, the Smiths mapped the curves of estrogen levels in both groups, and discovered that in nonpregnant women the levels of estrogen rose and fell in uniform curves. But in pregnant women, the levels fluctuated widely: the secretion of estrogen reached a peak at about the tenth week of pregnancy, then dropped off quite rapidly immediately before delivery.

By the 1930s, it was known that the ovaries produce two major hormones, estrogen and progesterone. In the ovaries of a woman of childbearing age, an egg matures each month. The egg is contained within a membrane in the ovary called the follicle, which fills with fluid during ovulation, while the ovary secretes estrogen into the bloodstream. After about two weeks, the membrane ruptures and expels the egg into the Fallopian tube, which leads to the uterus. The empty follicle then begins to produce progesterone.

A function of progesterone is to prepare the body for pregnancy. Its specific target tissue is the uterus, which it readies to receive the fertilized egg. If fertilization does not occur during ovulation, the level of both progesterone and estrogen diminishes, and menstruation begins. Estrogen production then goes up as the cycle starts again.

If conception does occur, the egg moves down the Fallopian tube and attaches itself to the wall of the uterus for nourishment. The ovary then begins to secrete large amounts of progesterone until the placenta begins to enlarge and produce its own progesterone. The primary purpose of the progesterone, it was believed, was to relax or "quiet" the uterus to accommodate the growing fetus. At about the third month of pregnancy, this production of progesterone by the placenta begins. It was known that many miscarriages occur during that crucial third month.

In March of 1938, in a paper published in the *New England Journal of Medicine,* the Smiths began to elaborate a theory of hormonal behavior in pregnancy. They noted that a rise of estrogen always preceded a rise in progesterone. From this they concluded that the presence of estrogen somehow stimulated the secretion of progesterone. The two hormones, in other words, depended upon each other to maintain pregnancy.

By 1940, the Smiths had refined this theory to explain certain disorders of pregnancy. In some cases of premature delivery, low estrogen levels had been found. This low estrogen level, they surmised, might be due to a low progesterone level. They used this hypothesis to speculate in the March 1940 issue of the *American Journal of Obstetrics and Gynecology* on the possibility of some sort of replacement therapy:

> The demonstration of hormonal imbalance involving an estrogen and progesterone deficiency has seemed to warrant the administration of these substances in the hope of reestablishing a normal balance.

But this was 1940, and the Smiths were forced to write:

> The administration of progesterone and estrogen as a therapeutic measure . . . is as yet of very limited clinical value for three reasons: 1) the large amounts required are not commercially available in sufficiently concentrated form and are still too costly, 2) the injections must be continued for at least six days before any effect can be expected, and 3) indications are that in cases of greater severity replacement therapy would be of no avail. . . .

This summarized the difficult position clinicians faced when trying to replace internal secretions with rare natural extracts.

. . . Evelyn has had four miscarriages. She suffers from what the medical profession terms "habitual abortion." When Evelyn became pregnant again, Dr. Ashton gave her ovarian hormone, because he thought it possible she was not sufficiently well provided with this essential to the development of a pregnancy. But it's expensive—$2 to $2.50 for each injection—and Dr. Ashton gave it to Evelyn for three months. . . .

M. Davis
"Most Women Can Have Babies"
Good Housekeeping
September 1940

By 1943, the Smiths had focused their attentions on the role of the placenta in aiding the growth of the fetus. They had decided that a deficiency of estrogen might cause a deficiency of production of progesterone by the placenta. This progesterone deficiency, they believed, was a primary cause of premature delivery and other pregnancy complications. As they had seen that estrogen levels fell rapidly immediately before delivery, and they had come to believe that estrogen stimulated the secretion of progesterone, they concluded that premature delivery was a condition in which the estrogen level declined too early, and the fetus was prematurely expelled from the womb.

By 1946, the Smiths were convinced that progesterone deficiency was a prime cause of pregnancy difficulties. They began administering doses of both estrogens and progesterone to women whose pregnancies were considered threatened by hormone deficiency. They decided that abnormalities in the production of hormones by the placenta often began in the second trimester, so stilbestrol therapy was started as early as the sixteenth week. Since it would have been quite impossible to replace the enormous quantities of hormones produced by the body in normal pregnancy with hormonal preparations, the Smiths decided that a more practical approach was to try to stimulate the placenta to secrete more of its own hormones. To give women specified doses of estrogens, the Smiths speculated, might cause the placenta to secrete more hormones on its own.

The perfect material for such experimental therapy had recently become available, a substance which fit the needs of the Smiths' theory so precisely it might have been designed for it:

There is reason to suppose that Stilbestrol, as well as being inexpensive and effective by mouth, might be a more useful therapeutic agent than naturally occurring estrogens. . . . It has accordingly been proposed, that the administration during the middle months of pregnancy of large amounts of estrogenic material . . . might forestall premature deficiency of estrogen and progesterone.

George Smith, Olive Smith, *et al.*
American Journal of Obstetrics and Gynecology
March 1946

They tested this hypothesis by giving a tremendous dose of stilbestrol to one woman patient, who was observed to secrete large amounts of hormone in her urine while getting the stilbestrol. The hormone level dropped precipitously each time the Smiths stopped giving her the stilbestrol. The Smiths prescribed to a certain "Mrs. K" the enormous dose of 135 milligrams per day for three weeks. She was observed to excrete the extraordinary amount of 150 milligrams of hormone in her urine in less than twenty-four hours. "It is possible that three weeks of such large dosages constituted excessive therapy," the Smiths bluntly admitted. But with the experience of this one patient and on the basis of their unproved theory, the Smiths were quite willing to draw what would become some rather influential conclusions.

Even with this tremendous dose, one hundred and thirty times more powerful than that prescribed for the alleviation of menopausal symptoms, the Smiths detected no remarkable effects other than grossly heightened hormonal secretion, which they took to be the prime indicator that their unusual therapy was working. In the March 1946 *American Journal of Obstetrics and Gynecology,* they wrote, "On the basis of these findings we are recommending the following regimen for prevention of late accidents of pregnancy—DES by mouth starting at the sixteenth week, thirty mg. daily with the daily dosage increased by 5 mg. weekly through the thirty-fifth week. . . . For this purpose, 25 mg. tablets may be supplemented by 5 mg. tablets to give the correct dosage."

The Smiths began a "five year study" to explore the efficacy of this novel treatment and enlisted the aid of clinicians around the country to cooperate in their investigations: "We would appreciate case reports from any others stimulated by this publication to try [replacement therapy]. . . . Our regimen is now being tried by a number of individuals throughout the country and their results reported to us. . . ." Clinicians were not the only parties stimulated to investigate the possibilities of the Smiths' new theory; drug companies began manufacturing a new, larger stilbestrol tablet to fit the Smith prescription: 25 milligram tablets were supplied by Squibb to give the correct dosage.

In May of 1944, Dr. J. S. Henry of Montreal had read a paper before the seventy-fifth annual meeting of the Canadian Medical Association, which was published in the July 1945 issue of the widely-read *Canadian Medical Association Journal*. The subject was estrogens and their use in the treatment of menopause. Henry wrote:

> . . . Since the chemical structure of the natural estrogens has been known, there have been warnings from both laboratory workers and clinicians that prolonged treatment with these substances, especially in large dosages, is not without danger. It is argued that they are essentially growth hormones specified for tissue of the reproductive organs, and that their prolonged use may lead to a pathological overstimulation of some of these tissues, and even to the production of malignant changes. . . . *Their close chemical relationships to some of the carcinogenic substances of coal tar justify such a warning on purely theoretical grounds,* and the results obtained in animal experiments make it imperative that clinicians should know the potential changes of the substances they are using in practice.

> . . . It has usually been stated that there is little to be feared in treating women with estrogens, since the amounts used in experimental carcinogenesis in animals are relatively so much higher than those used in medicine. It appears, however, that it is not always necessary to use large dosages in the experimental production of carcinoma in animals, and that the time factor is of great importance. The statement referred to is therefore a false comfort and is as such dangerous. . . .

Dr. Henry went on to report two cases of women who developed malignancies after prolonged estrogen therapy. One woman, aged forty-nine, had been given natural estrogens for three years for the control of menopausal symptoms, in this case irregular uterine bleeding. In August 1942 she was admitted to the hospital bleeding from the uterus; she was diagnosed as having a "hyperplastic endometrium," or changes of the lining of the vagina which "all five pathologists who have seen this specimen have agreed is at least precancerous, and one thought to be frankly malignant." It was also agreed that the excessive estrogen therapy had led to this "intense hyperplasia showing precancerous or actually malignant changes."

Another woman, aged fifty, had been given stilbestrol for three years also for the treatment of menopausal symptoms. She was also admitted to the hospital bleeding, and again "all were agreed that the process seen in this tissue is to all appearances a malignant one." Dr. Henry concluded: "It is probable that the endometrial changes originated in the prolonged treatment with Stilbestrol. . . ."

"If therapy is continued for many weeks and months, at any level of dosage which relieves the patient's symptoms," Henry continued, "sooner or later uterine bleeding occurs and this arouses the fear of carcinoma. . . . In other words, therapy has substituted one pathological condition for another, without curing the first. . . ."

By the mid-1940s such dire warnings were becoming increasingly frequent and insistent in tone. Dr. Henry had pointed to direct clinical experience implicating the use of estrogens in therapy in cancer development, but warnings based on the large body of animal data were far more common. In a widely read book on the subject published by the AMA in Chicago in 1942, entitled *Glandular Physiology and Therapy,* Edward A. Doisy, Edgar Allen's partner in the isolation of natural estrogen, had warned:

With every woman of forty years a prospective patient, an experiment of tremendous magnitude is in progress. The acute undesirable side-effects from . . . Stilbestrol have served as a definite warning that caution should be exercised. Furthermore, there seems during the last five years to be a definite trend toward massive dosage, with both natural and synthetic estrogens. Perhaps this will eventually prove satisfactory, but in the meantime it does not seem wise to be too incautious. . . . The increased incidence of malignant change following administration of estrogens seems a definite warning. . . .

It seems unwise to ignore the possibility of accelerating the growth of cancer in susceptible persons. . . .

In November of 1948 Dr. Olive Smith published in the *American Journal of Obstetrics and Gynecology* a preliminary report on her five year study, "still in progress," on the use of DES early in pregnancy. Dr. Smith divided her various patients into several categories: women observed to be "bleeding between the sixth and twenty-sixth week of pregnancy" who were considered cases of "threatened abortion"; women who had from two to five previous miscarriages who were "habitual aborters," and women with various other "late pregnancy complications." All these women were treated with DES in increasing doses; Olive Smith reported "significant" increases in successful pregnancies over the "average cure-rate" in each category. The increases were on the order of roughly fifty percent, with about three-quarters of the women "obtaining living babies," up from less than one-half usually observed in untreated threatened pregnancies. "Since the cases reported," Dr. Smith wrote, "received no supplementary therapy other than bed rest and sedation, the increased salvage must have been due to Stilbestrol and is highly significant."

"We have been concerned," Smith insisted, "about the theoretical dangers of Stilbestrol overdose. It is well known that estrogens in unphysiologic amounts are toxic to the fetuses of rodents [in fact it killed the fetuses]. . . . It seems likely that the continued administration . . . of Stilbestrol might inhibit placental secretion . . . and even do permanent damage to the secretory activity of this organ. . . ." In spite of this concern, "Twenty-eight patients were given what we consider overdosage prior to the twentieth week, and more than one-half of these developed later-pregnancy complications." Mrs. Smith concluded, ". . . the results are sufficiently alarming to convince us of the real danger of overdosage, especially during the early weeks when the placenta is assuming hormone production." It was precisely this early period of pregnancy during which the Smiths were recommending massive doses of stilbestrol.

The Smiths somewhat hastily concluded that stilbestrol increased estrogen and progesterone secretion from the placenta, "thereby providing a better maternal environment for the fetus so that when delivery does occur, it is in better condition than it would be if Stilbestrol had not been given. . . ." In other words, DES aided pregnancy regardless of the nature of the complications, because it apparently improved the general environment of the womb: "Several of the obstetricians noted that the placentas from Stilbestrol treated patients were grossly more healthy looking and the babies unusually rugged. . . ."

. . . It is exciting and encouraging to learn how much the medical profession has learned about mothers-to-be, and to know that today most wanted babies can be born without any trouble at all, even after some disappointments. . . .

M. Davis
"Most Women Can Have Babies"
Good Housekeeping
September 1940

In order to test their thesis that DES was helpful in virtually all pregnancies, the Smiths late in 1947 began an elaborate study at the Boston Lying-In Hospital. They gave 387 women who were pregnant for the first time stilbestrol in gradually increasing dosages, from the early stages of pregnancy to the thirty-sixth week, "as a prophylactic against complications of late pregnancy." These women were being given DES simply because first pregnancies, or "primigravidas," were known to have a statistically higher incidence of problems in late pregnancy than women who had successfully delivered babies before. In their nationwide study of DES in pregnancy published the preceding year, the Smiths had established no system of controls. In this study, published in the November 1949 issue of the *American Journal of Obstetrics and Gynecology,* the Smiths wrote, ". . . in order to eliminate all possible variables it was deemed important to have a synchronous control group from the same clinic rather than to depend upon the data from previous years or other clinics. . . ."

A control group is a group of patients who are treated in exactly the same way as the group who are given the drug, except that instead of the drug they are given either standard treatment or a placebo, an inert pill, usually sugar. The placebo tends to eliminate psychological factors in the testing process; the control group eliminates coincidental factors which might otherwise be attributed to the effects of the drug.

The most sophisticated form of control study at the time the Smiths were testing DES was the "double-blind" study. Neither the patient nor the physician knows in such a test whether the patient is getting an active agent or a placebo. The investigator is able later to compare results by means of a system of color-coding which remains secret until the test is over. This precaution is taken to further eliminate psychological influences on the part of patient or practitioner.

This study of DES in first pregnancy conducted by the Smiths at Boston Lying-In was neither a double-blind study nor a truly controlled study. In the Smiths' study the untreated patients were simply that, a randomly gathered sample of pregnant women coming in and out of the crowded prenatal clinic. The so-called synchronous control group was involved only by default. The patients who were taking something knew they were, the patients who were not knew they were not. The women who were given DES recall they were told only that they were taking "vitamins."

When all the results were in, "analysis on the data on spontaneous premature delivery revealed that the premature infants of Stilbestrol treated mothers were unusually large and mature. . . ." Of the babies born, only a single stilbestrol baby was seen to have an anomaly, whereas 7 of the 555 control were abnormal. "We knew of no reason why Stilbestrol . . . should reduce the instance of fetal abnormality, as might be inferred from these figures," the Smiths wrote. "It seems safe to conclude, however, that the use of Stilbestrol in the dosages prescribed by us is associated with no risk of maintaining an abnormal conceptus."

Evidence existed in the literature which would have indicated exactly the opposite. George Smith himself had only recently admitted that estrogens could be carcinogenic in certain patients:

Estrogen is known to be carcinogenic in susceptible animals. Conceivably, therefore, in the susceptible patient, it may tip the balance of unknowns in favor of endometrial malignancy. . . .

> George Smith *et al.*
> "The Ovary and Endometrial Cancer"
> *American Journal of Obstetrics and Gynecology*
> October 1948

Evidence was also available in the medical literature that this known carcinogen could pass through the placental barrier and expose the fetus to harm:

> . . . Estrogens can traverse the placenta, and so enter the fetal circulation. . . . Philip (1929) found estrogen in relatively large quantities in the urine of newborn babies. . . . In 1930, the observation that estrogen can pass from the maternal into the fetal circulation was confirmed by Courrier. . . .

> E. Burrows
> *Biological Actions of the Sex Hormones*
> Cambridge University Press, 1940

In the discussion following the presentation of the Smiths' final landmark paper at the Annual Congress of Obstetrics and Gynecology at Hot Springs, Virginia, in 1949, some listeners were skeptical as to the universally palliative effects of DES in pregnancy. Dr. Ernest Page of San Francisco said, ". . . It is difficult to believe that such a potent drug as Stilbestrol will prove to be—like an essential vitamin—necessary for the most successful outcome of normal pregnancies. . . ." The Smiths had concluded that DES had "rendered normal pregnancies more normal"; Dr. Page questioned this on "philosophical grounds," and went on to reinforce his doubts with a challenge to the Smiths' testing methods: "Is it possible that some unconscious factors of selection could have operated in the production of these differences? Does the fact that the control sample is forty-three percent larger than the experimental sample indicate that whatever disturbance occurred in the planned . . . cases might likewise have disturbed the complete randomness of selection?"

Dr. Willard M. Allen of St. Louis wondered about the Smiths' theory that estrogen therapy improved the maternal environment for the fetus. He began by citing some well-known animal results: "In the pregnant rabbit . . . the administration of estrogen is very deleterious to the fetus. In early pregnancy estrogen will prevent implantation or produce abortion, and during the later stages it leads to the death of the fetus. . . ." Dr. William J. Dieckmann of Chicago brought up the issue of testing methods again: "I gather that the essayists have not used a placebo which I think is important. . . . I am also curious as to how they know whether or not the patients take the Stilbestrol. . . ."

Dr. George Smith replied, ". . . We were not trying to sell Stilbestrol; we were trying to find out whether our idea was correct. The selection of patients was made by an elderly, retired school teacher; she had no experience whatsoever with medical problems; one woman looked just like another to her as regards pregnancy. . . ."

In spite of the somewhat skeptical reception their report was given at Hot Springs, the distinguished reputation of the Smiths and their respected Harvard background allowed the success story of DES to generate considerable excitement among the gathering there. From that day on many prominent Ob-Gyn men, particularly those around Boston who knew the Smiths by reputation, were willing to accept that stilbestrol did all that was claimed. Stilbestrol became, for those who believed the Smiths, the "drug of choice" in the prevention of miscarriage. Many of the nation's obstetricians were equally willing to accept the Smiths' conviction that stilbestrol, like a vitamin, could be useful in normal pregnancies.

6

The war was over when Victor Needham came home. He'd been in the Navy four and a half years. Mary was just starting her sophomore year when she met him. They were both studying pharmacy at Drake in Des Moines. They married almost immediately; both were Catholic and had a great many things in common.

Victor was having problems. His credits had been all messed up after his time in the service. In the Navy he'd had a year of pharmacy at Purdue, and before that one year at Dowling, a Catholic school. But transferring all the credits was too much for the bureaucracy, and Vic was spending more of his time untangling the mess than studying pharmacy.

Mary had her problems too. She almost got thrown out that sophomore year because she was carrying twenty credit hours while working for her room and board every night at a drugstore. She was on a scholarship, but she needed money for her expenses; she was getting tired and her grades were slipping. So the dean said, "Quit phys. ed., you're totally exhausted." She quit, but she didn't want to; her father had been an athlete. She was only studying pharmacy because she'd tried to get into nursing school but couldn't pass the physical.

Mary's mother was against her marrying Vic because she was sure Mary would have to drop out of school. Vic's family was against him marrying her, because she wasn't Irish. Mary was Catholic, but her mother was a Lutheran. To the Needhams that was a terrible thing, and the fact that she'd gone to a public and not a Catholic high school was pretty terrible too.

Mary had been raised in a very liberal household. Her father had been a coach with Iowa State for a while, and they'd always had athletes through their house. They had had people of every sort of race and ethnic background coming in and out: black, Chinese, Jewish, Russian; her father had lots of friends, most of whom were Swedish or Greek. The Needhams were one of those Irish families that thought they knew everything, but none of them had ever won a scholarship anywhere. She used to look at them and think, "My father would have laughed them off the face of the earth."

Mary's father had died when she was very young, and though her mother wasn't a Catholic, Mary had always remained one. When Mary was little she was injured, and her father would carry her to Mass. She was the youngest of a family of four, and her brothers were all athletes like her father. She always thought she should have majored in phys. ed. but she wanted something solid that would support her.

Victor and Mary were married, and they went to live in a trailer. It was very unsatisfactory. The water from the refrigerator dripped into the trailer, the little kerosene heater hardly worked, and you had to walk a block to the john. Vic had been working at a sundry store, which was a drugstore that sold no drugs: only over the counter remedies. The man who owned the store wanted to sell it, so Mary said, "Let's buy it." It cost $4,500. They scrounged up a thousand for the first payment and moved into the back.

Mary's mother was very upset. Vic's parents were very upset. But you could do anything, Mary believed, if you cared enough; when you quit caring, you killed people. They had a tremendous time. They were lucky because they were nice and warm, they had lots of good food, and Vic could come home to study if he wanted to. He didn't feel he needed to study, because he'd been in the Navy. For a lot of the fellows coming right out of service, it was a difficult time. They'd come back from combat and found themselves in a classroom with a lot of kids. The men were utterly bored; you could see it in their faces. They'd been fighting, and now that they were home, they couldn't sit still.

Victor and Mary worked hard that first year, because both of them were attending classes from eight in the morning until four or five in the afternoon. Mary tried to keep up the classes for a while, but they just didn't have enough money. So just as her mother had predicted, she dropped out to run the sundry store from nine in the morning until ten at night, seven days a week.

She got pregnant with Cathy almost immediately, and soon she was this huge lady behind the counter. She had a small frame, and it all seemed to come out in the front. They lived in that store over a year, and though there was work they were happy.

Mary was twenty. Vic was twenty-three. Vic took his degree in 1947, and after his State Board exam he was offered a job with a drugstore chain called Ford-Hopkins, in Des Moines. At that time, they sold their sundry store for not much more than they paid into it. They stayed in Des Moines for three years, until Ford-Hopkins made Vic a good offer to manage their new store in Park Forest, a suburb just south of Chicago.

> It is wonderful news . . . that medical science can now supplement the supply of vital hormones, when a mother's body does not produce enough. . . . In placing yourself under the care of a doctor who will guard against the possibility of any harm, you have done your part. Medical science stands ready to do its part. Between the two of you, you can insure the baby's safe arrival into the world. . . .
>
> Dr. Herman Bundesen
> "Miscarriage: Why It Happens and How to Avoid It"
> *Ladies' Home Journal*
> October 1952

In 1947, DES was approved for use in the prevention of miscarriage. Because the Smiths and others were not recommending the use of a new drug for a new purpose, but a new use for an old drug, the manufacturers involved maintained they were not required to perform any supplementary testing in animals or humans to prove it was safe for this purpose. DES had been put through its clinical trials in 1941; it had already passed its animal tests. The FDA's role in monitoring this "new indication" was limited to reading published material, such as papers by the Smiths, and modest studies initiated by the drug companies, many of which claimed definitive results by testing DES in a dozen or fewer women.

DES had been on the market for nearly a decade, without any observable serious side effects other than occasional nausea and irregular uterine bleeding caused by estrogen "withdrawal." By the provisions of the 1938 Food, Drug and Cosmetic Law, a drug which had been approved for selected purposes as "safe" did not have to be submitted to the same extensive testing as a new drug, even if it was intended for use in an entirely new set of circumstances. For the prevention of miscarriage, the doses involved were ten, twenty, and often a hundred times stronger than those prescribed for the alleviation of the symptoms of menopause. But nothing in the 1938 law required that the drug companies redefine the exact levels of safety, in the face of this new opportunity for danger.

By the 1938 law, a drug was required simply to be proven safe, not effective. Judgments of efficacy were left up to the drug companies and were considered the province of the practicing physician. For decades it was accepted that to market ineffective drugs was potentially dangerous, because a patient could conceivably be prevented from receiving more effective treatment. But the drug companies successfully defeated proposed legislation to redress this shortcoming on the grounds that such governmental intervention would interfere with the right of the practicing physician to prescribe the drug of choice.

If DES had had to be proved effective to prevent miscarriage, instead of merely safe, it would have had to go through much more extensive testing than it did immediately prior to 1947. If DES had been an entirely new preparation, it would have been tested extensively in pregnant women and in pregnant animals. Levels of safety, not only for the mother but for the fetus, would have had to have been established.

DES was the perfect drug introduced for the perfect purpose at the perfect time. World War II had recently ended. The veterans returning home were settling into a popular dream of family life, togetherness, growth, peace, and prosperity. The birthrate would soon be higher than that of India, Japan, Burma, or Pakistan. The number of American women with three or more children would double over the next ten years. DES would be the logical antagonist to birth control in a new form of family planning. *Good Housekeeping* estimated in 1949 that close to 20 percent of all pregnancies still ended in spontaneous abortion. Now women who apparently were biologically incapable of bearing these large families could have their uterine environments synthetically enhanced. Just as Americans dreamed of acquiring bigger and better

houses, bigger and better cars, now this latest wonder drug promised bigger, better families grown from bigger, better babies.

Park Forest was a brand-new town. The average age of the
villagers was about twenty-four, and most were moving up in big
companies. It was one of the first planned communities, built by a
man named Klutznick who had been with the housing administration during the war. It was said in the town he'd bankrolled the
place using all federal money, but the layout was attractive, and
everything was fresh and new. The Needhams were the second
people to occupy one street; the first couple had moved in two
days before. They moved in over muddy roads and duckboards.
The moving men carried the furniture in right across the mud.

About a year after moving to Park Forest, Mary knew she
was pregnant again. She'd been pregnant four times and mis-
carried twice. She always knew when she was pregnant because
her breasts would get sore and swell. Cathy was five and Victor Jr.
was two. She was very anxious not to lose this baby because she
only wanted three children and she'd lost that third child twice.
After six weeks she went to see Dr. Abrams, the only gynecologist
in town.

Mary told him she had had two miscarriages. Both times it
had been pretty traumatic; aborting when you want a baby is very
bad. It didn't seem to upset a man like Victor as much, because he
wasn't so physically involved. When a woman becomes pregnant,
an emotional as well as a physical change begins, and a man just
can't be attuned to it. Because she'd had the miscarriages, Dr.
Abrams didn't do a vaginal. He just wrote out two prescriptions,
one for a prenatal vitamin and the other for a new kind of pill. He
said, "This will keep you from losing the baby," and he called the
drugstore.

The marketing of "ethical" or prescription drugs is unique in
contemporary industry, because the buyer does not pay the bill
but simply orders the product. The practicing physician is "targeted" by the drug industry to be bombarded by a formidable
complex of magazine advertising, free circulars, and various creative promotional activities: he is invited out to educational lunches
and dinners to learn about new drugs, his mail is stuffed with
novelties bearing pharmaceutical imprints to remind him of brand
names and specific preparations, and almost every day he is visited

by drug salesmen known as "detail men," who circulate through hospitals, doctor's offices, and pharmacies pitching their company's products to physicians, hospital administrators, and pharmacists.

Detailing is a costly form of door-to-door salesmanship in which no money changes hands. Detail men do not take drug orders, but are charged with preaching the gospel of their compounds to all those whose job it is to listen. Detail men usually have little or no training in pharmacology and rarely have more than a limited understanding of what their assigned drugs do. In an investigation of the drug industry entitled *2,000,000 Guinea Pigs* (G. P. Putnam, 1972), John G. Fuller cited the example of the Parke, Davis detail man who testified before a Congressional hearing, "I told the doctor things I knew nothing about; since he knew nothing about what I was talking about, we were on very equal terms. That made us comfortable. Just how comfortable the patient was, no one will ever know."

The practice of detailing came under considerable fire in the late '50s from the Congressional committee under Senator Estes Kefauver investigating the drug industry. In their final report, the committee concluded:

> . . . The specific problem raised by the detail men is the difficulty, if not the impossibility, of checking for accuracy the information which they pass on to physicians. . . . If the physician regards the firm as a "good" company, and if the detail man has built up a "good" relationship between himself and the doctor, the opportunities for the transmission of misleading information are very real indeed.

The most widely available reference work in which the practicing physician may find out about prescription drugs is The Physicians' Desk Reference. The PDR is simply a compendium of entries written by the drug companies listing the manufacturer's description of a drug, some information about its chemical makeup, its known or admitted effects and side effects, its indications and contraindications. The PDR has been called the Yellow Pages of prescription drugs, because these entries are not data objectively arrived at by some independent body but paid advertisements placed by the drug companies presenting a tailored and official history of a drug and its effects. Unfavorable data and findings can easily be left out or deemphasized, studies can be erroneously interpreted, and just as with the detail men, "the opportunities for the transmission of misleading information are very real indeed." The PDR entries are really a form of labeling, resembling the material in package inserts to be read by interested physicians. All such material is prepared by the medical departments of the drug houses, and is further approved by the marketing divisions as part of an entire promotional package.

Because stilbestrol was a specialty drug, to be used only by obstetricians familiar with its specific properties, the DES manufacturers did not advertise their product in medical journals intended for the entire profession. They depended upon circulars, the PDR, package inserts, and detail men for its promotion. But in the case of DES, the drug companies were unusually fortunate in having the unqualified support of two such prominent people in the field as the Smiths. Their widely publicized series of papers, which amounted to personal endorsements of this controversial drug, were sufficiently powerful testimonials to sell the drug on their own.

Acceptance of this new drug and its novel therapeutic use was indeed immediate. Data published from two medical centers in the early 1950s indicate that DES was given to 5 to 10 percent of the pregnant women who entered. It is now assumed that close to 2 percent of pregnant women in the United States were given DES for various reasons. Total sales figures, with sales peaking in 1953, suggest a DES-taking population from 1947 onwards of between one and two million women.

By the mid-1950s DES was considered no longer a new drug. Companies interested in producing and selling DES no longer had to file New Drug Applications. It is claimed that more than two hundred companies began marketing DES for the purpose of preventing accidents of pregnancy, most of them received supplies from about a dozen companies licensed by the FDA. The number of DES-related drugs began to multiply throughout the '50s. These were sold under various brand and trade names, in various doses and forms. There were DES tablets, capsules, suppositories, creams, jellies, and liquids. Just as the number of product types began to proliferate, so the methods of administration, dosage schedules, and theories of use began to multiply, and depart from the comparatively sober and orthodox theories of the Smiths.

Some researchers recommended DES to be taken alternatively with progesterone; others recommended far higher doses, given at different times; some women were given DES early in pregnancy, others received it late. The average doses began to range widely over a less than coherent spectrum: one group of women tested were found to have received doses ingested throughout pregnancy ranging between 135 and 18,200 milligrams total. Close chemical relatives began to appear, which had similar biological effects but could be marketed as distinctive from basic stilbestrol. Two of the most common forms, Dienestrol and hexestrol, were both members of the original chemical group discovered by Dodds, but a confusing number of other DES products flooded the market throughout the '50s and '60s.

Stilbestrol was originally marketed as a generic drug, but various DES-related drugs were soon introduced under an array of registered trade names for sale to a rapidly expanding number of women.

DES-TYPE DRUGS THAT MAY HAVE BEEN PRESCRIBED TO PREGNANT WOMEN*

Nonsteroidal Estrogens

Benzestrol	Diethylstilbenediol	Mikarol	Stilbetin
Chlorotrianisene	Digestil	Mikarol forti	Stilbinol
Comestrol	Domestrol	Milestrol	Stilboestroform
Cyren A	Estilben	Monomestrol	Stilboestrol
Cyren B	Estrobene	Neo-Oestranol I	Stilboestrol DP
Delvinal	Estrobene DP	Neo-Oestranol II	Stilestrate
DES	Estrosyn	Nulabort	Stilpalmitate
DesPlex	Fonatol	Oestrogenine	Stilphostrol
Diestryl	Gynben	Oestromenin	Stilronate
Dibestil	Gyneben	Oestromon	Stilrone
Dienestrol	Hexestrol	Orestol	Stils
Dienoestrol	Hexoestrol	Pabestrol D	Synestrin
Diethylstilbestrol	H-Bestrol	Palestrol	Synestrol
Dipalmitate	Menocrin	Restrol	Synthoestrin
Diethylstilbestrol	Meprane	Stil-Rol	Tace
Diphosphate	Mestibol	Stilbal	Vallestril
Diethylstilbestrol	Methallenestril	Stilbestrol	Willestrol
Dipropionate	Microest	Stilbestronate	

Compiled by The National Cancer Institute.

All during Victor Needham's years as a pharmacist, detail men would come around. These detail men would show up at two- to three-week intervals. There was "Jim" from Lilly, and "Charles" from Abbott, and countless others whose names and faces Victor can't recall. The man from White Labs was slender, with dark hair and glasses. There was nothing distinctive about him, no accent, no special jewelry, no special cut to his clothes. Nothing stood out about him at all. He wore a tie, but then again, they all did. He carried a white card. The white card just said, "White Laboratories," right in the center.

The man from White had a pill he called "Dienestrol." This was a form of DES, the formula changed slightly in an attempt to reduce nausea. Dr. Abrams, a local obstetrician, suddenly began asking for tablets of these to prevent miscarriage.

The dosage Dr. Abrams prescribed called for increasing numbers of 25-milligram pills. These White pills came in little brown bottles, with off-white screw-on caps. The pill was a buff color, round, with a beveled edge. It had a score across it. It was uncoated. About a third the size of an aspirin tablet.

Victor was in his store behind the counter on the morning in October that Mary went to see the doctor. She stopped in right after her appointment with Dr. Abrams, with a prescription for some vitamins. Victor remembers himself saying, "Just a minute, honey, I'll type out the label." He typed out, "One tablet daily," took the big brown bottle of a thousand tablets, and carefully poured out a mound into the counting tray. He scraped just thirty off the pile and poured the surplus back into the bottle. He hadn't touched the pills with his hands.

7

Most important, however, is the deletion of stilbestrol . . . hormones have been widely used in recent years on the theory they help provide a healthy environment for the ovum. When . . . patients who went without them fared as well or better than those who took the hormones, they were eliminated entirely without affecting the rate of success.

> "Found: A Way to Prevent Miscarriage"
> *McCall's Magazine*
> May 1950

In the early 1950s, with sales of DES reaching their highest level since its introduction, amid a highly charged atmosphere of excitement and enthusiasm surrounding the Smiths' work, some researchers began to entertain apprehensions that the sudden and widespread infatuation with stilbestrol on the part of many clinicians might be obscuring genuine questions as to its usefulness.

In what amounted to something of a dissident movement on the part of some investigators, studies were initiated in response to the Smiths' unqualified endorsement of stilbestrol in pregnancy. In regions far from Boston, where the Smiths' Harvard background was less likely to inspire a dangerously uncritical awe, certain skeptical clinicians set out to test the Smiths' conviction that stilbestrol prevented a broad range of pregnancy problems. In

California, New York, Chicago, and New Orleans, stilbestrol was put through a series of rigorous trials, all of which insisted on comparing stilbestrol's usefulness to that of more traditional therapy, such as bed rest, sedation, and simple, proper medical attention.

The first of these studies was conducted at the U. S. Naval Hospital at Long Beach, California, by a naval commander and obstetrician named R. E. Crowder. In a report published in the *American Journal of Obstetrics and Gynecology* in the October 1950 issue, Commander Crowder introduced a salient fact which the recent enthusiasm over hormonal therapy had apparently begun to obscure: "Because 87% of all abortions are caused by defects in the ovum or other unavoidable maternal causes, only in 13% of abortions may the outcome be altered by therapy." With DES beginning to be routinely prescribed at the slightest hint of complications, or even sometimes without one, large numbers of obstetricians were knowingly exposing a sizable portion of their pregnant patients to the potential hazard of a controversial drug, from which less than 15 percent could even hope to benefit.

One hundred pregnant women who entered the clinic of the Naval Hospital at Long Beach, all diagnosed as cases of "threatened abortion" (defined by Crowder as suffering from "uterine bleeding in a pregnancy of less than 21 weeks duration") were selected for a test. Half were given large doses of stilbestrol on the Smith schedule. The other half were given nothing at all, simply the routine therapy of bed rest and sedation. At the end of the study, the women on stilbestrol had a "salvage rate" of only 51 percent. Of the women given bed rest and sedation, 57 percent carried their pregnancies to term. Crowder succinctly reported, "The results of our study indicate that stilbestrol did not increase the number of pregnancies salvaged. We have therefore concluded that stilbestrol is of no value in the treatment of threatened abortion."

In his discussion, Crowder pointed to recent evidence that effectively impeached the Smiths' fundamental and supporting concept:

> According to the Smiths, the mechanism through which stilbestrol prevents abortion is the stimulation of increased production of progesterone . . . that such is not the case

was shown by Davis and Fugo. If stilbestrol does not stimulate the increased production of progesterone, its use in threatened abortion has no theoretical basis.

Crowder also mentioned, in the conclusion of his striking report, the rather ominous cases of two women who "had to be curetted for continuous vaginal bleeding; the pathological diagnosis in these cases was 'endometrial hyperplasia,'" a condition known to be possibly cancerous. Crowder commented matter-of-factly, ". . . Probably the direct result of prolonged stilbestrol therapy." Crowder had rather diffidently planted here a warning sign to clinicians: Stilbestrol was not only of questionable merit in preventing miscarriage, it was potentially dangerous as well.

The next articulate voice of dissent emerged from New York City two years later. Drs. Robinson and Shettles of Columbia University's College of Physicians and Surgeons began a study in 1948 on DES, at the Sloane Hospital for Women of the Columbia Presbyterian Medical Center. In their report, published in the June 1952 issue of the *American Journal of Obstetrics and Gynecology,* the two doctors began by lamenting the current uncritical acceptance of stilbestrol:

> The synthetic estrogen, diethylstilbestrol, has recently become a popular form of therapy in threatened abortion. The public has been so frequently told of the virtues of this drug through articles appearing in lay journals, that it now requires a courageous physician to refuse this medication. The mass of pharmaceutical literature, extolling the wonders of this drug, has also rendered most practitioners amenable to his patient's demands. The understandable desire to do something positive toward rescuing a teetering pregnancy has resulted in the widespread use of stilbestrol in threatened abortion.

Fifty-one women entering the Sloane Hospital diagnosed as cases of threatened abortion were treated with stilbestrol. Forty-two identical cases were treated with "no specific therapy." At the end of treatment, Robinson and Shettles were in agreement with Crowder that stilbestrol had been of no use to prevent anything. In an attempt to provide a context for this conclusion, they wrote:

Threatened abortion is not a single disease entity. . . . It is an expression of multiple agents. . . . To expect, on theoretical grounds, that diethylstilbestrol should remedy all these factors appears inconceivable. The present study indicates that diethylstilbestrol is, in fact, a dismal failure in the general treatment of threatened abortion.

Between October 1950 and May 1952 an obstetrician on the staff of the Charity Hospital in New Orleans named James Henry Ferguson conducted the first truly controlled trial of the use of DES in pregnancy. Ferguson began his presentation in the March 1953 issue of the *American Journal of Obstetrics and Gynecology* with this blunt introduction:

A comparison will be made between a widely used dosage schedule of diethylstilbestrol and a placebo in their effect on pregnancy. Evidence will be presented that stilbestrol in these dosages has an effect that is extraordinarily similar to that of the placebo.

Ferguson did little to disguise his opinion of the Smiths' and other DES proponents' investigative methods. He wrote,

Much of the work done with stilbestrol can be challenged because of the poverty of controls. This delays the establishment of the true place of stilbestrol therapy in women. There seems to be a great deal of reluctance to match stilbestrol against the sugar pill. . . .

"It is impossible," Ferguson continued, "to give the same obstetric care to women treated with special medicine, as you give to patients who do not receive that medicine. The special group will inevitably receive more careful thought, more time, more sympathy, and unconsciously, decisions of management may be swayed." The Smiths had claimed that a comparison between two such groups was scientifically valid; Ferguson was implying here that the Smiths' unusually positive results in their stilbestrol-treated group could as well have been due to the heightened medical attention as to the stilbestrol itself.

At the conclusion of Ferguson's study, the effect of stilbestrol on pregnancy was clear-cut: "Stilbestrol had no effect on prematurity, fetal weight and survival, or the size of the placenta." As to the Smiths' highly publicized claims of a generally improved "stilbestrol-baby," Ferguson issued a simple denial: ". . . Stilbestrol babies did not seem to be any better than placebo babies."

The first respondent to Ferguson's study, Dr. R. Green of Chicago, found it difficult to restrain his satisfaction. His views appeared in the same issue of the *American Journal of Obstetrics and Gynecology.*

> Dr. Ferguson has demonstrated clearly and unequivocally that stilbestrol does not have the miraculous or even beneficial results claimed for it when administered to the normally pregnant woman. Furthermore, it does not cause babies born of treated mothers to be larger, healthier, or happier. Dr. Ferguson has, I believe, driven a very large nail into the coffin that we will someday use to bury the extremely outsized claims for stilbestrol.

Four months later, the fourth and most ambitious attack on the privileged and seemingly impervious position of stilbestrol was mounted at the center of the American obstetrical establishment. At the seventy-sixth annual meeting of the American Gynecological Society, at Lake Placid, New York, on June 16, 1953, Dr. William J. Dieckmann and associates at the University of Chicago presented the results of a double-blind study on the use of stilbestrol to prevent problems of pregnancy.

Dieckmann explained the motivation of conducting such an elaborate test on DES in the introduction to his paper published later in the November 1953 issue of the *American Journal of Obstetrics and Gynecology:*

> The laboratory experiments which provided the background for this interesting concept of the Smiths have lacked confirmation by other investigators. Davis and Fugo in two reports . . . noted that diethylstilbestrol did not result in an increased . . . output of progesterone . . . Sommerville, Marrian, and Clayton confirmed these observations. . . .

Following the path of Ferguson and others, Dieckmann went

on to criticize the Smiths' 1948 study, largely but not exclusively on the grounds of dubious methodology:

> The most severe criticism of this study is the lack of adequate controls. Subjects to whom medication is administered inevitably receive more scrupulous study and medical care than other patients cared for simultaneously. . . .

But more significant in Dieckmann's view than the Smiths' faulty methods was the fact that grander, more extravagant, and mostly illusory hopes were largely responsible for stilbestrol's stunning ascendancy:

> To prevent, postpone, or ameliorate some of the common hazards of childbirth for mothers and babies is certainly a worthy goal. That all this can be accomplished by the daily consumption of a few tablets is indeed enticing. . . .

Dieckmann and his colleagues had a total of 2,162 patients participate in their study, evenly divided between those who took stilbestrol and those who received placebos. The results, when finally computed, were as clear-cut as Ferguson's:

> Stilbestrol did not reduce the incidence of abortion, prematurity or postmaturity. Premature babies of stilbestrol treated mothers were not longer or more mature . . . than comparable prematures of placebo-treated mothers. . . .

In the following discussion, Dr. George van Siclen Smith attempted to meet this latest challenge to his and his wife's most cherished conclusions by displaying an elaborate sympathy for Dieckmann's "failure" to achieve "positive" results: "I realize how disappointed Dr. Dieckmann and his associates must be at getting negative results after putting so much thought, and expense into their carefully planned and well-carried-out experiment. . . ."

Smith shifted easily into the adversary position. He tried to question Dieckmann's conclusions by maintaining that his study was not really comparable to his. Because Dieckmann had admitted some women who were not pregnant for the first time into his test, while the Smiths' final study had selected only primigravidas, Smith insisted:

> The negative results reported and those recently published by Dr. Ferguson mean to us that not enough truly heterogeneous pregnancies were used. To break down such a series into truly comparable categories is difficult, if not impossible. . . . We too are disappointed, and apologetic, because we were instrumental in putting them to so much trouble in acquiring results that are still inconclusive. . . .

Whether Dieckmann's results were genuinely inconclusive was certainly a matter of Dr. Smith's opinion. But he did finally include the grudging admission: "We wish we had given placebo to our controls." Smith still persisted in viewing his omission of the placebo as relatively insignificant, and he concluded his remarks with a ringing endorsement of DES as the preferred preventer of miscarriage:

> Our experience with the use of stilbestrol continues to be satisfactory and to confirm our previously reported clinical results. We have never claimed that it is a panacea, but after ten years of careful study and observation of patients with bad and even hopeless prognoses . . . we are convinced that it has reduced the complications of late pregnancy and saved many babies. We trust that the many obstetricians who have been following our recommendations . . . will realize that the paper presented this morning and the report by Dr. Ferguson fail to provide evidence to the contrary.

Smith then gave the floor to his wife, who began by lamenting, "There are two major difficulties that Dr. George Smith and I have encountered in the controversy that has arisen over our work with stilbestrol." The first of these was that their "claims and conclusions concerning its beneficial action have been frequently misrepresented. . . ." She contended that she and her husband had never claimed DES was effective for the "treatment of pregnancy complications," but only to prevent them; that they had never claimed it was effective for preventing premature delivery or unexplained stillbirths. Then again, neither Dieckmann nor Ferguson, or for that matter, Crowder, or Robinson and Shettles, had represented them as claiming such benefits either.

Mrs. Smith's "second difficulty" was one her husband already had made reference to once that morning: ". . . The failure of other investigators, in attempting to repeat our experiments, to realize the importance of following the procedures adopted by us." Of course, Dieckmann had not scrupulously attempted to repeat the Smiths' experiments; it was precisely his methodological and philosophical divergence from the work of the Smiths which had provided the motive for his investigations. For Dieckmann and Ferguson, the procedures were precisely the point. Mrs. Smith concluded, somewhat circuitously:

> Our rationale for stilbestrol therapy, therefore, is something more than a philosophy. . . . It is not a panacea, but a therapeutic agent for the rational use of which there exists a sound rationale. . . .

A drug which had been so widely used across the country, on so slim a basis, had been exposed as entirely ineffective for the purposes for which it was marketed. Dr. Willard Allen of St. Louis, Missouri, commented:

> The one general conclusion to be drawn from this very painstaking study by Dieckmann . . . must be obvious to each of us; stilbestrol is no panacea. The original work of the Smiths in which estrogen was found to be useful . . . has, of course, been widely publicized. Many practicing physicians have come to believe that stilbestrol is a panacea. . . . It would seem to me, therefore, that these results [Dieckmann's] indicate that stilbestrol for routine use has little value.

It had been proven beyond reasonable scientific doubt, in a statistically significant, meticulously controlled trial, that DES did not do what it was supposed to do. The response from the DES manufacturers was equally simple: They did nothing. A drug was not legally required to be effective to be marketed. If they had a moral obligation to disclose the news to their customers, or to the medical profession, none of the DES makers elected to assume it.

They elected instead, to have the information suppressed.

66

This did not require intrigue or special tactics. They simply would not give notice; the news would be confined to the medical journals and to professional word-of-mouth. Of the normal channels open to the practicing physician to learn about drugs, the PDR, the package inserts, the detail men, and the medical journals, only the last was not a direct production of the industry. And only through that single channel did the bad news leak out.

None of the entries in The Physicians' Desk Reference were altered; none of the package inserts or instructions to the detail men revised; no circulars were circulated or "Dear Doctor" letters posted, to inform the public or the physician of the newly revised truth about DES. From the point of view of the practicing physician, left to his own resources, unable to perform his own tests or keep up with all the medical literature, nothing whatsoever had happened. As far as his PDR, his labeling material, and his friendly detail man would tell him, stilbestrol was still the most effective available prevention for the complications of pregnancy.

Sales peaked in 1953, the year the Dieckmann report was released. For those in the medical profession who had never believed in stilbestrol, Crowder's, Robinson and Shettles', Dieckmann's, and Ferguson's papers were simply vindications of a protracted skepticism. But for many practitioners, under pressure from anxious mothers to save their babies, some sort of program of relief was needed. Except for costly progesterone, DES was the only approved preventer of miscarriage on the market. In Dr. Dieckmann's well-chosen words, "That all this can be accomplished by the daily consumption of a few pills is indeed enticing. . . ."

Still, DES gradually fell out of favor with large portions of the medical profession as news of its inefficacy slowly spread. A feeling for the growing consensus in the upper echelons of the medical profession of the worthlessness of DES in pregnancy may be gleaned from a memorandum sent in 1950, three years before the Lake Placid conference, to Squibb's home office by one of its detail men. Misgivings of this high order were blithely ignored by the drug manufacturers:

> I got into a discussion today at Jewish Memorial Hospital
> with a group of outstanding Ob & Gyn men. . . . These
> men were all in agreement that the Smith and Smith ap-

proach to the problem of threatened abortion is of no value at all. Dr. Goodfried has been in touch with outstanding men all over the country and he says they hold the same opinion. . . . I don't know whether this kind of report is of any value to you. As for myself, I will continue to plug Stilbetin. . . .

Irving Sider to M.W.R. McGargue
November 17, 1950

Outstanding clinicians from all over the country were not overly impressed by the track record of DES. But these were merely opinions, exchanged privately among the elite of the profession. Mr. Sider's protestations of loyalty to his company and to his assigned preparation were just the permitted and established means by which the pharmaceutical industry was able effortlessly to override such an expanding consensus.

8

The Needhams found out about Anne's biopsy the first week of March. It was a very tension-filled time. There was nothing to say and nothing to do. They didn't have any big, tearing-apart discussions. They didn't tell the younger children. On Friday night, when the call finally came, Annie was home and Mary was home, and no one else was there. Annie answered the phone when it rang, but Jerry Warren wanted to speak to Mary first. Mary got on and he said, "Mary, we've got a serious problem here. It has to be taken care of immediately." There was a long pause, during which Mary said nothing.

Jerry said finally, "Mary, it's very bad news," and he told her what Anne had. Mary kept calm and said, "What should we do?" and Jerry told her, "I've called a radiologist, he's a specialist from the city in these sorts of cases. He'll be calling you in an hour." The specialist from the city called around ten. Annie was still in her room, and Mary couldn't disturb her. The specialist said he was very busy and he couldn't see them for several weeks, but if they wanted they could come to a technical seminar he was holding in the city and they could see what was commonly done in cases of this type.

Mary pulled herself together long enough to ask, "Will you see my daughter at that time?" There was a long pause at the other end. Mary went on: "Should she bring her clothes for the hospital?" and there was another pause. Mary asked, "Will you see her? Will you see her at that time?" and the specialist from the city cleared his throat and said, "Uh, probably not." At that point

Mary felt like breaking down but instead she sighed, "I don't know what to do." The specialist said, "Who is it that's sick anyway, you or your daughter?" Mary could hardly believe this man. She thanked him very much for his time and hung up.

Monday morning Mary went to work at Marshall Field's. A woman named Betty asked if something was wrong. At first Mary denied it. She said, "No, no, nothing's wrong. I'm just not feeling well, that's all." But later Betty kept looking at her in this funny way and came over and said, "Mary, something is drastically wrong." And Mary said, "Anne has cancer." Betty said, "Oh my God." Then: "What are you going to do?"

Mary mentioned that next week she was supposed to go into Chicago to take Anne to a seminar. Betty asked, "Why don't you go up to Rochester?" Mary knew she meant the Mayo Clinic. She shook her head and said, "I don't know anybody there. I don't know what to do." Betty told Mary her brother had had lung cancer and they'd called Mayo's that summer, and they took him right in and operated, and now he was fine. Betty put her hand on Mary's shoulder and said, "The less time you waste, the better off you'll be." It was then eleven in the morning.

Mary took her break, went home, and called the Mayo Clinic at noon. She called the main switchboard because she didn't know whom to contact. They put her right through to the gynecology clinic. The woman there told Mary not to be upset, they'd make an appointment right away. She told her to be at the clinic early Wednesday morning, before eight. Mary hung up and felt so much better for having made that one simple connection.

The next twenty-four hours went by. The point was to get Anne to Rochester, and that was all anyone was thinking about. On Monday night Annie went to Marshall Field's to get a nightgown for the hospital, because she had absolutely nothing to wear. She went in and saw her boss and told her she was going to Mayo's. One of the store detectives, a big woman, came up during the discussion and asked, "What do you mean you're going to Mayo's?" Anne said, "I'm going up to take some tests," and this woman asked, "Tests for what?" Anne looked down at the nightgown she'd just picked out and it came right out: "Possible cancer." Of course, Anne knew what it was but she had hesitated because she didn't want this woman blabbing it all over the store.

When they left for Rochester Tuesday afternoon, they were

late getting started. Mary called Dr. Warren's office in the morning and didn't even ask if he was there. She just left a message with the girl: "I'm taking Anne to Rochester." It wouldn't have mattered anyway what he'd said; if he'd told her she and Anne would be killed on the road it wouldn't have made any difference. They were committed, they were leaving, and at least it felt like finally something was being done. They left and were driving half an hour when Anne said, "Oh, Mom, I forgot the pathology slides." They had to turn right around and go back.

It's over three hundred miles from Park Forest to Rochester. They didn't get going again until after three. They drove west out of Chicago on 90, then north on 90 into Wisconsin. It was almost dark as they passed the state line, and they started running into snow. The expressway was clear but the land off to the sides was all snow and ice and mud. The spring thaw was just setting in, and everything around had been melting.

They were driving along and suddenly something was wrong —the car wheels were spinning but they weren't going anywhere. They had momentum but no power. It was just getting dark and Mary was driving because Anne had been feeling kind of faint. They pulled off the highway in a tiny little town in Wisconsin and looked for a gas station. The first place they stopped was closing. The man was just turning off his lights and he said, "I can't help you anyway, try across the road. They've got a mechanic."

They looked across the road at this terrible place. It was a little roadside joint with some gas pumps off to the side. Mary thought, "I don't want my daughter in some place like that." It had filthy windows and practically no paint, and mud and snow were plowed all around it. You could hardly see inside, the windows were so dirty. Mary told Annie to stay in the car and roll up the windows and she got out to take a good look.

The garage was a gray cement-block building. There was a truck stop next door with some big semitrailers parked all around it. Inside, a couple of young kids were working on a car. They paid no attention to her, but finally a man came up and Mary said, "I have a very difficult problem. My car isn't acting right and I have to get my daughter to Mayo's by eight in the morning. She's critically ill."

He was young, thin, without much hair. His hands were dirty, his green uniform was dirty. But Mary felt strength in him, right away. He asked, "What's the matter with your car?" Mary hung her head and said, "The car hangs in mid-air. It doesn't have any power."

He walked straight over to the car and got right in. Mary didn't want a strange man alone with her beautiful daughter, so she got in too, in the back. Anne was slumped down in the front, moody and completely despondent. She didn't seem to care what was going on, whether she'd ever get there or not. They drove a little ways, and the mechanic said, "You've got a bad bearing."

He drove the car into the garage, and right away he had all those young fellows working on it. Anne got out, obviously disgusted with the place, and Mary said cheerfully, "Let's go get something to eat." From the moment Mary knew Anne had cancer, she hadn't once let sadness slip into her voice. The mechanic said, "The soup over there is really great." Mary said brightly, "Oh, what a good idea."

They went into the truck stop and sat down at a booth. They ordered soup and sandwiches. When the food came, neither of them could eat a thing. They just sat there sipping soup and coffee and staring out the window. They did that for at least two hours. When they got back, the men were still working on the car. The mechanic had had to send one of his men off somewhere else to get a spare part. Mary went up and said to him wearily, "We have to do something. I have to get my daughter up there by morning."

The mechanic didn't even stop working. He just said, "Don't worry, lady, we'll get you there." Mary leaned over him and whispered, "It's only just a matter of time. I don't want my daughter to know how desperate we are. She has cancer."

He didn't even nod or blink. He said quietly, "I know she has cancer." He quickly opened his shirt and pointed to a long thin red seam down his chest. "I had lung cancer," he said. "I went up to Mayo's and they saved my life." He told her he had been in Vietnam, and then right after coming home he had gone through that. He went right back to work on the Mustang; Mary loved that Mustang.

After working another hour and patching a tire, he filled up the car with gas and finally got it going. He put his hand on Mary's shoulder. "Don't worry," he said. "She'll be all right." Mary asked him what they owed him and he named a figure so low it was practically nothing. He looked at Annie and then at

Mary and said in a low voice, "I don't know if you're ever coming back here, lady, but I'll sure pray for you." Mary started to cry, and said, "We'll pray for you too." She said if she was ever driving through again she'd stop and look for him. She did stop, several times, but each time she stopped at that place he was never there.

They were driving again—it was past one o'clock and they were less than halfway there. Annie turned to Mary and said, "Mom, I think we ought to go home." Mary asked, "Why, Anne?" She said, "Maybe God's trying to tell us something. We forgot the slides and the car broke down and maybe He just doesn't want us to get there." Anne was thinking there was probably nothing they'd be able to do. She thought it was too far gone. In Chicago, they were saying, "Maybe we can do something with radiation"; it all seemed so up in the air. Mary looked out the windshield at the road and said, "We've gotten this close, we've got to keep going." That was the end of that.

They got into Rochester after four. They went first to the wrong place. They had a reservation at a Holiday Inn just outside of town but they got off at the exit for downtown Rochester and went to the wrong Holiday Inn. When they finally got out to the right place it was nearly five, and even after they got into bed, neither of them could sleep. At about six they started getting dressed to go to the hospital. They'd been told to be at the clinic before eight to check in. They were there before seven.

The clinic is a tall building in downtown Rochester, right by the Methodist Hospital. The first floor is nothing but a huge reception area with a reception desk and a large contingent of staff people. They had to go through that screening area to get their assignment for a floor. They were the first ones in the waiting room. Anne got her little cards and paper, and they sat there until after eleven when they were finally sent up to a floor.

They waited in a second room for another few hours. It was after one when Anne had her first interview. Mary got up a few times to walk around, but Anne stayed slumped in her chair. She didn't feel much like walking around. She had been fasting because she knew she was going to have to take tests. She hadn't had as much as a drink of water all morning. Neither of them had had any sleep, and they were physically and mentally exhausted. A doctor came out and finally interviewed Anne in his office for about forty-five minutes.

He took her case history. She gave him her slides. He took another biopsy. The clinic has seventeen floors, and all the tests were on different floors. Anne's tests were programmed into a computer so they could be taken in proper sequence. They kept her moving all day from level to level, up and down in superfast elevators.

Some of the tests were so painful she could hardly walk. Mary decided they couldn't stay so far away from everything, so while Anne was in taking tests Mary checked out of the Holiday Inn and moved their things to the Kahler Hotel, catty-corner to the clinic. Because the winter weather in Rochester is so impossible, the hospitals and hotels in the downtown area are connected by tunnels. If Anne got really sick Mary could put her in a wheelchair and take her from the hotel to almost anywhere downtown without going outside.

Anne went to Ten West to meet Dr. Symmonds, the head of the Gynecology Department, who would be her surgeon. He came into the plain white office where Anne was sitting and said, "This is probably what we're going to do with you." He was holding a small plastic mold with which he demonstrated the operation. He explained the structure of the vagina and said they would probably be removing a large section of it and most of her female organs. He wanted Anne to know there was a strong possibility they'd have to do some radiation therapy after surgery. But he was hopeful they'd be able to eliminate the tumors without it.

Afterwards, the doctors examined her again with the colposcope, an instrument used to examine the vagina. They did some staining, which was incredibly painful. Anne was in such a daze it hardly mattered, but she must have had fifteen or twenty doctors coming in to look at her when she was being examined. Dr. Symmonds said hers was the third case of that cancer they had had at the clinic. The doctors kept coming in and telling Dr. Symmonds, "She's such a good patient." But Anne kept thinking, "What am I supposed to do?" She knew it was a learning experience for them. The parade of doctors didn't phase her a bit, which was strange because she'd always been so modest. She had always been the one to lock the door to the bathroom, so no one could even come in to get something.

Wednesday's procedures didn't end until after five. Anne could barely stand up. As she hobbled back through the tunnel to the Kahler, she was glad her mother had changed hotels. She was allowed to have something to eat, the first thing all day. But she felt so bad all she could get down was a little cup of soup, then she went upstairs to bed. She knocked herself out with a sleeping pill because of the pain from the tests and because she had to get back over there first thing in the morning for another round of tests.

Thursday was more of the same, but there was a good deal more blood. Many of the procedures were hard on the body; she had never felt pain like that. The whole time she just kept trying her best to tune it all out, the pain, the blood, the thoughts. She couldn't help thinking about the operation ahead, even though she tried not to. Mostly she was frightened they wouldn't be able to cut it out. Dr. Warren had told her he'd found two ulcers, one the size of a dime, the other the size of a nickel. But when Dr. Symmonds had described them he'd used different coin sizes: one was a nickel, the other a quarter. Anne couldn't help but keep thinking, "It must have grown that much in a week." She couldn't help but keep thinking, "It must be attacking other organs."

They called Mary in that afternoon just as Anne was getting dressed. There were three or four doctors in the room. Dr. Symmonds picked up a plastic cross-section of the uterus and showed her exactly what they were going to do, and how they were going to do it. He said, "We'd like her to go into the hospital right now." Mary stood there for a moment and said, "Now?" He said, "Yes. Today." It was just going on a quarter of four, and he wanted them in before five.

Anne was standing out in the hall wondering, "What are they telling her in there?" She was in awful pain and dying for someplace to sit down. Mary came out trying to pronounce this word to herself: "adenocarcinoma." She was sure she must have heard it wrong. She thought her mind was just not absorbing the name. Here was her daughter whom she was afraid God was going to snatch right away any moment, and they were telling her it was this whatever it was. Mary thought, "They're kidding me." They went back and picked up Annie's things and went over to check into Rochester Methodist Hospital. Anne got a nice room and a nice roommate, a sweet woman from South Dakota. She and Mary talked about Europe.

Anne had to be up at six in the morning to be on the table by eight. They told Mary to be there by six, so she was there at five-thirty. They came in and put Anne on the cart, and they gave her Demerol, and atropine to dry up secretions. They had a piece of tape across her forehead, and she was flying pretty high. When she finally got downstairs she tried as hard as she could not to go to sleep. She was going to stay awake as long as she could, until the last minute. She was scared that when she went to sleep, she wouldn't ever wake up.

She was lined up in a waiting room with three other women. They all just lay there gabbing. One little girl who was getting her tonsils out kept asking, "Are *your* walls moving?" A little old lady about sixty years old kept moaning and muttering, and there were two more women Anne couldn't make out. It was like they were lying in some little room all high on drugs.

It was the sixth of April, 1960, and Vic and Mary were on their way to Des Moines to go to a seminar. Mary knew she was pregnant again, with her seventh child. In the car she was sure she was going to miscarry, she got that terrible heavy feeling and she lay down in the back seat most of the way to Des Moines.

In the morning instead of going over to the campus she went downtown and called up her old obstetrician. She said, "I've got some problems here. Can you see me?" He said, "Come down right away." Mary went down and he started the exam and he cussed a few well known phrases. He said, "Don't let them kill you, Mary, don't let them do this to you." He didn't even bother to finish the exam. "Go ahead, get your clothes on," he said. It was as if he was disgusted at her for letting herself be forced into this situation of having more and more children. He told her she would be able to carry her child, but she shouldn't leave that hospital until the hysterectomy was performed.

Mary went home to Victor's parents' house, the big old house the Needhams had, and she went in. There was Vic sitting in the kitchen with his mother, drinking tea. Mary stood in the door with them staring at her; she was very upset.

Mary said, "The doctor says I have to have that repair work done right away."

Vic's mother looked at her like she was crazy, and said, "Ah, you just don't want to be having more children."

Victor looked away from her with a dark face. He muttered, "You won't be a woman anymore."

Mary walked straight to the river. By then it was dark and she walked along the river, sure she was going to throw herself in. All she could think of was Vic and his mother and she didn't see any reason to keep going. It was early in April but it was very cold, and Mary stood a long time looking at the water. A nicely dressed man came up and asked, "What's the matter?" Mary just shook her head and wouldn't say anything. The man looked her right in the eye and said, "Nothing is ever that bad." He didn't say anything more, but he took her by the arm and walked her away from the water.

On Friday morning, March 9, Dr. Richard Symmonds performed a radical hysterectomy, making a wide clearance of the malignancy by removing a large block of tissue: the uterus and cervix. A partial vaginectomy followed, comprising the removal of most of the upper part of Anne's vagina: 80 percent of the vaginal tract. The cavity created by this massive removal was packed with gauze to prevent its closure. The packing was allowed to remain in the opening for about ten days. In that time the residual vagina would heal. The lymph nodes showed no signs of malignancy, so they and the ovaries were preserved intact. The operation took the entire morning and most of the afternoon.

Mary stayed upstairs in Anne's room. She was afraid to leave because something might happen. About four in the afternoon, Dr. Symmonds came to where Mary was waiting in the hall, right down the hall from Anne's room. He said, "We'll have to go back in to do some more surgery. We're waiting until Anne gets a little stronger." Mary took him aside and whispered, "I have to tell you something." Dr. Symmonds looked concerned and asked, "What is it?" The tears started running down Mary's face, she wasn't making any noise but the tears were running down, and he said, "What's the matter?"

Mary said, "I don't have any money." He said lightly, "Oh, that's all right." Mary told him very slowly: "I don't think you understand what I'm saying to you. I don't have *any* money." The doctor took Mary by the arm and asked, "Mrs. Needham, do you have a problem?" and Mary said, "Yes. I do." Dr. Symmonds asked, "What is your problem?" and Mary said, "My daughter is ill." He asked, "Nothing else in the world matters, does it?" and she said, "No." He smiled and said, "That's the way I feel too. We don't have any problems at the moment except to get Anne well."

About an hour later two nurses came up and said, "Mrs. Needham, we have to take you down to Pathology." Mary asked, "Is it necessary?" and they said, "Yes." Mary thought maybe she'd see Annie. Maybe they had her down there. They went down to the second floor, and they walked along the corridor one nurse to each side of her, and they kept asking, "Are you all right?" and Mary kept saying, "I'm fine." She even tried to joke with them a little, but the jokes she made were pretty lame.

They walked into this little room, about six feet wide by ten feet deep. Mary was standing by the door and a big man wearing a mask came up. He was so big he had to bend over to see her. He said in a deep voice, "Mrs. Needham, will you come over here?" She went over there. He turned and walked across the room to get something, and he came back holding a platter, a china platter.

The platter had a big piece of gauze over it. He set it down on the counter in front of her, and Mary said, "Oh no. *No!*" He said, "Mrs. Needham, will you look at this?" and she sat down on a chair and said, "I guess that's what you brought me down here for. I'm all right now, I'm sorry." He pulled back the gauze and showed her the part of Anne's vagina that had the cancer in it. It was very clean, there was no blood. It was just like a piece of meat. He said, "This is what we took out of Anne. We just wanted to show it to you so you would know what we're dealing with here." It was like a huge mouth all swollen. Shooting out all around it was the cancer, radiating.

They brought Mary down to the Recovery Room. Anne lay there on her rolling bed, tubes out of every arm, out of her nose, and out of her mouth. Two tubes came out of her middle: one from her stomach, another from her vagina. She was completely out of it, but she knew her mother's voice. She kept moaning, "Mom, Mom, I've got bedsores." Mary said, over and over, "You can't have bedsores, sweetheart, you've only been here two days."

The next morning a nurse came in and made Anne stand up and walk around the bed. It was like some sort of nightmare, where she had to keep walking uphill with long needles stuck in her middle. She'd never felt pain like that. It was just for her body, to keep it functioning, but her mind could hardly take it. All the time as she made those circles around the bed she was on the point of crying.

The nurses were all wonderful. Some of them were mothers who would sit and cry right along with Mary. They'd put their arms right around her and say, "I know just how you feel." There were a couple of beautiful young nurses there who felt so much for Anne, they'd sit and talk with her for hours. Some got so attached to her, they gave her twenty-four-hour nurse service without thinking anything of it. They stayed with Mary and they stayed with Anne, and they did every little thing they could.

For three days Anne kept waking up and saying, "Mom, Mom, my butt still hurts." Finally Mary insisted that the doctors take a look, because no one knew what it was. No one could see because her body was encased in bandages and packing. She was in terrible pain down there. They finally found what the sores were about when they took the bandages off.

They had used two kinds of Merthiolate to cleanse the area. They had started above the chest with red Merthiolate, and continued below the waist with white. For the first surgery they had put her in stirrups with her legs way up and her rear down, and they took the white Merthiolate and poured it all over her. Her rear had lain in pools of white Merthiolate for hours. She developed terrible burns.

No one had known she was allergic to white Merthiolate. Soon they found she was also allergic to red. The second day after the surgery, she broke out in hives on her chest, where they had swabbed the red Merthiolate. Then it became clear she was allergic to the adhesive tape: when they tried to pull the tape off, her skin just came up with it. With the burns and the hives and the skin chafing from the bandages, the pain was almost worse than the pain from what they'd cut out.

It might have been partly from all the medication, but Anne was having terrible nightmares. They were mostly about insects, bugs, and crawling things. Anne would wake up screaming at night, and there'd always be a nurse sitting there, holding her hand. She would be so terrified, the nurses would sit and talk and calm her down. It was partly because her body was so creepy with the hives and the burns, it always felt like giant insects and crabs trying to get her.

Anne developed claustrophobia. They kept giving her oxygen to breathe. She'd fight off the mask because it made her feel enclosed. She was so cramped down, her arms were tied down, she could hardly move a muscle. The doctors had been having problems with the IVs, which kept slipping and popping out and losing the vein, and her arms would swell up horribly. They started taping her arms to a wooden board so she couldn't move. She had a catheter and drainage tubes and a tube up her nose and one down her throat, so she could hardly breathe. It got so bad she felt she was suffocating, and for months after the surgery she couldn't ride in a crowded elevator without panicking.

Ten days after the first operation, they performed the second surgery. On March 18, they reconstructed the vagina using a skin graft. Dr. Symmonds took a split-thickness graft; he shaved a partial thickness of skin from her left buttock and pulled this skin over a foam rubber mold which was inserted into the cavity left by the first operation. That mold was removed in a third operation ten days later and replaced with a clear polystyrene one she would wear for up to a year.

Anne thought Dr. Symmonds was a real sweetie, but he had two young doctors working with him, and one of them was a real jerk. When Dr. Symmonds would come into the room, he was always really breezy: "How's this beautiful young girl doing?" But when this one young assistant was taking Anne down to her second surgery, he asked, "Did they start you on your hormones yet?" Anne said, "What hormones?" She was drugged and going along on the cart. He said, "They took your ovaries out." Anne got upset and shouted, "They didn't take my ovaries out! What are you talking about?" She was just going under the anesthetic but she thought maybe they were keeping something from her. It later turned out he was completely wrong; he was just mixing up cases.

The other young doctor was really nice. He was handsome and charming. He was also concerned; he'd come up to sit and talk. He started coming around so much Anne's mom started saying, "Why don't you put some makeup on?" But Anne wasn't really up for socializing. Still, this young doctor coming up and being attentive made her start to feel a little better about herself. She'd come out of the second surgery thinking about what her dad had told her mother when she was about to have her hysterectomy: "You won't be a woman anymore." Now it had happened to her, and all she could think of was that line: that was the first time she cried.

After the second surgery, Anne started turning down shots. The doctor came in to administer the shot, and Anne said, "I'm just too dopey, can't you give me some sort of pill? I'm higher than a kite." So he tried some Darvon Compound 65, but it just didn't work like those Demerol shots. She ended up throwing in the towel on that. Being high as a kite wasn't so bad, but her eyes couldn't focus in to read a book. Her degree of concentration seemed to fade, until she just wandered around in her mind.

It was sad that she couldn't read things. She was getting thirty to forty postcards a day. She was able to get one arm free, and she'd try to pick up a card and read it. But most of the time her eyes wouldn't focus and her mother would read them to her. All their friends from Park Forest, and all the people from Marshall Field's, the ones that knew Anne and even some that didn't, wrote. Anne was fuzzy.

John called all the time. One time she was lying on her side, and she told him, "I'm just getting a shot right now." She got the shot and she could hear herself saying slowly, "I think I'd better . . . go. . . ."

After the surgery, she started feeling more positive about life. She started seeing things differently. For one thing, it just wasn't as easy to take things for granted. She started cherishing special moments, times, and things. She started feeling almost like a baby, the way every little thing makes a baby happy. She started looking around herself, and thinking, "I'm all right. I'm here. I'm fine."

The flight path of the Canadian honkers is right over Rochester. When Anne went into the hospital at the beginning of March, it was still winter. By the time she got out, it was spring. There was a lake not far from the hospital where the Canadian geese would swoop down and land. Anne would sit up in bed by the window and watch them fly by for hours. They were gorgeous, just hundreds and thousands of them taking off and landing. They are big, with long necks and big bodies and an enormous wing span. It wasn't grass and trees out there; just a parking lot with apartment buildings off in the distance. But she would watch those big beautiful birds fly by and think, "They're beautiful, just beautiful."

PART II

9

In 1966, a fifteen-year-old girl walked into the Vincent Memorial Hospital in Boston, a division of Massachusetts General Hospital, complaining of continuous and irregular vaginal bleeding which had been going on for at least six months. Her past history, as far as the examining doctors were able to tell, was entirely unremarkable. There was no immediate sign of infection. Her previous doctor had prescribed estrogens to control the bleeding, but they had been ineffective. He had never performed a vaginal examination. Two months before she was admitted to Vincent Memorial, she began suffering more heavy bleeding, accompanied by an unpleasant discharge.

At that time, she was referred by her doctor to a hospital where she underwent a complete vaginal examination under anesthesia. A tumor was located near her urethra on the vaginal wall. The doctors removed this nodule and found under a microscope that it revealed signs of being an extremely rare form of cancer known as "adenocarcinoma." The girl was referred to Massachusetts General Hospital for further treatment and possibly further surgery.

The doctors at Mass General were surprised and baffled by the appearance of such a rare tumor in a girl so young. Vaginal cancer is extremely rare, comprising less than 2 percent of all female reproductive-tract cancers. And of these, vaginal adenocarcinoma represented an infinitesimal quantity. When it had occurred in medical history, it had always appeared in women over fifty. Here the girl was only fifteen, and the doctors were forced to consider her a tragic but rather fascinating medical anomaly: not a single case of this disease had ever been seen at Massachusetts General.

The only measure left to be taken was taken. She underwent immediate and radical surgery. The first step was a radical hysterectomy: the removal of the uterus and cervix, including a great deal of tissue adjacent to the bladder and rectum. This was followed by a vaginectomy: the complete removal of the vagina. In a second operation, the vagina was replaced by a skin graft which was inserted stretched over a plastic mold. Two years after this surgery, the girl possessed a new, functioning vagina and was diagnosed as being entirely free of tumors.

Clear-cell adenocarcinoma is a type of cancer in which glandular cells of a malignant nature have grown in the vagina. It is characterized by the presence of glandular cells, tubules, and cysts. The benign form of this disorder is called "adenosis," where spots of glandular tissue infiltrate the vagina. The mass of malignant tissue removed from the girl's body contained numerous scattered glands, and three lymph nodes on her right side had become afflicted by the cancer. The girl was released from care and lived, a medically rare specimen, an anomaly: a young girl who had a rare, almost unheard-of disease years before any doctor could have reasonably expected it.

A few months later, another fifteen-year-old girl entered the clinic at Vincent Memorial complaining of similar symptoms. She too had been suffering from an unpleasant and frequent vaginal discharge which had been ongoing for about six months. After examination she was found to be suffering from a tumor occupying two-thirds of her vaginal wall. Under a microscope it was identified as adenocarcinoma. It was removed without the need for radical vaginectomy, but for a year after the operation, the girl was required to wear a plastic mold around which her residual vagina could heal.

The appearance of two such medical rarities in one city and at one hospital simply might have been an astounding coincidence. But the anomaly enlarged to a full-blown mystery when yet a third young girl, sixteen years old, entered the Vincent Memorial clinic with an eighteen-month history of severe and unexplained vaginal bleeding. As with the two other girls, her past history before the onset of the present illness was not unusual. But in her case, the physician consulted when the bleeding began had put her on cyclic hormone therapy for one year to control the bleeding. As with the first girl, estrogens did nothing of the kind. Other drugs were substituted, but the bleeding continued. She began to complain of incessant fatigue and abnormal pains in her legs. In the three months before she was finally hospitalized she lost eleven pounds. In the eighteen months during which she was under a physician's care, the doctor did not perform a vaginal exam.

After she was admitted to Massachusetts General Hospital, she was found to have a large mass of malignant tissue entirely filling her vagina. A biopsy was taken which showed adenocarcinoma, and when they explored her abdomen, it was found that her cancer had spread from the pelvis to the diaphragm. Surgery at this stage was impossible: she was discharged for chemotherapy, but after six months, the girl died.

From 1966 to 1969, in less than three years, four more young women who had been referred to the Vincent Memorial Hospital were diagnosed as having clear-cell adenocarcinoma. Each woman entered complaining of irregular vaginal bleeding. The next was only eighteen, a student nurse, and was successfully operated on after her biopsy revealed "sheets and nests of large cells . . . bizarre, hyperchromatic nuclei . . . ," all malignant cells.

Each of the women seen at Vincent Memorial in that three-year period was under twenty-two. In all of medical literature only seven cases of adenocarcinoma could be found; most of these reports were found in older, foreign publications and were extremely sketchy. And in none of those cases was the patient under fifty; that is, below menopausal age. So little was known about this disease that the doctors at Mass General were understandably bewildered as to how so many separate incidents could possibly have surfaced at one hospital in so brief a time: three years had produced a clustering of cases denser than that reported in all of medical history.

Dr. Arthur L. Herbst, a clinical associate in obstetrics and gynecology at Harvard Medical School, was in charge of some of these cases at Massachusetts General and had written extensively on vaginal cancer. Joined by a pathologist at the Harvard Medical School, Dr. Robert E. Scully, he began to prepare data for a report on the strange case of these seven girls all in the same city, all struck by this frightening unexplained malady. They published their preliminary findings in the April 1970 issue of *Cancer,* in which they simply stated the mystery and rendered the seven perplexing case histories.

They began by pointing out that in each case, "Hormonal therapy delayed the correct diagnosis, which was not made until vaginal examination was performed." They were highly critical of the widely accepted clinical practice of treating such bleeding routinely with hormones, without a full investigation of the cause. In the case of the girl who died, it was obvious that eighteen months of consistent bleeding without a complete physical check had so delayed a correct diagnosis that the girl's life had been forfeited.

Herbst and Scully discussed their preference for surgery over radiation in the treatment of these tumors. Here again, the doctors had little in past medical history to go on: "There are few cases of vaginal adenocarcinoma documented adequately as far as therapy is concerned," they wrote. In the case of these seven young girls, the surgeons in charge had elected to perform immediate surgery precisely because the patients were so young, and "the use of surgery avoids large cancerocidal doses of radiation to the pelvic viscera, and an artificial menopause." Also: "The vaginal canals that were constructed became soft, flexible structures, and were preferable to the scarred canals . . . that may occur after heavy irradiation."

Still, such notable if tragic success in treatment of these exotic cancers only emphasized a corresponding lack of success in locating a cause for their mysterious appearance. After the seven original cases had been documented, Herbst and Scully heard of an eighth identical case treated at another Boston hospital. This rare disease was assuming the aspect of a minor epidemic.

When such a bewildering concurrence of medical cases occurs, physicians consult an epidemiologist, who is literally an expert in epidemics. Since cancer is not a contagious disease, the services of an epidemiologist in a cancer study might be considered something of an irrelevancy. But one of the most perplexing characteristics of cancer is that it can often afflict persons of a specific background, or who live in a certain location. Because cancer is so often caused or stimulated by a wide variety of environmental, geographic, and genetic factors, a cancer epidemiologist will look at a cluster of cases and attempt to analyze all available data which can be gathered concerning the patients and the disease.

Herbst called upon Dr. David Poskanzer to be the epidemiologist on the project. Armed with the eight case histories and practically nothing else, Herbst and Poskanzer set out to find out what it was that had struck down these girls, and why it had struck only them. Dr. Howard Ulfelder, chief of the Department of Gynecology at Vincent Memorial, had published several papers with Herbst on vaginal carcinoma. He joined the investigation team. Dr. Scully, as a pathologist, did not participate in the epidemiological study.

Two of the most striking and significant similarities in the cases were age and the practically simultaneous appearance of symptoms all within three years. Since all but one of the cases were found to display some evidence of accompanying adenosis, the existence of glandular tissue of a distorted but benign nature, attention was initially focused on that. Historically, adenosis had only appeared in older women; now it was appearing in young girls. But little more was known about adenosis than about its malignant cousin, adenocarcinoma. The investigators had to look for some common factor in the histories of these girls which would point them toward the origin of both.

That did not prove easy. Each of the seven living patients was questioned closely as to the use of or exposure to substances which might reasonably have led to the initiation or spread of malignancy. None of the girls were found to have been exposed to the same intravaginal irritant, douches, or tampon. Only one of the girls had had sexual experience, so sexual activity had to be ruled out. Before the beginning of the vaginal bleeding, none of the girls had taken birth control pills.

Since the medical histories of the girls themselves apparently could not provide any help or clue to the cause of their misfortune, Herbst, Ulfelder, and Poskanzer decided to conduct a classic retrospective, case-control epidemiologic study. In such a study, a control goup is selected which corresponds as closely as possible to the group under investigation. Herbst and his associates went to the hospital where each of their eight subjects was born. They examined birth records and selected females born within five days of each of their seven girls and born also on the same type of maternity service, ward or private.

The thirty-two young women who could be located were joined by their families. The failure to obtain any significant common factor in the girls' own medical histories indicated that other unknown factors might be involved: genetic and other inherited characteristics, personal habits of the parents, environmental factors. The investigators cast a wider exploratory net in the hope of uncovering some common factor which might be a clue to the cause.

Herbst, Ulfelder, and Poskanzer drew up a standard questionnaire to be answered by the girls and their families. The questionnaire drawn up by the team included a wide range of possible factors. They asked both the control and the patient groups about birth weight, age at onset of menstruation, childhood diseases of both mothers and patients, history of tonsillectomy, childhood ingestions of all kinds, household pets, notable illnesses of both daughters and mothers, cosmetic use in daughters and mothers, cigarette smoking in parents and patients, alcohol consumption in parents, breast feeding, and intrauterine X-ray exposure.

Analysis of all these factors revealed no significant difference between the control group and the patient group in any of these categories. The possible exception was cigarette smoking: seven out of the eight patients with cancer had mothers who smoked at least ten cigarettes per day before the birth of their child. But it turned out twenty-one out of the thirty-two control group mothers smoked at least as much.

The investigation might have ended there. But one day the mother of one of Howard Ulfelder's patients mentioned something in a hospital elevator: She had taken something while she was pregnant with her daughter; some sort of vitamin, or hormone. The investigators cautiously added prenatal hormones to their list of questions.

When the results came back, there was reason for both congratulation and alarm. Out of the eight mothers of the girls struck by the cancer, seven had definitely taken diethylstilbestrol during pregnancy. None of the thirty-two control mothers had taken estrogens during pregnancy.

All the mothers who had taken stilbestrol had begun taking it in the first trimester of pregnancy; some had received a constant dose throughout, some had been given a gradually increasing dose almost to term, as in the Smith and Smith recommendations. The initial mystery of causation had apparently been solved, for which the investigators could be congratulated; but a new and alarming mystery had been introduced: how great a risk did this surprising factor pose to how great a population?

Herbst and his associates had found a likely cause for this cancer. But scientists may not employ the term "cause" to describe a connection such as that uncovered here; since it is not known how cancer develops, such a carcinogen as stilbestrol could only be termed a "primary factor" in the development of these tumors; the term Herbst scrupulously used was "association." The degree of association between the treatment of mothers with diethylstilbestrol and the development of adenocarcinoma in their daughters was described by Herbst and his team as "highly significant."

In order to calculate the risk of development of these tumors in the female offspring, Herbst and colleagues requested the records of a special high-risk pregnancy clinic of the Boston Lying-In Hospital for the years 1946 through 1951, the years in which the affected girls were born. Out of about 14,500 deliveries, stilbestrol had been prescribed to 675 ward patients, or about 1 out of 21 patients. Herbst and his team concluded, "Whatever the risk of tumor development in the exposed offspring, it appears to be small." But unfortunately, no one had any idea how many women in the United States had received stilbestrol during pregnancy: estimates ranged from 500,000 to more than 2,000,000.

Herbst sent his material as soon as it could be organized to the *New England Journal of Medicine* for immediate publication. He then took his raw data sheets and requested that the editor of the *New England Journal* send them immediately to the FDA. The paper was due for publication in April of 1971. In early March, Dr. Franz Inglefinger, editor of the journal, sent the manuscript and data to the FDA in Washington in the expectation that the agency would act. A few days later, he received a phone call acknowledging receipt of the letter and requesting more information. Early in April, Herbst sent more data. He and Inglefinger patiently waited for something to happen.

The publication of the Herbst study in the *New England Journal of Medicine* on April 22, 1971, marked the first time in scientific history that a specific cancer had been so authoritatively linked to a specific environmental source. Because adenocarcinoma is so extremely rare, positive identification of the offending agent was possible: If stilbestrol had caused a much more common form of cancer, such as cervical cancer, the connection could never have been so definitively made.

Herbst's link of stilbestrol ingestion to cancer in the female offspring was also a scientific first, because it was the first time that a carcinogen had been found to pass through the placental barrier and affect the fetus growing in the womb. Science had in past decades been learning more about an action described as "teratogenesis," which means, literally, "monster-making." A teratogen is a substance capable of passing through the placental barrier, from the maternal into the fetal circulation, to exert changes on the growing fetus. A great deal of scientific attention had been directed toward understanding teratogenesis and uncovering possible teratogens since the notorious thalidomide disaster of the early 1960s, in which a nonnarcotic sedative known as thalidomide was found to produce horrifying birth defects in the infants of mothers who took it. Though the efforts of a dedicated FDA inspector, Dr. Frances Kelsey, prevented thalidomide from ever being approved for marketing in this country, the catastrophe in Europe caused a considerable furor on both sides of the Atlantic.

Herbst did not discover that stilbestrol was a carcinogen: that had been known and suspected for decades. Neither did he prove that stilbestrol passed through the placenta: Dr. Burrows in his endocrinology text of 1945 demonstrated that that had been known since 1930. He did not even discover that stilbestrol was a teratogen: that had been known since 1959, when a paper by Dr. Alfred Bongiovanni and colleagues at the Children's Hospital in Philadelphia appeared in the *Journal of Endocrinology* describing the bizarre, "paradoxical" effects of stilbestrol on the growing fetus.

These doctors reported four very rare cases of masculinization in the female fetuses of mothers who took stilbestrol during pregnancy. Four female infants had been born with clitorises so enlarged they resembled small penises; one female infant was a partial hermaphrodite. These effects were termed "paradoxical" because this feminizing hormone was shown to exert masculinizing effects on some female fetuses.

What Herbst did discover and report in 1971 was that stilbestrol was a "transplacental" carcinogen in man; that bathing the fetus in a powerful solution of stilbestrol suspended in the maternal bloodstream and passed into the fetal circulation exposed the fetus to the known carcinogenic effects of the drug. Herbst's findings simply confirmed what might have been predicted from available literature dating from the 1930s and '40s. But this was no longer suspicion, prediction, or speculation. This was fact: stilbestrol exerted a carcinogenic effect on the fetus which only surfaced after puberty; fifteen to twenty years later.

The Herbst report was released on April 22, 1971, in the *New England Journal of Medicine*. It was accompanied by a prominent editorial. Under the bold headline, "NEW ENVIRONMENTAL FACTOR IN CONGENITAL DISEASE," Dr. A. D. Langmuir wrote:

> This issue contains an original communication of great scientific importance and serious social implications. The highly significant correlation between the appearance of adenocarcinoma of the vagina in teenage girls and young women, a very rare disease, and the ingestion of diethylstilbestrol by their mothers . . . adds a new dimension to the whole matter of what drugs are safe and unsafe to administer to pregnant women.

He also reiterated the most obvious conclusion to be drawn from the Herbst findings:

> It seems prudent for physicians to use caution in prescribing estrogenic substances during pregnancy. Indeed, physicians must think more seriously before administering any drug to a pregnant woman.

He wondered whether the cancer link indicated might indeed be harder and faster than Herbst proposed:

> The authors have been conservative in reporting their observations as merely an "association" . . . the epidemiological evidence indicates a direct etiologic relation. . . .

He concluded by calling for the establishment of a clearinghouse for information on this rather astonishing phenomenon, in which cancer in human beings had been demonstrably caused by human beings themselves.

Herbst acted quickly to establish just such a clearinghouse, which he called the Registry of Clear-Cell Adenocarcinoma. The registry actively sought complete information on all cases of the disease detected throughout the United States and around the world. Herbst and his colleagues sent off urgent letters to numerous state, university, and local medical and cancer centers, with appeals for information on all known cases of this rare disease.

Meanwhile, they heard nothing from FDA. After the preliminary phone call routinely requesting more information, the agency in Washington remained unforthcoming as to proper steps to be taken about the DES hazard. No appeals were sent out for information, no warnings were posted, no letters were sent out, no studies were mounted or investigations begun, to learn more about the problem, to take whatever steps might be necessary to contain the spread of the disease, or to detect it early where it might surface.

Dr. Peter Greenwald, director of the Cancer Control Bureau of the New York State Department of Health, was not content to ignore or dismiss the social implications of the Herbst report. Without waiting for word from the FDA, Greenwald resolved to immediately mount his own investigation of the DES situation within the natural bounds of his bureau's jurisdiction: all of New York State excluding New York City.

Greenwald, a physician and an epidemiologist, a graduate of the Harvard School of Public Health, and a former epidemiologist at the Boston City Hospital, began his own independent study taking Herbst's conclusions as his starting point. He requested from the New York State Cancer Registry reports on all cases of adenocarcinoma detected in New York State, exclusive of New York City, from 1950 through 1970. In those two decades, five adenocarcinomas had been reported in patients under the age of thirty. Greenwald developed a standardized form to collect clinical data from hospitals and physicians, and followed up the questionnaire with inspections of prenatal and delivery data from hospital and obstetrical records.

The five cancer cases reported were all born in the years

1951, 1952, and 1953. These dates alone were sufficient to arouse Greenwald's suspicion that these were DES-related. When the questionnaires came back, his suspicions were confirmed: all five mothers had taken DES during pregnancy. Three of the five DES daughters had died of advanced disease.

Greenwald had selected a matched control group to compare these results, and none of the mothers in that group had a history of stilbestrol ingestion. Greenwald found that the mothers had been given stilbestrol over many months and in large doses. He therefore concluded:

> The clustering of the vaginal cancer patients by date of birth within a three year period when synthetic estrogen therapy for threatened abortion was common suggests that the cancer was related to maternal therapy rather than to threatened abortion in the absence of therapy. . . . In fact, the true risk of miscarriage in some of these cases may have been quite low.

Greenwald sent his results to the *New England Journal of Medicine,* which accepted them for publication in their August 12 issue. But he was not satisfied, as a public health official for the State of New York, because nothing official was being done to ban DES from use during pregnancy and nothing official was being done to locate and treat DES daughters.

Greenwald sent his results to Hollis Ingraham, the New York State Commissioner of Health. Ingraham was sufficiently alarmed by Greenwald's report to authorize a letter, dated June 15, 1971, to be mailed to the 37,000 practicing physicians in the state. He wrote to FDA Commissioner Charles Edwards, advising him, in part, that New York State was taking this unprecedented action:

June 15, 1971

Charles C. Edwards, M.D.
U.S. Commissioner of Food and Drugs
Arlington, Va.

DEAR DR. EDWARDS: A study published in the New England Journal of Medicine (April 22, 1971) associating adenocarcinoma of the vagina in seven young women with the administration of diethylstilbestrol to their mothers during pregnancy suggests a new mechanism in the development of congenital neoplastic disease. The journal also noted editorially the great scientific importance and serious social implications of these findings.

The Cancer Control Bureau of the New York State Department of Health has surveyed its extensive statewide cancer registry to determine whether department records confirm the association report. The registry records five cases of vaginal cancer, the mothers of all five girls had received synthetic estrogens during pregnancy.

We feel this is adequate documentation that the administration of synthetic estrogens during pregnancy leads to an increased incidence of vaginal adenocarcinoma in female children resulting from that pregnancy. It appears from the data that adenocarcinoma of the vagina is extremely rare except when induced by estrogen administration in utero, since our registry discloses no cases of this cancer which did not have such a history.

On the basis of our findings, we are officially notifying all physicians in New York State of the danger of estrogen administration during pregnancy.

We also recommend most urgently that the Food and Drug Administration initiate immediate measures to ban the use of synthetic estrogens during pregnancy. . . .

Sincerely,

HOLLIS S. INGRAHAM, M.D.
Commissioner of Health

A week later, this letter was sent to all practicing physicians in New York State:

STATE OF NEW YORK
DEPARTMENT OF HEALTH,
EXECUTIVE DIVISION.
Albany, N.Y., June 22, 1971.

DEAR DOCTOR: The New York State Department of Health Cancer Registry has gathered reports of five teenage women throughout the State with adenocarcinoma of the vagina. Their mothers had been given stilbestrol or dienestrol, both synthetic estrogens, during pregnancy to prevent threatened abortion, raising the suspicion of a cause-and-effect relationship. . . .

The patients were 15 to 19 years old at diagnosis. Vaginal bleeding was commonly the first symptom. Three patients died of advanced disease and two are doing well postoperatively.

These findings demonstrate that synthetic estrogens are contraindicated in pregnancy. Young women with persistent irregular bleeding should have careful intravaginal inspection to rule out possible neoplastic disease. . . .

Sincerely yours,

HOLLIS S. INGRAHAM, M.D.
Commissioner of Health

Ingraham's appeal for action from the FDA was met with seeming indifference from Washington. A few days after Ingraham's letter of June 15 was mailed, his office received a phone call from the FDA acknowledging receipt of the letter.

A month went by, and at the beginning of August, the FDA requested more information. DES prescriptions continued to be written, DES daughters with cancer continued to surface around the country, while other unknown numbers of DES daughters remained untreated, undetected, unwarned. From March 1971 to November 1971, DES remained available to prevent miscarriage. One estimate suggests that as many as 20,000 unborn females may well have been exposed during that period.

Greenwald's confirmation of Herbst's findings was published in the August 12, 1971, issue of the *New England Journal of Medicine,* accompanied by another editorial. Dr. Judah Folkman wrote:

The cluster of cases described in Herbst's original report exceeds the number of cases in the entire world literature. . . . If a hidden factor were operating . . . there should have been many cases before 1945. It thus appears that exposure to stilbestrol and vaginal carcinoma may have a cause and effect relation. . . .

He theorized that the development of these tumors only after puberty may be due to hormonal changes in the body during the reaching of sexual maturity, when hormones surge through the body and stimulate vaginal tissue:

> . . . A single fetal cell in the future vaginal tissue undergoes malignant transformation because of stilbestrol. . . . This genetic defect might not be disclosed during prepubertal years when cellular renewal is sluggish. . . . At puberty the vaginal epithelium responds to surges of hormonal stimulation and depletion. . . . This provides the opportunity for a lurking defective cell to display its malignant nature.

He concluded with the sober realization that this was a medically caused catastrophe, an "iatrogenic," or physician-induced, disease:

> The Herbst and Greenwald reports bring into sharp focus the realization that man may produce neoplasia in himself. . . .

On August 10th, two months after Ingraham's letter reached their office, four months after the appearance of the Herbst report, five months after they first received raw data from Herbst through the *New England Journal of Medicine,* the FDA released its long awaited response to this pressing public health problem. James D. Grant, deputy commissioner to Charles Edwards, wrote to Ingraham simply acknowledging receipt of his letter, and requesting additional information:

> Thank you very much for your letter on June 15, 1971. As you know, the study published in the New England Journal of Medicine suggested an association between [DES and vaginal cancer]. . . . Whether this condition would occur with any estrogenic substance remains to be defined. We have obtained and are actively evaluating data from the study. . . . In response to your kind offer to provide information, I would appreciate complete medical records of the five cases.

10

Anne sat on the airplane leaving Rochester for Chicago, trying desperately to sleep. The residue from all the drugs she'd been taking still lingered in her body and it made her head fuzzy. Mary Needham sat wide awake in the seat beside her, looking out the window, glancing occasionally at a magazine, but Anne kept floating uneasily between sleep and wakefulness, wrapped up in her own thoughts.

Anne's mother had picked her up that morning at Methodist Hospital and taken her on a bus to the airport. Anne had been in a wheelchair the whole time.

The steward had carried her onto the plane. It was March 28, 1974. Anne was going home after just under a month at Mayo's. Ten days before she had undergone the third surgery, a vaginal reconstruction using a skin graft. She'd been released that morning wearing a plastic mold she would use for the better part of a year.

Anne was scared about leaving Mayo's. She had built up a routine. Life in the hospital had been pretty dull, but all the simple things had been taken care of. Now she was worried that each step on the way to getting better would be painful. Even little things she'd once taken for granted, like sitting down or walking, were painful. She wanted to sleep, because thinking about where her life would go from here wasn't easy either. They'd given her some Darvon but it wasn't doing much. She closed her eyes and tried not to think about unknown things.

Right now she had more immediate problems to deal with.

The worst two were wearing that mold and her lack of bladder control. Both were major sources of frustration and humiliation. The mold, for one thing, just wouldn't stay in. Anne had tried to work up all these crazy rigs to keep it in, but it just kept falling out anyway. The bladder problem was even worse, because it was not just painful, it was embarrassing. She hated having her private problem be public; the humiliation was far worse than the physical pain. She had no real control, and she had had several accidents already. She knew she was in store for many more before her condition improved.

Being in the hospital had allowed her to settle into an artificial set of habits, and she knew when she got home things would be different. She'd have to deal with people: with her family, with friends, with John.

She didn't know whether people would be able to see her as normal. She was afraid they wouldn't be able to deal with her in the old way, that they'd be uneasy and strange. She knew it was partly that she considered herself so completely different, after all she'd been through. But she didn't want other people to know it: she wanted to be the same.

Later that night, Anne sat in bed, dimly aware of people quietly coming in and out, one at a time. Nicky was home, Mary was home, Pammy was home, and they all came in and hugged her and said how good it was she was back. Patrick came in alone a little later; they had always been particularly close. He stayed outside at first, almost as if he was scared to go in. Finally Anne saw him coming into the room. He just came right in and put his arms around her, and hugged her for a long time.

The light came on at one point, and there they all were, standing in a circle around the bed. Anne was completely beat, she could hardly stay awake, but they talked for a little bit until she slipped off into sleep, and everyone just stayed there for a while. Anne slept so soundly she didn't have any of the creepy dreams she'd been plagued with in the hospital. She was home again in her own bed, in her own bedroom; she slept late the next morning.

She woke up the next day with the sun shining in the window. She was feeling pretty good. In fact, she sat up in bed, got up and walked around a few steps, and started feeling really good. She felt so good she thought to herself, "Gee, I could do anything." But there was nothing to do. No one was home, every one was at school or at work.

In the hospital, there'd been a routine, there'd always been lots of people around. Now she felt lonely and a little useless. But she walked around a bit and decided things looked bad in the house. She was used to helping out with the housework, she'd done it since she was small. She started cleaning up and immediately felt better, now that she had something to do. She was doing well for about three hours, when she got unbelievably tired. She went back to bed for a little nap and didn't wake up until almost evening, when she felt terribly sore.

For dinner that night they had her mom's special pot roast. She always cooked it slowly and added things to it along the way, and Anne had a plate and it made her sick. She didn't know what was happening, but she couldn't eat her favorite foods without getting cramps. It felt like sharp stabs in her intestines, and she couldn't digest anything with meat or grease, like stew. What with the strain from the cleaning and the pot roast at dinner, she felt worse that night than she had in days. It felt like her insides were all jumbled.

Anne was depressed once she got home, because she couldn't do anything for herself. She didn't realize what good care she'd received at Mayo's until she got home, when everything became so much harder. She'd been waited on hand and foot at the hospital, but she hadn't thought of the nurses as waiting on her. She didn't like to be waited on by her family. She'd always been the one to help get dinner, to help out around the house, to do things for other people. Now any time Anne tried to get up to get something, people would say, "Here, I'll get it for you."

Her family didn't know how to make her happy. But Anne didn't want them to try. If she moved oddly or seemed at all tired, her family would turn concerned and uneasy. They were all so worried she might pass out or fall down suddenly, they stayed with her all the time. For the first few weeks when she took a shower someone would always be with her. When she got sick from the pot roast that night, Pammy went with Anne to the bathroom. Anne appreciated the care and the effort, but at times she felt like she needed more privacy, to be alone with her own thoughts and feelings. It wasn't a big house, and she didn't have much space of her own within which to sort things out.

She knew the situation in some ways was not as hard on her as it was on people who were close to her. They didn't always know what was going on, they had to try to guess at the way she was feeling, they had to deal with the frustration of not being able to do anything substantial, of not being able to offer any practical help. The best they could offer was moral support, and Anne found that difficult to accept. Part of it was that so much remained unsaid in her family, emotions were mentioned but not revealed. Nothing was said in the house about her cancer for fear it would upset her. Her illness was never directly discussed, it was only something in the background.

She had to depend on people, even though she resented that dependence. She had to depend on John for support, but she worried about leaning on him too much. She was a little apprehensive about that before she saw him.

John came over for dinner the second night Anne was home. It was really touching to see him. He was shy at first, but he sat with Anne in the living room, and they talked for a long time. He'd never been able to make it up to the hospital because he couldn't get the time off. But they'd talked on the phone almost daily, and one of the first things he said, in his joking way, was, "Man, is my phone bill ever going to be high." At the time he wasn't making that much money. Of course, the bill came in eventually and his father never even showed it to him.

They didn't discuss the cancer much. They talked about other things. Anne talked about her sense of frustration, of not being able to do things, of not being able to walk fast, of not even being able to stand up straight. When she came home from the hospital she was walking around completely doubled over, like a little old lady. When she walked, she just hobbled around. They talked about the mold, how Anne hated having it in her, how she kept fighting it and it kept coming out. She talked about the bladder problem, about how she couldn't go anywhere without leaking. She felt, she told him, like one of the old ladies she used to take care of at the nursing home, who were so infirm they couldn't do anything by themselves.

She didn't want to feel like an invalid with John, she didn't want him to have to take care of her. But as he sat on the blue settee looking concerned and even a little frightened, kind of nervous, Anne's heart went out to him. He was just so glad she was home, she could tell, he was just happy she had pulled through. They couldn't talk much about all that stuff. But she sensed then that he'd had a really bad time when she was away. She could tell from his reserve that he had been completely scared and out of touch and out of control of everything that was going on with her life. She felt as if he'd been sure things were worse than they were: that she was going to die. John said at one point, "You know, you always said things were fine on the phone, but I knew they weren't, Anne."

He couldn't tell what she was thinking or feeling, except what she chose to tell him. She had to pretend things were better than they were, so as not to let everything get too depressing. He had to put on an act too. He had to act as if everything was fine, that she hadn't had cancer, that there was no chance it would come back. They had to put on this skit with each other, but at times the skit would break down. Anne would feel sorry for herself and often get nasty and sharp. John would stand there and shake his head, and by his eyes Anne would know he realized it wasn't her talking, but the fear and frustration coming out.

Anne knew from the way John acted that he loved her. She knew it would be a long time before they could have sex, and they would never be able to have children. Neither of these problems came up much in their talks, partly because there wasn't a whole lot to discuss. They both knew that the first problem would heal with time, and the second they could do nothing about. Anne continued to depend on John for emotional support, and to the best of his abilities he was there.

The first Sunday he had off from work he came over to the house. It was a nice warm spring day, and Anne hadn't been out yet. They sat around her place for a while, until John said, "Hey, let's go over to my house." Without another word he picked Anne up, carried her out to his car, and deposited her gently in the right bucket seat. Even with his help, it was terribly painful getting in and out of the car, because the seats were so low. He drove her straight to his parents' house. They sat around his living room for about twenty minutes, until she got terribly tired. He picked her up, put her back in his car, and drove her straight home.

John's behavior gave her assurance that if other men might not find her appealing, at least he did. That still left her with the problem, "What man will want me," if something should happen to him. Her confidence in herself was shaken, and though John's devotion was a wonderful help she was still deeply disturbed by the prospect of losing him and being left with no one. "What other men would want me," was a recurrent theme in her worries; it was a question she couldn't answer.

After her mother had her hysterectomy, her father hadn't thought of her as a woman anymore. That idea continued to haunt Anne, of her own father's love for her mother vanishing after she was no longer able to bear children. Anne had always admired her mother, and when she was young she'd always thought she'd have seven children. Now neither of them could bear any children, and the parallel was there: She had tremendous anxiety that any man she married might eventually draw away because she couldn't have a child. She always thought sadly to herself, "I'm not much of a woman anymore."

Within two weeks of coming home, Anne was back up at Mayo's. She'd come up for her six-week check, which was figured from the date of her first surgery. It was the middle of April. Anne dreaded going back there. It brought on a lot of memories, but it also made her afraid they'd find something new. Doctors, she worried, could always find things when they were really looking.

They ended up at the Holiday Inn on the outskirts of town where they'd stayed upon first arriving in Rochester. Anne woke up early the next morning and reported to Ten West for tests and an interview. She had to have kidney X-rays, lung X-rays, blood and urine samples. The doctor there, whom she'd never seen before, updated her file and took her most recent medical history. The question was always: "Any complaints?" Anne complained mostly of stomach problems, about wearing the mold and the problems keeping it in, and about the bladder control.

The bladder control, the doctor said, should improve as the muscles in the area began to tighten up and regain their strength. The mold had to be kept in constantly, and the doctor had no specific suggestions about improving the process. The stomach problems, the doctor said, were due to damage done to the mucous membrane of the intestines in the rearranging. The membrane needed time to re-form.

Anne was sent to the various stations of the clinic for tests, and afterwards her mother said, "Let's go back to the hospital." The idea was to visit and thank everyone there who had been so good to them. Anne was in the elevator heading up to the floor where she'd stayed when she was hit by a claustrophobia attack. She was suddenly suffocating, gasping for air, fighting for air, trying to breathe. She instantly flashed on an image of herself after her surgery fighting off the oxygen mask. She felt she was about to pass out when the elevator stopped at their floor.

Anne got out gasping for breath. She'd never felt anything like it. She stood in the corridor, just past the elevator banks, trying to pull herself together. She'd always been a stable person; she'd never been given to fits or seizures. The panicky feeling and shaking through her body was something alarmingly new. She told herself it was all right, everything was fine. Mary Needham stood right by and watched this all impassively. She had a sense of what Anne was feeling, but she said cheerfully, "Let's go see the nurses."

There was one nurse who had been really good to Anne. All of them had been great, but this one woman had been very special. Anne knew that nurse was on duty. She knew other nurses were. She started walking down that bare white corridor, fighting off a thick, clammy fear which surfaced in her gut and seemed to be threatening to strangle her.

She got up to the nurse's station, and she found herself stopped dead in her tracks. It was fear as she had never felt it before, a solid thing like a separate person opposing her. What was stopping her was the sight of the nurse's station itself, and the corridor beyond, where her room had been. She couldn't force herself past that spot any easier than if she'd tried to jump out a window.

She found herself running down the hall toward the elevator banks, her mother following behind her flabbergasted. "What's the matter, Annie," her mom said a couple of times. Just like in one of those nightmares, Anne wanted to say what was wrong, but she couldn't say it. She ended up by the elevator banks, shaking, as if she'd caught a terrible chill. Finally she turned to her mother and said, "Mom, we've got to go."

Mary Needham didn't ask any questions, but simply said, "All right Annie, let's come back some other time."

11

In November of 1971, FDA Commissioner Charles Edwards was called before a special hearing of the Intergovernmental Relations Subcommittee of the Committee on Governmental Operations to defend his actions, or lack of action, in the matter of DES. Congressman L. H. Fountain's subcommittee had long maintained a lively and skeptical interest in the regulatory behavior of the FDA, and the burgeoning issue of DES was the latest in a series of subjects on which the FDA had been called upon to testify.

In March of 1971, this same committee had heard testimony on a growing controversy: the use of DES as a feed additive for beef cattle. At that time, cattle industry representatives and FDA officials had defended the use of DES in animal feed, admitting that though it was known to be a carcinogen in animals, it posed no real hazard to the public health when present as residue in meat. With the publication of the Herbst and Greenwald reports on DES, the entire matter was transformed. Now DES had been demonstrated to be a powerful carcinogen to humans, and a genuine health problem. The committee heard testimony for two days on the issue, beginning on Thursday, November 11, 1971.

Congressman Fountain called the hearing to order and briefly summarized the latest developments in the DES story:

> During the March hearings, the subcommittee was informed by government witnesses that DES was a carcinogen in experimental animals, but they knew of no instance of human cancer caused by DES in the thirty years

since the drug has been administered to men and women. Recently, however, DES has reportedly been linked to cancer of the vagina in young women whose mothers took DES during pregnancy some 15 to 20 years ago. If this is true, we are confronted with a startling development, the implications of which have yet to be unraveled. . . .

Dr. Arthur L. Herbst was called as the first witness, to begin the necessary unraveling. He summarized his recent findings and described the establishment of the registry to centralize information on the subject. By the time of the hearings in November, the number of known cancer cases had swelled to sixty-two.

Fountain questioned Herbst closely on the FDA's response to his warnings of danger:

Fountain: Did you receive any communication from the FDA in connection with the journal, or in reply to it, or any comment upon it?

Herbst: I received an inquiry from them, and on April 14 submitted to them our raw data sheets, which dealt with the study I just reported to you.

Fountain: You received no other communication?

Herbst: . . . I did not have any further connection with them until recently.

Dr. Peter Greenwald testified about his independent investigations confirming Herbst's findings on the DES hazard, about his successful attempts to notify physicians in New York State, about his futile attempts to elicit some responsive action on the part of FDA.

Fountain: When did you notify the FDA?

Greenwald: June 15 . . . A phone call came two days later acknowledging receipt of the letter, at the end of July or the beginning of August they requested more detailed information. . . .

Fountain: Do you see the need for a large-scale case-finding

> program to identify as early as possible these young women?

Greenwald: Yes, I think it is especially important . . . in order that we get the best possible treatment for these women, and for the education of physicians . . . it is important to our knowledge of how cancer may be induced, to our basic knowledge about cancer. . . .

FDA Commissioner Charles Edwards testified on action taken by the FDA. The FDA had taken no action until the week the congressional hearings began. Two days before, on Tuesday, November 9, Commissioner Edwards had placed in the Federal Register (a daily publication issued by the General Services Administration giving notice of changes in Federal regulations) a warning against the usage of DES during pregnancy.

Congressman Fountain raised the question of the FDA's inconclusive letter of August 10 from FDA deputy commissioner Grant to Hollis Ingraham. He remarked:

> It seems to be that two months was a pretty long time to end up by acknowledging the letter and forwarding of case histories. This ought to have been done in a matter of days.

Edwards: . . . I must say that I do not agree with Dr. Ingraham's action. I think he was premature. I think there were others he should have consulted prior to his taking the actions he took. Not that his actions are necessarily wrong, but I think he could well have studied it a little more than he did.

Fountain: . . . may I point out that only after extensive inquiries of FDA from our own staff was the letter answered at all.

. . . I am sure it was coincidental that the response followed the subcommittee's inquiries. . . .

So it surfaced that the only reason the FDA had answered the letter at all, after two months, was because of pressure from a congressional committee that some action be taken. Congressman

Fountain asked Edwards why nothing had been done more quickly; why did DES remain on the market to that day, for that dangerous indication?

> *Fountain:* I have right in front of me in The Physicians' Desk Reference [a drug] called Synestrol, and the present instructions to the physicians is that it is indicated for this purpose [threatened abortion]. Would you agree that this constitutes a serious situation, in view of the action you have initiated?

> *Edwards:* In view of the fact that it was published yesterday [the warning in the Congressional Register] I would expect these products not to be properly labeled.

Dr. Delphis Goldberg of the committee staff asked Edwards some questions about the efficacy of DES for the purpose of threatened abortion. Edwards stuck literally to the record:

> The National Academy of Sciences in its review of these drugs . . . rates this particular claim for the drug "possibly effective."

But Goldberg countered with what the panel had actually said:

> "The panel feels that estrogens are not harmful in such conditions as threatened abortion but that their effectiveness cannot be documented by literature or its own experience. The company should be asked to supply further evidence to substantiate the claims in question."

> *Goldberg:* Have the companies provided further evidence to FDA that this is not an ineffective drug?

> *Edwards:* No.

> *Goldberg:* If there is no documentation in the literature and no information otherwise available to the panel to demonstrate effectiveness, is not the drug actually ineffective under the terms of the Kefauver-Harris Act?

For a safe response to this straightforward question, Edwards was forced to turn to FDA chief counsel Peter Barton Hutt, who replied:

> It means to me as a lawyer that it is less than effective, but it does not necessarily mean that it is ineffective. . . .

To this Commissioner Edwards helpfully added:

> These were practicing physicians, bright men, who were well aware of the fact that there must be at least some evidence of possible effectiveness of this drug because of its widespread use in the medical profession. . . .

The panel of the National Academy of Sciences which had evaluated DES as "possibly effective" had been enlisted to carry out a national drug efficacy study to determine what preparations marketed prior to 1962 deserved to remain on the market. The results of the enormous study on 1,600 different drugs had been completed in 1967; DES had slipped through the regulatory net once again.

> *Goldberg:* . . . it may very well be that the panel . . . decided for their own purposes to throw the drug in the "possibly effective" category, knowing that the manufacturer would have more time to try to come up with some evidence. . . .

Henry Simmons, director of the Bureau of Drugs for the FDA, tirelessly reiterated the adage of the "tried and true" preparation, which might not be scientifically defensible but which physicians continue to prescribe because it seems to work:

> Dr. Goldberg, I think it's very important to point out that the panel knew of respected and very able clinicians who had used the drug for that purpose and felt it was successful. . . .

Fountain pressed Edwards on why DES had not been correctly evaluated in the '60s, and why the public had not been advised of its hazardous potential immediately in 1971:

Edwards: The initial evidence of Dr. Herbst did not come until the spring of this year.

Fountain: What was the reason for delaying . . . after that information came to light?

Edwards: . . . It is one thing for Dr. Herbst to publish this in a journal, which he obviously should; it is one thing for the New York State Health Department to make certain observations. But I think when the FDA passes judgment on anything, it is not only nationwide, it is worldwide.

. . . In this particular case you might argue that we were too slow and perhaps we were, but nevertheless there were lots of analyses which had to be carried out on these figures before we felt we were prepared to act. Perhaps we did not act quite as soon as we should have, nevertheless, I think we have the responsibility to be sure. . . .

Fountain did not accept this:

But where you have a situation where the dangers are of an imminent nature, it seems to me that every effort should be made to expedite action, whatever action is considered appropriate. And you did have information indicating that this was not found to be an effective drug. . . .

Bureau of Drugs Director Simmons promptly interjected:

And the only drug available for this condition, Mr. Fountain. There are only two drugs of even this level of efficacy. If none of these drugs are available, there would be nothing available to make it possible for a woman who wanted to have a child, to make it possible. . . .

Committee staff physician Goldberg:

If it is only possibly effective, how in the world can you justify in view of the hazard which was certainly delimited very, very sharply by the findings in Massachusetts and New York—how could you justify not warning physicians immediately?

Simmons waffled neatly:

. . . Neither we nor the experts throughout this country know it is not effective. I do not think we can make that judgment. . . .

Goldberg: Does FDA have evidence of the effectiveness of DES for the treatment of threatened abortion?

Simmons: We do not. But we do not have evidence of its ineffectiveness.

Goldberg: How can you say it is effective if you have no evidence?

Commissioner Edwards raised this circuitous exchange to new heights:

Edwards: Because the National Academy of Sciences rated it "possibly effective."

Goldberg: My comment was prompted not by the consideration of whether this was possibly effective, or whether it was ineffective, but rather by what was very evident, that there was a singular situation developing when you got the warning from Dr. Herbst, Dr. Ingraham, and Dr. Greenwald about the association of this drug with vaginal cancer. Now did this not call for a warning?

Edwards: We have issued a warning.

Goldberg: What warning have you issued?

Edwards: Well, have you read the Federal Register?

Goldberg: Do physicians read the Federal Register?

Simmons then tried to explain how and why the agency had failed to adequately warn of danger, and how it had been possible for DES to remain on the market for so long in view of an admitted hazard, in view of dubious efficacy.

> *Simmons:* I would like to go back to a further point about the "possibly effective" labeling for this drug. Prior to the knowledge that Dr. Herbst presented to the world in April, there were two drugs rated "possibly effective" for threatened abortion; they were progesterone and diethylstilbestrol.
>
> At that time, and continuing to today, there are no other drugs which have any rating of effectiveness for this condition.
>
> As a benefit-risk situation, there are women in this country who lose many babies continuously through an inability to conceive.
>
> I suspect that some women would feel the risk of use of such drugs was warranted, with the hope of producing a live child, even though that live child, now on present evidence, may have a possibility of producing another action. . . .
>
> Now this is the benefit-risk situation that is always considered by this agency and considered by every physician in the country. . . .

Simmons was presenting the remarkable claim that the division under his jurisdiction did not take any immediate action to deal with a known danger to the public health because the hypothetical patient, not the physician, might choose the risk in order to attain some doubtful benefit, even if she had no authoritative knowledge that the drug was in fact dangerous, or ineffective. The PDR certainly contained no information to allow anyone to make such a decision, the drug companies showed no signs of independently electing to warn the public or the practicing physician. Only the FDA had such a capability, indeed only the FDA had an explicit mandate to do so.

Goldberg finally allowed a tinge of indignation to invade his civil tones:

> Dr. Simmons, when you have a drug which is known to be carcinogenic in animals and when a link to hu-

man carcinoma has been established . . . I fail to see how you can talk of a benefit-risk ratio. . . . What you are doing is weighing the possibility, without any evidence of effectiveness, that a drug may be effective and may be helpful to that woman, against the possibility that she may deliver a daughter who will develop cancer of the vagina.

Simmons: At the price of having a daughter which she might not have had, Dr. Goldberg.

Edwards concluded by expressing more anxiety over a possible "cancer-scare" than over any hazard to the public health:

I think we have to be very careful in our activities and our pronouncements not to create an emotional crisis on the part of American women. The average American woman probably does not know if she threatened to abort what her doctor might have given her. I think this is one of the responsibilities that has to be laid directly at the doorstep of the American doctor.

12

It was the first week in May, and Anne was getting ready to go out to a bar. It wasn't going to be a big night on the town, but she was apprehensive. Denny's band was playing down the road at Dettmering's in Matteson and people she knew would be there.

Anne wanted to see people, but she didn't want to have them keep asking, "Anne, are you all right?" People can get such an attitude, Anne thought, they look at you forever with these sad, puppy-dog eyes. The thought of having people she knew and didn't know feeling sorry for her was extremely intimidating. Anne spent a good deal of time thinking about what to wear, about how she would look: She didn't want to seem pale or sick or frightened. She wanted to be happy-go-lucky, casual, confident, but she had to cover up her anxiety. She stood at the mirror in the bathroom, distractedly brushing her hair. Was her skin pale? Was her face blotchy? She put on more makeup.

She planned to wear her brown corduroy pants because they were old and worn out, and her jeans were too tight across her stomach. She was wearing the mold and her stomach was still swollen from the surgery, so the cords, being softer and looser, were much more comfortable. She was worried she had gotten thin. She'd been on IVs and a bland diet in the hospital, and she hadn't been eating well recently because of the cramps. She hadn't really lost much weight, but that didn't stop her from being anxious that she seemed too thin: She didn't want anyone to be able to look at her and think, "Wow, that girl's had cancer."

John rang the bell and Anne met him at the door. The band was going on late, but Anne didn't feel like sitting around at her place. She wanted to be out of there. She'd been resting and resting, and she was finally sick of resting. She knew she must have been feeling better lately because she'd been so bored. She deposited herself gingerly in John's bucket seat and opened her window all the way. It was a cool, breezy night and she wanted to feel the wind in her face, to feel like she was going somewhere.

When they got to the bar, it was like she'd never been away. Nothing had changed: the cars in the driveway, the lighting inside, the bar in the front with the TV behind, and the small bandstand in the corner with a few spotlights above, where Denny and his band were still setting up. Here and there at the bar and at the few small tables were faces she recognized. But no one jumped up to greet her or made a big fuss. A few people nodded naturally, and as she and John went up to say hello to Denny and his friends, no one acted different or strange.

Of course, Denny and his girl friend Lynn were Anne's two best friends, and they'd been over to visit already. The guys in his band knew all about it, but nobody gave much of a sign. It came over Anne like a revelation that people weren't all that concerned. Her own problems didn't occupy their minds; and though that was a relief it was also a letdown, because her going out obviously seemed like such a production only to her. To the rest of the world it didn't matter much; that was something she'd forgotten, as if when she'd been away she'd developed an exaggerated view of herself.

The one thing a few people did mention was how John had taken the whole thing. One woman said really seriously, "I was worried about John when you were sick. He was really on edge. He just wasn't himself." Apparently he'd been very withdrawn, had really tied one on a couple of times, and had seemed out of it pretty much the whole time. That didn't surprise Anne, but she was surprised at how much of that disturbance he'd kept to himself.

She had to hide so much from others. She'd always been a private person, with only a small circle of friends with whom she'd been close, but now that circle was even more constricted, and even with them she couldn't tell everything. In the end she felt more alone than she'd ever felt before. Leaning on people bothered her, she didn't know how to confide in them without becoming dependent. If she accepted people feeling sorry for her, she had to accept her own permanent sickness. People would call up and say, "Anne, how you doin'?" Anne would say, "Fine, just fine." They'd say, "I know you're not, Anne, *how are you?*" in this deep, solemn voice. After a while, Anne couldn't take it. She'd ask them about everything under the sun, just so they wouldn't ask her any more questions.

They sat around and had a few drinks, and then she and John drove home. Anne couldn't believe how much better she felt now that she'd been out in society and society didn't seem to care. She realized how much the concern people had felt about her had been both a support and a burden. As time went on and she started to recover, the most important thing was for her to get back on her own two feet again. Having people around mooning over her just made it that much harder.

Early in May there was a stretch of warm weather. Anne started doing a little gardening. Not at the house, but at a small lot the village let out, where she and her mom took a plot. That was the first year they had one together, and they grew cantaloupes. They weren't at all hard and mealy like some people's, they turned out sweet and soft.

She spent time in the garden, trimmed the bushes around the house, baked, made cookies and dinner, and tried as hard as she could to read. Her eyes still wouldn't focus. She'd had the same problem in the hospital, and the condition had never improved. She was sure the drugs she'd taken then were still having some effect, because she still couldn't read more than a line or two. Her eyes wouldn't concentrate, they'd drift right across the page.

She couldn't concentrate on the future. Trying to look ahead at all, to plan out her life, became a mental and emotional effort beyond what she could bear. Planning the future just didn't excite her. Her ambitions for nursing, which she'd held on to up until the day she went into the hospital, had been shattered by the experience of not even being able to visit her own nurses. Going into the medical field seemed preposterous now, after what had happened; she had always hoped to work in a maternity ward.

The questionnaire arrived one day in May, in a plain white

envelope with a Mayo Clinic letterhead, addressed to Mary Needham. It lay around the house for a few days because Mary didn't want to deal with it. One Sunday afternoon when Vic was home Mary finally decided she'd better open it. She remembered Dr. Symmonds at Mayo's asking her something after the first operation. Symmonds had asked, "Did you take any medication when you were pregnant with Anne?" Mary had answered, "Yes, I did." He had asked her what it was, and Mary had answered honestly that she had no idea what it was. Dr. Symmonds had asked her to ask Vic about it, but when she talked to Vic that night on the phone she didn't even think of it because Anne was in such excruciating pain. She was under oxygen, and all Mary had been concerned with was that Anne should know that there was someone with her: she would rub Anne's hand or her arm or anything, just so she would know it.

By the time Anne got home from the hospital, Mary already feared that the cause of Anne's illness might have been something she had done. She didn't want to face up to it, the prospect was just too frightening. It wasn't even a decision she made, she just somehow did not remember to ask Vic about it. Mary stood motionless for a second after having torn open the letter. She went to the dining room table.

Dear Mrs. Needham:

Enclosed you will find a form, which we would appreciate you completing to the best of your ability.

Recently, it has been noted that some of the patients with the type of medical problem your daughter, Anne Elizabeth, had have been exposed to certain hormone drugs before birth. It would be of great interest to us to know if this was the case in this instance. . . .

Kenneth L. Noller, M.D.

Mary was in the dining room, Vic was in the den. Mary called in to him, "Vic, what was the name of the pill I took when I was pregnant with Anne?" At first Vic didn't answer. Mary got up and went to the door and asked him the question again. He was in his favorite chair, dozing with his reading glasses on, a book spread out flat against his lap.

Anne was in her room only a few feet away, lying on her bed resting and thinking, with her door open. She got up to go into the kitchen for something to drink, walked through the living room, and passed her mother, who was sitting at the dining room table. Her mother had a form spread out on the table, and she kept calling into the den with questions: "Vic, what was that again?" and "Vic, what about this?" Anne went into the kitchen and got a glass of water, and as she came back into the room she had a funny feeling in her stomach: they were talking about her. Anne stood in the doorway, actually feeling queasy. She asked, "Hey, what are you guys talking about?"

From where she was standing in the kitchen doorway, Anne could see past the living room and into the den beyond. Her dad was in his chair in the corner, with his reddish hair and his short, red moustache, with a book in his lap and his feet up. Finally he came in and sat down heavily on the blue settee. Anne sat down next to him. Her mom was getting confused by some of the questions, and she hadn't all the names and spellings right. Mary said, "What was that drug I took." Victor said, "Dienestrol."

Anne had never heard that name before. Mary remembered that it was some kind of vitamin. Anne remembered that when she first had arrived at Mayo's, they had asked her, "Did your mother take any drugs during pregnancy?" Anne had answered that she didn't know. Anne was thinking, as if it had nothing much to do with her, that if this was the drug they were asking her about, then she'd given the wrong answer. She felt vaguely uncomfortable, as if she'd done badly on a test for school.

For Mary, it confirmed her worst suspicions that she'd done something horribly wrong. No mother can bear to see any of her children hurt. If they fall down, if they're sick or injured, it's about the worst feeling a mother can have. For Mary, she had to say to herself, "I am the reason my child was injured."

From that day on Mary felt completely and personally responsible. She knew she could say, "It's not my fault, it's the pill's fault," but the fact was that she had done it, and if she hadn't taken those pills, Anne never would have had cancer. What was so immediately upsetting was that she had only taken the pill because she so desperately wanted that child. Annie had come along at a very bad time in her life, when her marriage was in a particularly painful phase, and she had had to hang on to the fact that God had given her this wonderful girl to help and to keep. When Mary thought that Annie had almost been snatched away because of that drug, it made her physically sick.

Victor didn't seem to find the issue all that important. Anne didn't seem to be that concerned herself. But for Mary, that letter was the beginning of a long period of guilt and self-recrimination, which wouldn't be dispelled for years.

Mary found it difficult to accept that her daughter had been made ill because of a drug. Mary loved the drug business. She had always trusted the drug companies, she had always thought they were gods. Mary had worked in drugstores since she was a little girl, and she'd always thought of pills and drugs as the greatest healers of people. During Mary's two years of pharmacy college the miracle drugs were saving countless lives around the world. It was her profession, though she had never taken her degree, and her husband's profession, in which they had worked so long and hard and met so many wonderful people. She had met lots of the drug company people, and so had Vic, and they had been fine people, nice people, the kind you'd be happy to invite to your home. But now these same people had hurt her daughter, and that hurt Mary Needham.

Mary sat at the dining room table, watching her daughter sitting so silently across the room. She'd been through so much, it was hard to believe how much, so quickly. Anne had always been a carefree girl, happy and cheerful, prepared to help out anyone. She'd never had to take anything from anyone. Now she'd been forced to accept people's sympathy, which absolutely galled her. Now Anne was often despondent, moody, and irritable, and no one could blame her. Everyone had to forgive her, she had to be treated differently.

Mary was worried that Anne was stagnating at home. She could well have been a concert harpist, that's what her harp teacher in seventh grade had said. But that big beautiful harp Anne had once played just sat by the sofa in the living room, its strings untuned and the pedals dusty. It broke Mary's heart to see Anne having so little to do for herself, and having so little to look forward to. Mary herself couldn't imagine any life without children. When Mary went to Mass she didn't pray for herself, but to thank God for giving her her children. Now she prayed to God for having given her back her Anne.

Given all that had happened, Mary thought Anne was doing beautifully. Third children are very blessed children: first children you expect to be perfect, but they never are; with second children you think you're relaxed, but you're not; by the time you get to the third child, you're so used to it you can do the things you should have done with the first child. Mary had always thought of Annie as a very well-balanced child. She could handle just about anything. One thing Mary had always hoped to impress on her children was that if you face up to reality for what it is, you can take on the world. Anne, Mary had always felt, had best been able to absorb that information.

Still, Anne had had to deal with awful things. The worst were these terrible, frequent stomach pains, which had started right after she came home. Mary had come home from work one afternoon to find Anne crawling across the floor from the bathroom to her bed. She was in such pain she couldn't even walk. She was so brave, she'd never make a single sound out loud, she'd just cry silently. To watch your own child crawling across the floor because she is in too much pain to stand up makes you just about want to throw in the towel. Mary weighed about a hundred pounds at that point, and she couldn't possibly have picked her up.

They had to change Anne's bandages daily after she came home. It was a horrible area, raw and red, and Mary knew it was revolting to Anne. Handling the mold was revolting to Anne, and the dressing of the wounds was horrible. Mary didn't like it either, but Mary did it, and then it finally got to the point where Anne could do it.

They didn't discuss cancer in the house. Mary tried consciously and vigilantly to take Anne's mind off her troubles. She'd look for funny programs on TV, light entertainment, nothing sad, nothing deep. She'd put cheerful music on the stereo and act as nonchalant as possible. Part of it was pretending that nothing terrible had happened, which Mary knew went against her idea of facing up to reality as it was, but she had to admit that in this case facing up to reality wasn't turning out to be easy for either of them.

Anne was sitting on the blue settee, thinking about all sorts of things. She was thinking about going out that night with John, she was thinking that she needed a new pair of pants, she was thinking that she hadn't eaten much of anything all day. It really didn't hit her then that what had happened to her hadn't been random. Later on, she realized that she just didn't associate drugs and cancer. She wasn't aware of environmental factors, of agents outside the body, being able to cause her disease. It was 1974, and people hadn't heard much about toxic chemicals, or about cancer rates being higher in certain exposed areas. Anne had always thought of her cancer as something wrong with her, as something that had been in her body because of genes. It wouldn't be for some time that she would realize that she had been dealt a bad hand, not by nature, but by people.

The phone rang. Anne jumped up to get it. She realized the three of them had been sitting in the living room without talking for two or three minutes. That seemed strange, but she didn't give it much thought. John was on the line. He was coming over.

Two hours later, it was nearly dusk and the sky was turning cloudy. In the courtyard of the Needham house, which really was a blacktop turnaround onto which faced three or four small houses, Anne and John had played Frisbee.

Anne was in terrible pain, with severe shocks shooting right through her buttocks where the skin graft had been. A few times she had wanted to stop, but John had urged her, "Let's play a couple more minutes, you can do it," and strangely enough, Anne could.

John would come over and make Anne play on and on for hours, because he knew that physical exercise is a cure for a lot of things, both physical and mental. John would get her to extend herself physically, to get her moving, to show herself that she could do more than she thought she could. Anne had started getting tired and it had started to hurt, and John had kept saying, "Come on, keep it up," almost like a coach. Anne had gotten her second wind, and she'd started playing hard.

It had developed almost into a fight between them. She had started getting mad at John for making her keep playing. She'd started really winging the Frisbee, showing him she could throw it hard, trying to keep him from catching it. John was really good at Frisbee, and he'd catch them all, but Anne had started getting madder and madder, and started throwing the Frisbee harder and harder, and he'd throw it back at her hard and far away to make her run for it, and lunge for it, stretching herself and moving faster until she was dizzy and out of breath. He hadn't let her stop then, but had just kept throwing it farther and farther from her, and she'd even jumped for some and caught them, ones she thought she'd never be able to get.

Now she was standing in the soft pool of light from the lamp above the front door, on their small front lawn. It was really getting too dark to play, now that the sun had fallen back behind the trees. The cars in the driveways were hidden in shadows, and she was scared she'd run into one. John was panting and out of breath, with his long hair falling over his shoulders, and Anne felt tired and out of breath, and she had pains in her rear. But she felt great, better than she had in weeks. Throwing that Frisbee at John had expressed so much rage and frustration, not at him but at the world. She felt hungry, and tired, and a little sweaty; mostly she felt much stronger.

Soon it was summer, and Anne was at work. Everything seemed just the same: she was right back where she'd been, at Marshall Field's, in the "Young Chicago" section, junior clothes. She was standing behind the counter as a salesgirl, pleased to be doing something but at the same time a little depressed. She was grateful to Field's that they'd held her job for her. Still, it was quite a letdown. She knew it was practical, but that didn't make it exciting. It was only four hours a day, three days a week at first, and she knew it was convenient, and there was always somebody there, and they knew she was healthy now. With her medical history, who else would hire her?

Certain incidents would set her off. She would get sad over little things that didn't mean anything in themselves but represented something. It was summer and Anne was over at John's. They were playing Frisbee on the front lawn. A friend of theirs came by on his motorcycle and gunned up the driveway, shouting, "Hey, we're having a party, a picnic out in the country." Anne was wearing a pair of jeans and a halter top, and the jeans came down low, like hip-huggers, and her stomach was still swollen and you could see part of her scar. It was still red at that time, like a bright crimson seam right down her stomach that disappeared into her jeans.

This guy and John talked for a minute, he was still on his bike. He was trying to get them to come to this party, but at one point he looked down and his eye stopped right at the middle of Anne's waist. He said, "Gee Anne, that's a real nice scar." Anne just wanted to die. Before her first surgery she'd told the doctors, "Please, I've already picked out my bikini. Please don't scar me above it."

Anne knew the guy didn't mean anything by it. But she just stood there the whole time wanting to vanish, looking down at that awful scar thinking, "My God, when will it stop being red? When will it go away?" She knew it would eventually stop being red, but it would never go away.

Then it was fall. Anne was sitting in her room reading a woman's magazine. A woman her mom worked with at Field's had brought it in one day to show Mary, saying that there was an article in it which described something just like what Anne had had. Mary brought it home one afternoon in the middle of October, and Anne took it straight to her room.

She sat there on the bed for a long time with the magazine flat out on the bedspread. She found herself in the withdrawn state she'd become so comfortable in since her surgery, a feeling almost like dreaming, but more than partway toward sleep. The article was by a woman who called herself a DES daughter, and it was personal, not scientific or medical. Anne lay back on her bed and closed her eyes. The article had been about this woman's feelings after she went through her vaginal cancer. She suddenly remembered how she felt that night she'd lay there on the bed and Dr. Warren had said he was referring her to a radiologist. It felt just like that, the feeling made her body quiet and still.

What stuck in Anne's mind most about the article wasn't that a drug had caused the illness. That didn't interest her half as much as this woman's feelings as she went through the same things Anne had been through. She put the magazine down on the bedside table. It wasn't the facts she'd read that impressed her. It was the life of this parallel woman.

It was only then that what had happened to her really started to hit. Up until that point, the feelings she had been suppressing were safely buried. But the article brought so much pain and sadness up to the surface it made Anne want to gag. The article had something in it about the woman's feelings for her mother after she found out she'd taken DES. There was a picture of them both in there. So much hidden resentment and bad feelings about her own mother came up in Anne that it scared her. The whole subject hit her between the eyes, and afterwards she was bitter and mad.

In September Anne went back to Mayo's for her six-month check. She dreaded it just as she had her other visits, but now she wanted to find out something. She felt as if she'd never been given the whole story of what happened, and she felt like one of those people in the movies who go out stalking the murderer of their family. She was out to find out what happened. She was assigned to Dr. Kenneth Noller from that visit on, because he had written the letter to her mom with the DES questionnaire.

Anne went to see him, and it was while she was still sitting up on the table after her physical examination that he got a beep for a long-distance phone call. Dr. Noller excused himself and went to pick it up. It was from somewhere in the South, and it was another doctor requesting some information, some statistics that Dr. Noller had. Anne couldn't help but listen, and she heard those words she'd been hearing: "correlation," "stilbestrol," "exposure in utero." Noller got off the phone, and Anne was sitting right there. Dr. Noller said, "That man was looking for some statistics on DES. I gave him some of the information we've compiled so far."

Anne asked him what it was all about. Dr. Noller was in his thirties, about six feet tall, and looked like he could use a little exercise. He sat right down and looked at Anne sadly. He told Anne that at that time they knew of approximately 175 cases of confirmed DES ingestion by the mother and of vaginal cancer in the offspring daughters. There were some 250 other cases, he said, in which there was suspicion of DES or other prenatal hormone ingestion, but it could not be confirmed. Anne asked if DES had caused the cancer, and Noller looked a little uncomfortable before saying that there was a correlation between the two, that you couldn't really speak in terms of cause and effect. The discussion they had was very abstract, all about numbers and cases. Anne knew there were all these cases, but whether she was one of the confirmed 175 he had referred to was left unclear to her.

Anne left Dr. Noller's office feeling confused. She felt upset and angry, but she had nothing specific to direct her anger against. She was now convinced that her cancer had been caused by someone, but she didn't know who it was. She felt like she'd been cheated and abused, but it wasn't even her, it was her mother who had taken the pill. It made her feel very strange about her mother, and she became suddenly aware of why her mother had been acting so peculiar all summer since that questionnaire came in. Her mother felt terribly guilty but Anne had only dimly noticed it.

She wasn't angry at any doctors, she assumed they hadn't known what they were doing. She knew her mother had had problems carrying babies, that she had had two miscarriages before her, and more than that after she was born. She knew the drug had been said to prevent miscarriages, and she didn't know if she'd have been born at all if her mother hadn't taken that drug.

13

At nearly the same time doctors had learned that DES was a potent human transplacental carcinogen, public health officials were growing increasingly concerned about its presence in the nation's meat. DES had been demonstrated to pose a risk to a large but limited group of women whose mothers had taken the drug decades before. But DES in the food supply potentially threatened the health of every man, woman, and child in the country. Stopping the use of stilbestrol in pregnancy was a relatively simple step, once a reluctant FDA was prodded into action. Getting the DES out of beef proved a much more complex, prolonged, and difficult task.

In 1954, the FDA had permitted DES to be added to the feed of beef cattle. The stilbestrol supplements increased the body weight markedly, largely through a nutritionally useless but highly profitable increase in the amount of water and body fat. In 1955, the FDA approved an application to allow the implantation of DES pellets in the ears of beef cattle. At that time, tests detected no residues in the tissues of the beef itself.

In September of 1958 Congress passed an amendment to the Food, Drug and Cosmetic Act called the Delaney Provision, prohibiting the marketing of any food substance containing detectable amounts of any known carcinogen. But in 1962, under intense pressure from the cattle industry, Congress was persuaded to exclude DES specifically from that prohibition. The new clause was known as Section 512(d)(H), and it allowed the use of DES as a feed additive as long as no residues could be detected when the chemical was used according to instructions "reasonably certain to be followed in practice."

These instructions were certainly convenient: DES was to be withdrawn from feed forty-eight hours before slaughtering. Theoretically, all DES residues would be excreted from the animal in the urine during that time. But for fourteen years, from 1952, when DES was first approved as feed for cattle, until 1966, the United States Department of Agriculture, responsible for such testing, neglected to test any cattle.

In 1966, the USDA finally instituted a pilot testing program and found DES in 1.1 percent of 1,023 samples, a modest sample considering the relative size of the nation's cattle production: 30 million head per year. The next year, the USDA tested even fewer animals, 495, but the percentage of DES detected increased. In 1971, 6,000 animals were tested, and allegedly none had DES residues. That report turned out eventually to be false: some cattle actually had been found with large amounts of DES still in their system, but a lower level USDA official was found to have suppressed the information.

The Fountain hearings were called primarily to look into this problem. Both Herbst and Greenwald were questioned closely as to the danger posed to the public by DES in meat. Congressman Fountain had asked Peter Greenwald, "Has any animal residue constituted a potential hazard to the female fetus when ingested by pregnant women?" Greenwald had replied, ". . . Well, I would not want to give it to my wife during pregnancy." The FDA, for its part, represented at those hearings by Commissioner Edwards, Bureau of Drugs Director Henry Simmons, and chief counsel Peter Hutt, took a position in line with its generally hands-off approach to the entire question, maintaining that DES was no more carcinogenic than natural estrogens present in many plants and animals, and that if ingested in small enough doses even over a long period of time, the compound was still relatively safe.

Before April of 1971, the cattle industry had been able to claim that DES posed no harm to humans, even though it was known to be a powerful carcinogen in animals. But the Herbst report changed all that, as Congressman Fountain maintained in his opening remarks at the hearing. Now that DES had been confirmed as a human carcinogen, the question that became paramount was simply, What benefit does the public receive from involuntarily exposing itself to this proven hazard? The answer that emerged from the Fountain hearings was quite straightforward: The nation stood to save somewhere between $.03 (a government estimate) and $.10 (a cattle industry estimate) per pound on each pound of beef purchased.

The reason only extremely low residue amounts of DES were detected prior to 1966 was largely due to the coarseness of the analytical method used to locate DES traces. The methods gradually became more sensitive, but not until April of 1971 did a new method of gas chromatography begin to detect much more DES in meat than had previously been suspected. While Senator William Proxmire introduced a bill in Congress to ban DES immediately, the National Resources Defense Council sued both the FDA and USDA to remove DES from meat. In response to this considerable public pressure, FDA finally compromised by lengthening the period of withdrawal of DES from cattle feed from two to seven days.

That stopgap measure didn't work. DES was soon found in cattle fed under the new regulations. The seven-day period proved unenforceable and impractical for cattlemen to follow.

On July 20, 1972, the Senate Subcommittee on Health held a hearing in Washington, with Chairman Edward Kennedy presiding. Senator Kennedy opened the hearing with these chilling phrases:

> We are here today because DES, a known cancer-causing agent, is appearing on thousands of American dinner tables. . . . The latest figures show that 2.27 percent of all cattle tested contained DES residues after slaughter. . . . More than 660,000 head of cattle probably reach American dinner tables. . . .

> Six months ago FDA took the position that the residues could be eliminated by tightening administrative procedures. . . . It now seems the control procedures are unenforceable . . . incidence has risen from .5 to 2.27 percent. Yet DES is at the present time still not banned. . . .

Commissioner Edwards took the stand in justification of his agency's remarkable inaction in the face of the DES hazard.

Edwards: . . . On finding the incidence of violations [of the new regulations] increasing, we commenced appropriate procedures to withdraw approval for the use of DES.

Kennedy: Does that mean you have banned it or not banned it?

Edwards: . . . We proposed withdrawing approval for DES. . . . Under the procedures, there is a thirty day period for comments, which expired Friday of this week. . . .

Kennedy: The Secretary [of HEW] could declare it an imminent hazard, could he not, and stop it today?

Edwards: That is correct.

Kennedy: Are you prepared to make that recommendation to the Secretary?

Edwards: We are not . . . because we have absolutely no evidence that DES in animal feed has caused harm to human health.

Kennedy questioned Bureau of Drugs Director Henry Simmons on his reluctance to recommend a DES ban.

Kennedy: Do you think it is a bona fide carcinogen?

Simmons: Animal, not human.

Kennedy: How can you be so sure it is not human?

Simmons: I have no evidence.

In elaborating his position, Simmons made light of the DES danger:

Stilbestrol is not a carcinogen, period. It is an estrogen. . . . Estrogens are vital to life. And with a very high dose it can be carcinogenic. It has not been demonstrated in humans to be carcinogenic at a normal dose. . . . When we eat steak that is grilled I think the honest answer is if there is an imminent hazard, it is more from charcoal grilled steaks and fires than from DES residue. . . .

Kennedy replied that charcoal grilling was a matter of choice; a meat consumer's ingestion of DES was a matter of chance.

Duane E. Flack, chairman of the National Task Force Committee on DES of the American National Cattle Association, was present to give the cattle industry perspective on the DES problem:

> The beef cattle industry . . . is concerned. . . . Ours is a multi billion dollar industry. I think we rightfully have more sincere interest in the wholesomeness, purity, and quality of our product than all the scientists and legislators you could gather to discuss the subject.

Flack tended to dismiss a DES ban as unscientific, irrational, unenforceable, and impractical:

> . . . It has been stated on many occasions by competent scientific investigators that mankind, our environment, Mother Nature, could not comply with a zero attitude on anything.

DES was finally banned from animal feed on January 1, 1973. But the FDA left a gaping loophole in the new restrictions: DES was still permitted to be used in the form of pellets implanted in a cow's ears. The use of DES implants was almost as old as the use of DES itself, but they had fallen out of favor when the feed additive forms were deemed cheaper and more efficient. With the ban on DES in feed, DES implants achieved a new position in agricultural production. No matter how many times DES was banished from some use, the producers of this versatile chemical seemed always to come up with new purposes for it.

In his announcement of the ban, Commissioner Edwards defended his exclusion of the implants because the USDA had supposedly never detected a residue when implants were used as the sole source of DES. But Congressman Fountain later described this statement as false and misleading: false because a USDA inspector had found DES residues in beef liver (about 60 parts per billion) after the use of the implants; misleading because USDA had never bothered to extensively test for residues after implanting DES prior to the ban, so its not finding any traces constituted no real scientific conclusion.

The FDA's belated efforts to impose a ban on DES in feed were only temporarily successful. The cattle industry succeeded a year later in overturning the Federal ban. In April of 1973, when the initial ban had been in effect only three months, USDA inspectors began finding more and more DES residues in cattle treated with DES implants. By the end of April, as it had promised both the public and Congress it would do if residues were still detectable, FDA banned the implant method also, resulting in a total revocation of the drug.

The cattlemen then attempted in Congress to exempt DES from the Food, Drug and Cosmetic Act of 1938, which would have removed it altogether from the provisions of the Delaney Amendment. They failed, but they then filed a Federal suit on procedural grounds, alleging that the FDA ban was illegal because the agency had failed to hold an administrative hearing. They obtained a restraining order from a Federal court allowing them to resume use of the drug, and succeeded in further postponing hearings. In January of '74, the District of Columbia Court of Appeals, maintaining that FDA indeed had neglected its procedural obligation to hold a proper hearing, overturned the FDA ban, one year after its first imposition. One year later, by January of '75, DES residues were still being found in beef.

In 1971, a study of a thousand female students at the University of Michigan by a clinician named Lucille Kuchera produced results which led to the conclusion that DES was nearly 100 percent effective as a postcoital contraceptive. Though the mechanism of action was unknown, massive doses of DES theoretically inhibited implantation of the fertilized egg in the wall of the uterus. Widespread clinical interest in this miraculous "morning-after" pill inevitably followed Kuchera's positive report in the *Journal of the American Medical Association*. Within nine months of the FDA's contraindication of DES use in pregnancy (in November of 1971), total national DES sales had gone up approximately 4 percent.

It wasn't long before DES was available as a postcoital contraceptive at thousands of university health clinics. DES was given to many women without adequate counseling about carcinogenic potential or other effects, while its effectiveness was only haphazardly monitored with follow-up reports. This was a unique use for a drug which had received an extraordinary amount of public criticism only months before its burgeoning popularity as a contraceptive. Without any official approval or FDA investigation, the morning-after pill became an established if unofficial alternative to more traditional contraceptive methods for thousands of university-affiliated women who remained uninformed of its dangers.

This extraordinary situation was exacerbated in May of 1973, when the FDA sent out an erroneous drug bulletin to physicians informing that the agency had approved DES as a morning-after pill for emergency situations. In fact, DES had received no such agency approval, and the division of the FDA responsible for such approval did not even see the application submitted for marketing of this new dosage. For two years, the error was never corrected. Physicians and university health service staffers around the country eagerly dispensed DES as a postcoital contraceptive in the mistaken belief that it had been approved by the FDA for this indication.

On Thursday, February 27, 1975, Senator Edward Kennedy's Subcommittee on Health of the Committee on Labor and Public Welfare held a new hearing to look into what was being done about the DES hazard. With DES still being added to the national beef supply, with no official steps being taken to warn or find millions of DES daughters, and with DES now achieving a new position as the nation's only postcoital contraceptive, the hearings began on an indignant, exasperated, almost resigned note, sounded by Chairman Kennedy:

> DES is a drug out of control. It is known to cause cancer in the daughters of some mothers who took it during pregnancy. It is in widespread use in the United States as a morning after pill. . . . All experts agree that because it does cause human cancer it must be used with great caution and only in emergency situations. Most experts also agree that continued widespread misuse could present a major health hazard.
>
> It is ironic and disheartening that the FDA, through a major bureaucratic error, has contributed to the national confusion about DES. . . . In the real world doctors have been operating since 1973 under the assumption that the drug has been approved for emergencies. . . .

132

DES is also still being used as a cattle feed additive. . . . Now we are back where we started.

In order to effectively communicate to the Congress and to the public the real dangers of DES and the extent of the DES problem, Senator Kennedy called before the committee two DES mothers, who eloquently testified on the nature and extent of the injuries they had suffered from this drug. The first woman to come forward was Grace Molloy, of San Diego, California.

Back in 1955 when I was threatened to lose my baby the doctor gave me a little white pill to take. This was a miracle that was going to save my child, and I lost that baby in six months.

I became pregnant again about three months later and again started the spotting. And about the third month, the doctor gave me a little white pill, called diethylstilbestrol.

In December 1955, Christmas Day, I had a baby girl. When she was fourteen, I was reading the morning paper, and the morning paper had an article by Dr. Herbst, describing the dangers of DES, and stating that several daughters of mothers who were taking DES had vaginal cancer.

Of course, I became alarmed, and I took my daughter . . . to the doctor, and during the course of examination Marilyn was found to have vaginal cancer.

Three weeks later she had vaginal surgery in New York City. She was four weeks in the hospital. The doctors told me they had gotten all of it, there was no problem, everything was taken care of, the cancer rarely spread beyond the internal organs. . . . A year later she had cancer of the lung, and she had tumors on her trachea. And the doctors operated and removed the lung. They removed the tumors on the trachea and the bronchial tubes.

About four and a half months later, she started having severe head pains. The cancer had spread into her head. She had whole head radiation, and her hip started to hurt, and she had hip radiation, and eventually she went blind, and died two and a half years after we had discovered the cancer.

Kennedy: What kind of strain has this placed on you and your family?

Mrs. Molloy: I myself went into a fairly deep depression after her first surgery. . . . We are under constant pressure. It is a horrible, terrible thing to watch the child suffer, and eventually when she dies you think that this is a blessing, this is far easier to accept than the actual suffering.

Kennedy: . . . What would you say to the young women of the country who are using it indiscriminately?

Mrs. Molloy: Stay away from it, as far away as you can get.

Mrs. Albert Green, of Glen Cove, Long Island, spoke next:

I had a son in 1948, and two years later decided we would like another child. . . . One month I was a little late, and when my period came it was very heavy, and he said I think we ought to give you diethylstilbestrol, I think you have had a spontaneous abortion. My daughter was born on February 9, 1951. She was fine until she was fifteen. She hemorrhaged one day. I lived in a small town in New York called Glen Cove. And the doctors told me she had a very rare form of cancer. This was in 1966.

. . . She was fine for a while [after surgery], and then the cancer spread. She died when she was eighteen, in March 1967.

. . . Years later I received a call from Dr. Herbst, telling me there was a connection between . . . DES and my daughter's vaginal cancer.

I could not believe that something with any inherent danger would be given out so indiscriminately as that drug was given out in the 1950s.

. . . Many friends contacted me when this was publicly

known, and some that had taken it, and many of them were told by gynecologists oh, do not worry, your chances of contacting cancer, well you can get hit by an automobile faster.

. . . You know, if you take statistics, it is very meaningless unless that statistic is one of your own children.

Dr. Peter Greenwald appeared before the committee to update the members on the extent of the DES problem.

Greenwald: The last comprehensive registry report was 120 fully investigated. The total number is over 200 cases occurring. . . .

Kennedy: Do you think this is really the tip of the iceberg?

Greenwald: Yes . . . I feel that the incidence is still going up. We know from our data . . . that the incidence of vaginal cancer . . . is increasing. . . . On the basis of the study, the Mayo Clinic group estimated that the incidence of vaginal cancer among DES exposed persons could be as high as four per thousand. I do not think we should pass off incidence rates of this magnitude as trivial. Four per one thousand is equivalent to the annual death rate from heart disease in New York State, is forty-four times higher than the annual incidence rate for leukemia, and considerably higher than the annual incidence of breast cancer and colon cancer. . . .

Immediately prior to these hearings, the FDA had conditionally approved the use of DES as the morning-after pill, rectifying their earlier blunder. According to Senator Kennedy, "the knowledge of wide and inappropriate usage is, in part, responsible for FDA's recent decision to approve it . . . in emergency situations. FDA had defined such emergencies as rape, incest, or a similar tragedy." The primary purpose of these hearings was to seek and weigh public opinion on that recent decision.

Chief among the concerns expressed by health experts was the possibility of an undetected DES daughter receiving more DES as a postcoital contraceptive, an additional and massive jolt of hormones which could conceivably push affected cells from latency toward malignancy. Also, concern was expressed about the possibility of a fetus which survived the massive DES dose growing up with an extraordinarily high predilection toward vaginal cancer, as the dosage for postcoital contraception was many times higher than that used for prevention of miscarriage.

Belita Cowan, an instructor in health care at the University of Michigan, where the DES morning-after pill had first been introduced, testified to the enormous amount of carelessness, misinformation, and vague theoretical reasoning surrounding the emergence of this newest use for DES.

> DES is a drug that is abused, prescribed casually and carelessly to young women; DES is inappropriate therapy for rape victims; there is little scientific evidence to the FDA claim that the morning after pill is effective in preventing pregnancy.

Ms. Cowan had conducted a survey of women in Ann Arbor, Michigan, who had been given DES as a morning-after pill. She came up with some interesting, disturbing, but not altogether surprising results:

> 45% of my sample were not given pelvic or breast exams. 56% did not have taken a personal or family history. Only 26% were followed up to see if DES worked. 25% didn't take all ten pills. They became so ill from the DES they could not continue to use it.

A prime FDA justification for the recent move toward approval of the morning-after pill was its potential for treatment of rape victims. Cowan cited numerous reasons for treating the FDA's sanction of this purpose as dangerous, unrealistic, and impractical.

> FDA expects emergency room doctors to take full personal and family medical histories, pelvic and breast exams, counsel victims about cancerous and other effects, handle consent forms and do follow up work.
>
> If 10% of rape victims get pregnant we can offer

them menstrual extraction. Why give 90% of women a drug they don't need? Is the FDA so against abortion techniques that it will approve a known cancer-causing drug as an alternative?

Cowan sharply criticized the widespread acceptance of this drug after a single study proclaimed its supposed usefulness. It was the same old DES story all over again, with the medical profession eager to accept an exciting new remedy for an alleged problem, without proper regard for proof of efficacy, without proper regard for proof of safety. In this case, the FDA had so mismanaged the issue that thousands of physicians and health centers had gone ahead and used the drug without any real proof of either. Cowan testified:

Efficacy of DES is not 100% as FDA claims. Not one scientifically controlled efficacy study has been performed. Dr. Kuchera's study of more than 1000 college students at University of Michigan was retrospective. Many of these students were not even told they were part of an experimental study. Furthermore, many were not even followed up to see if they were pregnant. Dr. Kuchera's claim of 100% effectiveness is wishful thinking, and the FDA knows this.

Dr. Alexander M. Schmidt, Charles Edwards' successor as Commissioner of the FDA, was asked to testify at the Kennedy hearings about the FDA's recent decision to approve the morning-after pill, and about the current status of the agency's dealings on DES. Schmidt defended his department's conditional approval of the morning-after pill for "rape, incest, or other emergencies" as the only appropriate regulatory behavior which would control what had been an entirely uncontrolled and illegal usage:

What we have here is the widespread use of an approved drug for an unapproved use.

Schmidt insisted that to single out DES as opposed to other estrogenic preparations on the market, such as those used in the controversial oral contraceptives, would be unfair and unrealistic.

Senator Kennedy had begun these hearings with the words: "DES is a drug out of control." Schmidt represented a few minor changes in DES regulations as positive attempts to bring this uncontrolled preparation into some form of regulatory captivity.

Chief among the reforms offered by Commissioner Schmidt was a new set of labels for DES as a postcoital contraceptive. "These labels," Schmidt maintained, "stress the importance of limiting the use of DES to emergency situations." The new labeling phrase read as follows:

> If you find it necessary to use this treatment more than once, you should consult with your physician to obtain an adequate means of routine contraception.

As to whether or not emergency room doctors would be able to handle the difficulties of obtaining consent for prescribing DES or ensure that DES wouldn't be administered to DES daughters or women with personal or family histories of cancer, Schmidt had no response. About complaints that government agencies had abrogated their responsibility to set up a national program to aid and locate DES mothers and daughters, Schmidt had no proposals. The labeling changes, and the move to approve the pill itself, were all FDA had to offer consumers as regulatory safeguards to protect them from the DES danger.

The final testimony on the part of FDA officials came from Peter Barton Hutt, chief counsel for the FDA, whose chief experience prior to his entering service at FDA consisted of eleven years at Covington and Burling, a Washington law firm well known for its experience protecting private industry from inconvenient regulatory burdens. Hutt had been characterized at the time of his appointment as one of the food and drug industry's foremost defenders. He had assumed a position within the FDA considered second only to that of commissioner. And in his testimony, Hutt attempted to shift the blame for this whole fiasco away from the government once and for all:

> The problem is broader than DES. We have hundreds of drugs today that are on the market that the National Academy of Sciences has found to be ineffective but that remain on the market because of the statutory prohibition

against our taking them off the market until we have ruled on a request for an evidentiary hearing.

DES should be banned for other reasons [than as an imminent health hazard]; namely, the lack of assurance that it is safe. . . . The burden should not be on the government to prove it is a hazard. The burden should be on the industry to prove it is not a hazard.

14

In the fall of 1975, a friend of Anne's father started talking to the Needham family about the possibility of a lawsuit. He had read some articles about DES, and he was convinced that Anne should look into what might be done legally to compensate her for all she had gone through. Anne felt strange about it. She didn't much like the idea of hiring some men she didn't know to sue some other men she didn't know.

It was a bad time for Anne because she was in the middle of breaking up with John. It was a mutual thing. It didn't involve any painful recriminations, it was just one of those complex situations, and neither of them totally understood it. Anne knew she'd been feeling insecure about her own identity as a woman. Her general feeling of stagnation in her life seemed to encompass the relationship as well. She'd never gone out with anybody else in five years, a long part of her life. She knew that being unable to have children made her uncomfortable about settling down. Also, though they talked vaguely about marriage, about setting off and setting up somewhere, nothing had ever happened.

Anne had been feeling restless, she wanted to leave Park Forest. It had started seeming too small for her, everyone she knew knew her too well. They all knew what had happened to her. She had begun to associate the town with things she didn't like about her life: the sameness, the routine, the constricted feeling she'd never shaken since leaving the hospital, the claustrophobia she felt in crowded rooms and elevators.

Anne was scared about depending on John. She wasn't confident that any man would be able to support her emotionally over a long period. "What does he see in me," she would constantly ask herself; her own insecurity filled her with doubts. Their relationship didn't seem completely real, she had no idea anymore what it was founded upon. She wanted, she knew but didn't want to admit to herself, to go out in the world and find out how people beyond Park Forest might find her.

All these personal problems distracted Anne from thinking about going into a legal case, but the main reason for her hesitation was fear. She had finally begun to feel free of the immediate fear of a recurrence, and she didn't have any desire to relive what she'd been through by going all over it again with lawyers. She felt as if she was just now becoming something more than a medical case; she didn't want to become just a legal case.

What finally made her agree to see some lawyers was when her father's friend told her that the drug companies had known since the '40s that DES was a carcinogen. Anne found that hard to believe, but this man had read it somewhere. That finally got Anne mad. Anne wanted to know what the real story was. She felt strong enough to find out what had happened. She knew it was going to be one of the only ways to deal with it, short of therapy. She didn't believe in psychiatrists, but she knew what therapy was. She'd always been ashamed about running away from that nurse's station at the hospital. She felt like she'd spent almost two years running away from herself. Now she thought she'd go forward and find out what she could.

Early in 1976, Anne agreed to see a lawyer that her father's friend knew, Mel Cahan of Lurie and Cahan in Chicago. It was a Sunday afternoon in February, and Anne went down with her father to the firm's office in the Continental Bank Building in the Loop. Mr. Cahan was a large man, very impressive and businesslike. He had a young associate with him. Anne went off into a library with them, and they sat there and took down the facts.

Mr. Cahan was very intent on impressing upon Anne that time was running out. If she didn't act quickly, he explained, nothing would happen. There was a statute of limitations on cases of this sort, and the time period was exactly two years. They checked the dates, and they figured that the two years, if dated from the time of the surgery, was almost up. Anne felt pressured by this.

These men wanted her to go forward so fast. She didn't feel pressure from her father, he stayed pretty well out of it. She knew she had psychological conflicts over the whole thing, over confronting the issue or ducking away. She finally decided in that office that she'd not duck it again. They gave her some papers to sign, and she signed. Mr. Cahan said that in all probability the case would never see the inside of a courtroom. The chances were they would settle. That was just fine with Anne. She'd never even been in traffic court.

Anne left the office feeling scared. She had never had to deal with attorneys, they were an unknown quantity to her. But she also knew that if they were any good they should be able to help her out. She was scared by the power of the drug companies. As she walked between the giant buildings in the Loop, all housing major corporations, she felt as if she were taking on all of them. She wondered if there was enough power there to crush any opposition. She wondered, even as she knew it was all absurd speculation, whether she'd be spied upon, or somehow discredited. She felt like she was trying to solve a mystery, to fill in a puzzle; she felt almost like a detective.

Anne had never had much in the way of political ideals or convictions. She had never been a feminist. She had been against the Vietnam War when that had been fashionable, but she really had just been following the lead of other people. Political issues had seemed so abstract, but now this was her issue, and it positively burned her up. She actually felt good about her anger; it was the first positive, forward-looking feeling she'd had in years.

Anne Needham's complaint was filed on March 22, 1976. The firm assigned a young lawyer to her case, and she was supposed to contact him if she had any questions. But she had no questions, she hoped that in the early stages the case would take care of itself. She was busy with the first real change in her life to come in some time. She was leaving town, going somewhere new, and for the first time in a long while she was able to think of the future as having possibility, of something good hanging around the corner.

In May, Anne moved to Carbondale, Illinois, the home of Southern Illinois University. Her older sister, Cathy, was living up there, and Anne moved in with her. They found a cute little house on a noisy highway. Being a college town, Carbondale was full of young people, not only students, but people who had gone to school and stayed, or just people like Anne who moved there because the life was casual.

Anne knew getting a job would be tough because there weren't many. What there was didn't pay much because so many students worked for low wages. But Anne had some money saved and she just felt like relaxing. It was spring, and Cathy had a great group of friends. They went rafting and played in the sun. Anne made several girl friends. It was the first time in her life she had been close to other women, and she wondered if it might be because she'd gone through something that women could more easily understand. But even so, she didn't talk much to them about what had happened. The whole point of the move was to get away from all that. It was a breezy, easy, happy time; it felt good to be young, single, and away from home. She didn't want anymore to lean on her mother, her friends, or a man. She no longer wanted to settle down and have kids like her mother. In Carbondale, no one lived that kind of life. Park Forest, the baby-boom town with the small houses and the big families, seemed suddenly straight and strange.

The legal case couldn't have seemed further away. From time to time she talked on the phone to Mr. Cahan's associate about details, or if he needed some information from her. She wasn't that curious about the proceedings, she was vaguely aware there were motions to be filed, pleadings and briefs and summations and such, but she had little interest in them. She knew that when she would have to take part it would be difficult and painful, and she was trying not to let herself become frightened by the prospect. She had doubts and misgivings about having started it at all, and sometimes the whole idea that she should be suing some corporation seemed preposterous, and possibly pointless.

It was the fall of 1977. Anne was sitting on the train from Carbondale to Chicago, staring out the window at the fields and occasional towns. She was getting off in Homewood, near Park Forest, where her mother was supposed to meet her to drive into downtown Chicago. It was a chilly day, and Anne was heading into the city to have her deposition taken. She felt somewhat removed from the whole process, so much had happened since she'd first started the case, and it seemed a long time ago that she'd been lying there in pain at Mayo's staring out the window at the Canadian geese. Four years ago; she was surprised the case had happened so fast. They'd talked about it taking years and years and now it was coming right at her.

She'd lately gotten herself involved in another relationship, with a man she'd met years before in Park Forest, but had run into again at Carbondale. She hadn't really been interested in another heavy relationship, she'd enjoyed being free. But it had been an easy thing to get into without thinking much about it. He'd pursued it mostly from his end at first. He'd come into town to visit and pretty soon they had started seeing each other. At first she had resisted moving in with him because she didn't want to get dependent. He'd kept saying, "It's kind of stupid your paying rent down in Carbondale," but Anne had wanted to keep her own place. Finally she had given up, and now they were living together in Champaign.

He didn't like to deal with all the psychological problems she had from her illness. His indifference to that side of her life was kind of a relief, it made it seem finally in the past. He had no interest in dwelling on what had happened to her, in fact he gave no sign of wanting to deal with it at all. The strange thing was, Anne didn't mind. The way she was feeling, relaxed and casual about her life, she wasn't looking for any heavy examination of her own problems.

But the legal case brought that all back. She didn't much like the feeling. She rarely thought that much about the case, until lately, and when she did she kept it to herself. The case was a foreign, irritating thing to him, he assumed it had nothing to do with him because he hadn't known her then. He really didn't care about it, and he wasn't graceful at dealing with pain or disease. His mom had been having some kidney trouble at about that time, and once she had said to Anne, "He's terrible about people when they're sick. He just doesn't like it." It was true: All the time his mom had been in the hospital, he'd hated visiting her.

She still went back to Mayo's once a year. She tried as hard as she could to feel as if her medical case was over, at least she was hoping. Every time just before she went up there she'd have unbearable anxiety, but each time when she came back with a clean bill of health she would be elated for a while. Soon the five-year mark would arrive, and that was a thing to look forward to.

They said if you made it for five years after surgery, your chances of survival were good.

The scars had finally faded, and the pain was mostly gone. The incontinence was still a problem, but she'd slowly grown adjusted to it as it had slowly improved. She had all the reason in the world to feel confident about her life and her future. But she was unusually apprehensive on the train that morning in November. Her medical case might be ending, but her legal case was beginning. At times she wondered if the legal case might prove almost as painful as the medical. She was filled with a strange anxiety, as if something awful might happen.

She wasn't worried about the deposition. She felt she could handle it. It all seemed a long time ago, but she trusted her memory and knew she wouldn't have to distort anything. She knew they were going to challenge her version of events because of the statute of limitations. If they could prove that she knew about the DES while she was still in the hospital, or very soon after, she wouldn't have a case. But Anne knew exactly when she first was aware of the DES, and that was when the questionnaire came, in May. She didn't feel as if she needed much in the way of preparation before going in. Her lawyer didn't seem to think so either; he planned to meet with her briefly just prior to the taking of the dep. Hers was due to be taken at noon, her mother's was scheduled for eleven.

Mary Needham picked Anne up at Homewood Station, and they drove straight down to Chicago. Neither of them said very much on the ride downtown because they were both getting nervous. Anne began to think a bit about being under oath. She never had been under oath before, and the majesty of that was intimidating. Anne knew she was a lousy liar, so she was glad she wouldn't have to lie. They parked the car and headed for the offices of Baker and McKenzie, the attorneys for White Labs, in the Prudential Building, Suite 2700. They met their lawyer from Lurie and Cahan in the lobby and went right up to the twenty-seventh floor. Anne waited in the reception room outside.

Anne wasn't at all frightened until her mother came out at noon. She was white as a sheet, visibly trembling, and Anne stood up and went right over to her and said, "What happened? What did they do to you?" Mary Needham just shook her head and couldn't say anything. Anne got really upset, she felt like running out of the room. But Mary straightened herself up, took hold of herself, and said, "Don't worry Annie. Go ahead. I'll be just fine." Anne went into the conference room where all the men were waiting.

There was a court reporter on one side and three or four men from the other side ranged along one end of a long conference table. Harry J. O'Kane of Baker and McKenzie began asking her questions. They started out quite easily, about where she was born and where she lived. But after a while they started getting rougher and Anne started to get upset. He began asking about sexual relations; the questions kept coming, and the tone began to change into something harsher, like a sneer, and he kept asking about men and sex, and Anne got the strong impression this man was trying to make her out to look like a streetwalker or something, as someone kind of loose.

Nothing could be further from the truth. Anne was absolutely indignant. She'd gone out with one man for almost five years and never cheated on him. A lot of people were far worse, and Anne kept insisting to herself that she hadn't done anything wrong by her book. The insinuating tone of this man was infuriating and impudent. She was aware all the while it was a technique, a technique of humiliation. But the technique was amazingly effective.

He asked questions about marriage. He asked if she ever had planned to marry John. She replied that they had considered it. He asked if she planned to marry her current boyfriend. She responded in much the same way.

Q: You had never lived with John, is that correct?

A: That is correct.

Q: What were your reasons for not marrying him? He just wasn't your type?

A: Marriage is a big step. I didn't really know if it would work. I had my own doubts.

Q: About John?

A: He is a good man. I just didn't know if it would work.

Then he got to her current boyfriend.

Q: Have either you or he pronounced the opinion to marry?

A: We have talked about it possibly for some time in the future. But not for a while.

He moved to the fact that she wasn't working. It was because she had only just moved to Champaign and hadn't yet found a job. But the lawyer portrayed it as if she were unstable, as if she were some sort of a bum.

Finally he got to the medical questions, about her visits over the years with Dr. Warren. But he concentrated at first on how she had received birth control pills in high school for menstrual irregularity. He asked so many questions on that subject that Anne was convinced he was trying to suggest the blame for her cancer might rest on the birth control pills, not DES.

Finally, Mr. O'Kane got to the point Anne had been waiting for. He sort of snuck it up on her:

Q: In February of '74 did you tell [Dr. Warren] that you had a yellowish discharge that was odorous?

A: Yes. Then I was in for a physical.

Q: Did you then tell him the discharge was yellowish and odorous?

A: Yes.

Q: What did he say?

A: He placed me up on the table and gave me an exam and proceeded to get very excited.

Q: Proceeded to get very excited at that point in time in February of '74?

A: Yes. He said he had found something abnormal.

Q: Then what did he do?

A: He took a biopsy in the office. I proceeded to take it as I recall to St. James Hospital. He proceeded to ask me when I was still in the office—

Q: Could you speak a little louder? You took the material to St. James Hospital at his request for a biopsy, right?

A: Yes.

Q: Okay, what did you do, go home?

A: No. I went to a girlfriend's house.

Q: Okay. When Dr. Warren said he found something abnormal, did he tell you what he found?

A: Yes. As I recall, I think he said he found ulcers.

He asked how she found out about the biopsy:

A: I got on the phone when Dr. Warren called with the results . . . he asked to talk to my parents, and my mother got on the phone and I proceeded to get on the other phone. . . . I told him I thought I should be involved.

Q: Did he [Dr. Warren] tell you what caused the malignancy?

Anne knew this was a crucial question. She replied evenly:

A: No.

Q: Did your father then learn of it that evening?

A: He learned of something wrong.

Q: Did you and your father and mother discuss this malignancy and what caused it at that time?

A: No we did not.

Q: Did your father tell you at some point in time that it was allegedly caused by DES?

A: At some point in time he told me. It was after I was home from the hospital. And the clinic, Mayo's, had mailed out pamphlets or questionnaires for my parents or my mother to fill out. At that point in time we discussed the whole thing.

Q: You never discussed it before that? Your father never told you that this condition was caused by DES?

A: No, not until it was approximately May or April, possibly June. I do not remember when the questionnaire came out.

Q: And who told you then that it was caused by the DES, your father?

A: No. We, he and my mother were discussing, if I can recall this correctly, what pills she had taken.

Q: When was this?

A: When the questionnaire had come out from Mayo's Clinic.

Q: This wasn't before you went to Mayo Brothers?

A: No, this wasn't before.

Under questioning, Anne repeatedly demonstrated that she had not been familiar with her mother's taking prenatal hormones while still at Mayo Brothers:

A: We were questioned at the clinic of the possibility—I was asked if my mother had taken anything before I was born. And I responded I had no idea. I did not know.

O'Kane pressed her on whether her father had mentioned DES.

Q: You talked to your father over the telephone when you were up at Mayo's?

A: Yes.

Q: When was that?

A: When I was lying in bed.

Q: Did you talk to him before your surgery from the time you left your house in Park Forest?

A: I don't recall if we called that evening. . . . I don't recall if we did call that evening from a pay phone down the hall. . . .

Q: Do you know if you talked to your father?

A: My father worked quite a bit.

Q: Okay. Do you want to take a five minute break and compose yourself?

A: I will be okay in a second.

Anne had broken down. One thing her lawyer had told her was, "Don't let them get a pace going, don't let them start making the pace or you're finished." He told her to just break the pace, take a deep breath, think as long as she wanted, and answer the questions slowly and truthfully. Just then the pace had accelerated, the questions had started coming faster and faster, and her answers had started coming faster. And then he had started in on her father and whether she talked everything over with him, and she was sensitive on that point and she hadn't been able to handle it.

As the deposition dragged on it began to feel like the Spanish Inquisition. She started feeling softened up by what she interpreted as verbal abuse, and she began to feel wounded and punchy. She knew that was exactly how they wanted to make her feel, and she tried to keep her cool. She had kept looking to her own lawyer for some sort of support, but she knew he couldn't counsel her during the deposition. He was only empowered to object to certain questions. Still, she kept trying to catch his eye as the questions got worse, but most of the time he wasn't looking at her. All he could do was object to a question and have the objection on the record. But all through the thick of it he didn't raise a single objection.

Harry O'Kane had been particularly insistent about asking Anne whether she had ever discussed her case with her father while at Mayo's, or immediately before. Anne had indicated that her discussions with her father on the subject had been minimal at best. But over and over O'Kane had questioned Anne about her talking to her father, whether or not she called her father, etc. Victor Needham had given his deposition two months before, on September 12. In that deposition he demonstrated a distinct lack of clarity in his recollections of the events of late February and early March of '74, the period when Anne had her surgery. In particular, Victor was unclear as to whether he might have discussed Anne's case and its possible association with DES prior to her leaving for Rochester; some of his comments indicated that the subject of a link between Anne's cancer and DES might have come up in talks with Dr. Warren.

Q: When did you and Dr. Warren first discuss the fact that the cancer might have been caused by Dienestrol?

A: . . . I think after, it was after the surgery and Annie came home, or maybe she was still up there, that Mary and I— And then in between we talked with Dr. Warren. It was a possible relation between cancer and the—

150

Q: . . . Was it you who suggested to Dr. Warren that there might be an association with cancer through your wife's taking DES at the time of the pregnancy with Anne?

A: Quite frankly, it was in my mind, but I do not remember definitely bringing this up to the doctor. I think the doctor brought it up to us.

Q: . . . That would be between the time the biopsy report came back and the surgery occurred?

A: Yes.

Q: So that would be at the end of February, some time between February and March 8?

A: Yes, sir.

If White Laboratories was able to prove that Anne Needham knew about the DES causing her cancer while she was at Mayo's, or before, or even very shortly after her return, White would have had the right to have the case dismissed. Anne had filed her case in March of '76, almost exactly two years after her return from the Mayo Clinic. Anne insisted that she found out about the DES link at the time the questionnaire came from Mayo's in May. Victor's uncertainty about the time any such information might reasonably have become known to Anne put the case in jeopardy.

Q: . . . with regard to Anne, she was told either the same day the biopsy report came back or within a day or two, right?

A: Yes.

Q: Was she told about that association?

A: Yes. I believe we did.

Q: So all of this transpired between the time of the biopsy report and surgery at Mayo, correct?

A: Yes.

But when such a conversation might have taken place was unclear:

Q: And in that conversation that you had with Dr. Warren, he

. . . broached the possible association of Dienestrol with cancer?

A: Yes, sir.

Q: Then after that did your wife have any conversations or meet- ings with Dr. Warren?

A: I am sure they did, but probably after the—

Q: Surgery at Mayo?

A: Yes, sir.

In fact, neither Mary nor Anne discussed the case with Dr. Warren either while at Mayo's or immediately after.

Q: Do you know if your wife had [discussions] prior to the surgery?

A: I would assume so, but I am not sure.

Q: Do you know if your wife or rather if your daughter had any conversations with Dr. Warren?

A: I really don't know. I think so, but I definitely cannot say.

Attempts by the White lawyer to pin Victor down on when he might have mentioned DES to Anne in that hectic period proved futile. Victor simply didn't remember. O'Kane asked Victor about Mary calling him from Mayo's to ask about prenatal hormones.

Victor remembered distinctly telling Mary she had taken Dienestrol. But when asked to recall whether either Anne or Mary had been specifically informed of the connection between DES and Anne's cancer, Victor replied that he had no idea.

The case also hinged on Victor's positive identification of the product he had given his wife during her pregnancy with Anne as Dienestrol, a White product. On that, Victor was virtually certain.

Mary Needham finished her deposition feeling as if someone had been trying to strip the clothes right off her body. They had tried to make her look ignorant, she felt, and nobody wants to be made to look like an absolute ass. That lawyer White Labs had hired, Mary wanted to whack him right in the mouth for his impudence. They had tried to double-talk her, but Mary thought she had not done so badly under the circumstances. She had gotten confused, she had had trouble with her dates, but Mary knew she hadn't gotten anything factually or substantially wrong.

Mary was optimistic. She was sure they would finally win. She wasn't at all sure the pain and humiliation were going to be worth it, but the whole process turned out to be good for her. It began to relieve her of the burden of guilt she'd carried around for three or four years, ever since she realized it was something she had taken that had been the cause. She couldn't help but think it was all her fault. Getting involved in the case helped to transfer that burden to other people. She didn't feel quite as uncomfortable with Anne, and she felt as if Anne herself had transferred that blame, at least unconsciously, away from her and onto White Laboratories.

The ridiculous thing, Mary often told herself, was that if that drug company had come to them and said, "We'll pay all your medical bills, for now and in the future," they probably would have settled. They were having a terrible time meeting those bills, and though Mayo's was being very good about it, it put them under a deep financial strain. The Needhams didn't want some huge amount, they just wanted what was owed them, but once they got the case going, Mary wanted to really sock it to them. It felt good after so long to finally get your blood running. Getting into the case was great for Mary because it made her feel like a fighter again.

Giving the deposition was awful. It began sadly, with a long litany of births, and miscarriages. After what seemed like hours, Mr. O'Kane moved on to a question about her pregnancy with Anne. He asked about the medications prescribed to her at that time. With a slow, sinking feeling, Mary began to recall:

A: We had just moved to Park Forest. And when I became pregnant with Anne, as soon as I realized I was pregnant, I went to see Dr. Abrams. He was the only gynecologist in the town. And I went to him. And I told him I had two miscarriages. So, he did not do a vaginal. He just put me on a pill, a vitamin. The pill was to help me keep from losing the baby . . . I believe I took it once a day, and it was a small coated tablet. In the morning when I took my vitamins and juice. And I gave all of my kids their vitamins and juice.

Q: Did Dr. Abrams ever tell you what that prescription was?

A: I don't recall.

Q: You don't recall if he ever discussed it with you?

A: No.

Q: He just said, "Here is a prescription that will help you keep that baby"?

A: Words to that effect. I didn't want to abort again.

Q: I am asking you what he told you.

A: I don't recall his words.

Mary felt as if lost in a dream, floating back to when she was young and having children, twenty-three years ago. She remembered something:

A: It was not like an aspirin, soft.

Q: Not like an aspirin what?

A: An aspirin is not a coated pill. This was a coated pill.

He asked her when she learned what the pill was called. She said:

A: I can't give you a time, Mr. O'Kane.

Q: Well, was it at Mayo Brothers?

Mary said wearily:

A: I think I probably knew it years ago. I don't know. I have shut my mind to so many things.

Then she had to pull herself forward, to another time:

A: The doctor at the hospital asked me at Mayo's before Anne had her surgery if I had taken anything when I carried her. And I said, "Yes, I had."

Q: What did you tell him?

A: I told him I had taken a vitamin pill and a pill so I wouldn't abort because I had had two miscarriages before Anne.

Q: What doctor asked you this at Mayo?

A: Dr. Symmonds, I believe. Wait a minute, I had better qualify that. I think it was Dr. Symmonds. There were five doctors in the room and it was a very trying time.

He asked the crucial question:

Q: When did you first learn after Mayo Brothers what kind of a pill you took?

A: It was sometime later when the first letter from Mayo's came regarding any medication I had taken when I carried Anne.

Q: In other words, sometime after the surgery?

A: Sometime after the surgery to Anne, when she came home, yes.

Later:

Q: From the time that the biopsy report results were given Anne by you and the time you left Tuesday afternoon, did you and Victor and Anne discuss the matter?

A: To the best of my recollection there was just a very tense-filled time. And there was never any big tearing apart discussion. We had to move. We had to make decisions. So, they were made.

He asked if when she called Victor right after Anne's surgery, whether Victor had mentioned the drug she took by name. She said:

A: No, I don't recall that he did.

Q: And I imagine you asked him, "Do you remember my taking any medication?"

A: I imagine so, but I will tell you that I was in such a distraught state I don't remember what I did at that time. I was a basket case.

Later:

Q: Did Dr. Warren ever tell you that Anne's condition was
caused by the medication you took during your pregnancy
with her?

A: Dr. Warren never told me that, that I can recall. Never.

After Anne got back to Champaign, the deposition came in a
manila envelope. She didn't want to read it at first, because she
was sure it would be terrible. But finally she was just so curious
she opened it and began to read. After a few lines she realized it
wasn't hers. It was her mother's. She didn't read any further. She
put the pages back in the envelope and called her mother immediately. Sure enough, her mother had her deposition, and Anne felt
terrible for a long time. She didn't even ask her mother if she had
read it. She assumed she probably had.

Her mother never had known about her entire life, and now
suddenly she did. Anne felt as if she'd been caught doing bad
things, like a kid. It bothered her terribly that people she knew
would know about all that stuff. It was much worse than with
strangers or a jury, it was her own mother. She suddenly realized
how much exposure going into a case like this entailed. In the end,
she told herself it was going to be worth it, but having her mother
read her deposition was even worse than having to say all those
things to that room of men.

Anne finally got hold of her own deposition, and that, if possible, was worse. She had gone back home to switch the deps, and
she took it all the way back on the train to Champaign and never
once looked at it. When she got home she glanced through it fur-
tively, as if it were something she shouldn't see. She never finished
reading it, she just stuck it right back in the envelope and put it into
a bottom drawer under a pile of clothes. What she had read was
just like when she heard herself sometimes on tape recorders. She
seemed incoherent, unconnected, with every kind of idea and
phrase going off in different directions, loose words dangling on
strings. She was supposed to read it, sign it, and send it back, but
she was upset because she thought she sounded awful, like a bum-
bling idiot. She was most upset that now all of a sudden everyone
should know her whole life. As she put the dep deep into her
drawer, she knew she would just have to get it out again and send

it back to them. She had an impulse just to lose the thing, to get rid of it somewhere. But she knew there would be copies of it, copies everywhere, for everyone to read. She imagined copies and copies of this thing going through the mails, landing on all sorts of strange desks, being opened by strange hands. She felt somehow defiled and thought, "God, maybe I shouldn't be in this case."

15

The average American woman probably does not know if she threatened to abort what her doctor might have given her. I think this is one of the responsibilities that has to be laid directly at the doorstep of the American doctor.

FDA Commissioner Charles Edwards
The Fountain Hearings
November 11, 1971

If the medical profession created the epidemic, it also took strenuous if disconnected steps to stop it once it began. Initially, Herbst and his colleagues were able to rely on highly sophisticated epidemiological methods to learn of and assess the nature of the problem. They were able to obtain a grant from the National Cancer Institute, which sponsored the foundation of the Registry of Clear-Cell Adenocarcinoma. They were able to employ advanced surgical techniques to treat the cases discovered. But their attempt to enlist the aid of FDA in stopping the actual cause of the epidemic, namely the use of DES in pregnancy, broke down not only because of inefficiency and caution to the point of negligence on the part of the agency, but also because of a lack of proper channels for public policy to be informed by private opinion.

To effectively screen out, examine, and treat the entirely unknown numbers of DES daughters, to locate and trace all medical records, and then to mount the kind of program which would have guaranteed some measure of safety for the endangered women was so overwhelming a task that all parties conceivably responsible quickly shrank away from it. The medical profession, the FDA, and the DES manufacturers entered almost immediately into a dispute over which group should take the blame and do the awesome duty. The FDA gingerly passed the buck to the "American doctor," who for the most part rejected the responsibility and its complementary onus, while the drug companies were put immediately on the defensive and fought off all attempts to get them to fund any kind of DES screening programs, let alone provide compensation for the injured victims.

The response of leading members of the medical profession, as represented by editorials in the most prestigious medical journals, was one of shock and alarm. The *New England Journal* published weighty editorials with each of the Herbst and Greenwald articles. In England, both the *Lancet* and the *British Medical Journal* published equally grave editorials, but each pointed out that stilbestrol was never approved for use in pregnancy in England, the country of its origin, which made the DES-induced cancer epidemic a largely American problem.

As physicians around the world were alerted to the possibility of outbreaks of clear-cell adenocarcinoma in their own countries, some interesting results were obtained and sent to the registry.

A Danish physician, alarmed by Herbst's original report, rushed immediately to the national records for any reported cases of clear-cell adenocarcinoma reported in the previous twenty years. He found no reported cases, and was about to write to Herbst and Ulfelder that they must have come across some sort of medical fluke, when he happened to ask one of his colleagues whether DES had ever been used in that country to prevent miscarriage. The answer was no, and the Danish doctor was forced to write to Boston advising them that his findings demonstrated a very low chance of such an epidemic breaking out in any area where DES wasn't sold. Other reports from other countries, such as Great Britain and West Germany, confirmed a virtual nonincidence of clear-cell adenocarcinoma in countries where DES had never been given during pregnancy.

This was the largest need of the DES daughter: timely and

accurate diagnosis. In the first report in *Cancer* by Herbst and Scully on the original seven cancer cases, the problem had been apparent; many women could undergo an ordinary vaginal examination without having their adenosis or adenocarcinoma discovered. The one common symptom of cancer was irregular vaginal bleeding, but just as many cases eventually detected had been entirely asymptomatic. One of the first questions addressed by the medical profession was the establishment of standard methods of diagnosis and treatment.

Herbst and his colleagues generally recommended a manual technique known as vaginal palpation, which, when combined as necessary with staining with a chemical known as Lugol's solution, usually revealed any DES-induced changes in the vaginal lining such as adenosis or clear-cell carcinoma. A team of physicians at the Medical College of Wisconsin, Stafl and Mattingly, highly recommended the use of a colposcope, an extremely costly microscope adapted for use in pelvic examinations, which may be fitted with various filters and stereocamera attachments and which permits a magnified and illuminated view of the vaginal wall that can bring the subtle cellular changes caused by DES exposure into sharp focus after staining.

One of the great puzzles confronting physicians attempting to do something about the DES hazard was the nature of adenosis. Its precise origin was obscure, and a great deal of speculation arose early in the DES investigations about its development, evidently early in the fetal period, and about its relative benignity or malignancy. Since many of the known adenocarcinoma cases were found surrounded by adenosis, the presence of tube and glandlike structures on the surface of the vaginal wall, it was widely assumed that cancer developed from the adenosis, that adenosis was a premalignant, or precancerous condition. Others adopted more of a conservative attitude, and demured from considering adenosis an immediately dangerous condition. Unfortunately, though the latter view eventually prevailed, initially there were numerous cases of radical surgery being performed on young women suffering only from adenosis.

The question of adenosis versus carcinoma bore directly on one of the primary goals of DES research: determining the actual risk that DES exposure posed to the population. Unfortunately, this issue was greatly obscured by the almost total lack of data on

DES sales. If the DES manufacturers themselves possessed such information, none was released to medical researchers. The first full-scale attempt to compile DES sales figures, by O. P. Heinonen, was published in *Cancer* in March 1973.

The study was conducted by the Boston Collaborative Drug Surveillance Program of the Boston University Medical Center. Publication of the report simply reinforced the impression that accurate statistics were unavailable. Two pharmaceutical market research firms were consulted, and their figures were extrapolated on to arrive at a national figure:

> Both sources indicated an average of 2.5 million prescriptions for DES written per year between 1960 and 1970, of which approximately 100,000 were written for women who were pregnant.

But the unavailability of figures for before 1960 made these estimates almost inherently misleading, because a separate attempt by Herbst in which he did receive sales figures from one major drug company indicated what most observers had suspected, that DES sales went from a relatively low level in 1947 to a peak in 1952–53. Presumably the publication of so many negative reports on efficacy caused those figures to decline after 1955, until they were down to less than 50 percent of the peak by 1959, back to the previous low of 1947.

Another issue of contention within the medical profession, and later in the legal profession, was whether DES could be said to "cause" cancer. What lawyers and laymen refer to as "cause" is in science always a matter of probability. In biology, particularly in that obscure arena of carcinogenesis, the notion of cause is almost literally an invitation to protracted dispute. In an absolute scientific sense, nobody knows what "causes" cancer.

Herbst and his colleagues elected to term the link between maternal ingestion of DES and the appearance of clear-cell adenocarcinoma in offspring daughters an "association." They attempted from the beginning to correlate both dosage ingested and time of ingestion to the probability of cancer. Though it proved impossible to come up with a dosage below which cancer would certainly not strike, it did become virtually certain that the danger was greatest with the earliest possible exposure: In all reported cases of cancer, stilbestrol exposure took place before the eighteenth week of pregnancy.

If one of the more controversial aspects of the crisis was the issue of causation, its eventual settlement rested largely on national sales figures which proved impossible to obtain. Even with the obstacle of these elusive sales records, the extreme rarity of the illness involved matched with what was known about DES sales produced a precise profile of the cause and spread of the clear-cell cancer epidemic.

The first phase of the hypothesis based on DES sales was simply that the diseases of clear-cell cancer and adenosis had practically not existed before DES. A researcher named Sandberg who had studied adenosis extensively prior to the outbreak of the DES issue had been able to locate fewer than fifty documented cases of adenosis in the world's medical literature. The nonincidence of clear-cell carcinoma was likewise well known. The additional information that clear-cell carcinoma was virtually nonexistent in countries where stilbestrol had not been prescribed for miscarriage was for some investigators a particularly convincing reinforcement of the theory. Not until some years later was the DES-causation hypothesis additionally confirmed by Herbst's partial sales figures, which gave a peak for DES sales for the years 1952–53. Calculating a latency period of twenty years for the cancer to develop, which was the statistical average for the cases on record, Herbst found a corresponding peak in the cancer incidence for the years 1972–73. This constituted for some observers final proof that DES was the primary cause.

Throughout this controversy, physicians, government officials, and scientists alike were far more comfortable encouraging and undertaking research projects to "find out more" about the dangers of DES than they were trying to do anything substantial for the victims involved. Of course, to find out how many victims there might be, what risk they would have to live with, and what should be done clinically to treat those who succumbed to illness were all worthy goals of accelerated research. But while the DES controversy sparked an enormous number of research projects, the comparative poverty of programs to directly aid affected persons became increasingly evident as time went on.

An editorial which appeared in the *Journal of the American Medical Association* on December 6, 1971, only a few months after the issue became public, was characteristic of the response of organized medicine. The organization, it seemed, existed to prevent further organization:

> The responsibilities of the physician are clear-cut. However, an organized effort by the medical profession to inform all women who were given estrogen therapy of the possible tragic consequences for the female offspring is of questionable advisability.
>
> Although the extent to which diethylstilbestrol and other synthetic estrogens were administered in high risk pregnancies is not known, available data suggests that the risk to offspring is small. . . . Meanwhile, the fact that the risk exists should be known to the physician, and should guide him to act in a careful, responsible fashion, according to the needs of the individual patient. . . .

This, then, was the editorial response from the American Medical Association: that while the physician should be informed of the danger, it would be best for the patient to remain unaware; that any "organized" effort to warn patients of the "possible tragic consequences" would only lead to unnecessary panic; that since the risk was thought to be small, it should be up to the individual physician to respond each in his purely personal, private fashion. The official attitude toward the patient could be easily summarized: What they don't know won't hurt them.

In September of '72, Herbst and Scully released new findings from their extensive examination of numerous DES daughters. In the journal *Obstetrics and Gynecology,* they wrote:

> During the course of examination . . . we encountered frequent gross and microscopic abnormalities of the vagina and cervix other than carcinoma. These changes include: vaginal adenosis (glandular epithelium in the vagina), cervical erosion (the presence of glandular epithelium on the portio of the cervix) and transverse vaginal and cervical ridges. . . .

A new focus had developed in DES research; attention was being directed toward DES daughters free of malignancy but not free of other changes. Using colposcopes, staining, and other sophisticated techniques, researchers began uncovering significant and potentially dangerous abnormalities in many DES daughters. Adolf Stafl of the Medical College of Wisconsin, a leader in the clinical use of the colposcope, and his colleague Richard Mattingly wrote in the November 1972 issue of the *American Journal of Obstetrics and Gynecology* of the importance of the colposcope in detecting these subtle changes. In sixty-three young women whose mothers had taken DES, 23 percent had lesions suggesting adenosis. In many of these cases, routine examination had been completely normal; when the colposcope was used, they commonly found: vaginal hoods, comprising a circular fold in the vagina which partially obscured the cervix; a cockscomb-patterned anterior lip of the cervix, with a frequently inflamed, granular surface and adenosis in a third of the cases. Stafl and Mattingly concluded:

> vaginal adenosis is clinically unrecognizable in most cases by conventional diagnostic methods. . . .

In the May 1974 issue of *Obstetrics and Gynecology,* Barber and Sommers of New York's Lenox Hill Hospital wrote:

> If clear-cell adenocarcinoma of the vagina definitely proves to be related to the mother's use of DES . . . the situation will be unique in that it will be a self-limiting cancer, that will disappear within one generation. It will represent a cancer restricted to the twentieth century.

The first comprehensive attempt on the part of any public health agency to reach out to DES victims came toward the end of 1974. At that time, the National Cancer Institute Cancer Control Project contracted with several university health centers to set up DES programs. The program, with headquarters at Baylor University's Houston campus, enlisted four centers, at Baylor, Harvard, the University of Southern California, and the Mayo Clinic in Rochester, Minnesota, to test 1,000 DES daughters at each center. Though this represented a significant coordinated effort jointly managed by government and several academic institutions to set up a national DES program, it still was limited to a pilot test of a few thousand women.

This lack of response on the part of government, the medical profession, and industry, set the stage for much citizen agitation and litigation for more aid to DES victims. Some early lawsuits sought to force the drug companies to fund such programs, while citizens' groups, particularly women's health action groups, desperately lobbied for more government involvement, even special legislation to deal with the cancer epidemic. The ensuing organization around the country of groups with names like "DES Watch" and "DES Action" was largely a by-product of protracted corporate and government apathy and inaction in the face of a clearly defined hazard. DES rapidly became a national women's health issue, and the focus of a great deal of critical attention directed on the part of many women's organizations against the national reliance on artificial estrogenic preparations in oral contraceptives.

The medical profession continued to find out more about the natural history of adenocarcinoma and adenosis, and to institute real innovations in therapy in the treatment of detected cancer cases. The research went on as the legal battles began. As DES became a major legal issue, the reaction of the medical profession subtly began to change. Though individual physicians were rarely even considered as defendants in DES cases, appeals by DES Action and concerned citizens' groups asking doctors to send out mailings to patients with recorded DES prescriptions caused numerous cases of office records mysteriously disappearing and doctors unwilling or unable to inform DES mothers and daughters about their risks and their possible options.

DES researchers were soon subjected within the profession to a great deal of criticism. In the May 1, 1977, issue of the *American Journal of Obstetrics and Gynecology,* Dr. Raymond Kaufman released important findings of a study conducted as part of the National Cancer Institute DESAD (National Cooperative Diethylstilbestrol Adenosis) Project at a screening clinic established at Baylor University in Houston, Texas. He found that forty out of sixty DES daughters had "changes in the uterus which differed significantly from those seen in the past." In 36 out of 40, he discovered "gross defects of the cervix"; in a majority, he found a "T-shaped uterus," which constituted an undiscovered potential for pregnancy complications, birth defects, and fertility loss.

Herbst reported in the same issue the latest findings of the DES registry, which by December 31, 1976, had complete information on 333 clear-cell cancer cases. Cancer risk to DES daughters was clearly estimated at 10 to 20 times that in the general population. The risk was computed at .7 to 1.4 cases per thousand of cancer developing in a DES-exposed female through the age of twenty-four. The peak age incidence, and thus the year of greatest danger for the DES daughter, was figured at age nineteen.

Some doctors seemed far more concerned about the adverse publicity of DES affecting their practices than about adequate treatment of DES daughters. Dr. David Decker of Rochester, Minnesota, remarked in a discussion reported in that same issue:

The emotional impact of this malignancy on society in general is certainly well known, and the avidity of the news media for information concerning this problem needs no emphasis. It would seem that the time has come when only factual, solidly based information rather than further speculative efforts on our part should appear on this subject.

Dr. John Isaacs of Evanston, Illinois, responded:

The author is now apparently of the opinion that DES is not a complete carcinogen . . . this attitude seems more appropriate than his previous statement in 1971, implicating a highly significant association. . . . It is likewise more appropriate than his statement made in 1972 that ". . . a review of the Registry has corroborated earlier reports linking *most* cases of vaginal adenocarcinoma to intrauterine exposure to stilbestrol. . . ."

Dr. Isaacs continued, with thinly concealed dismay:

We are indebted to Dr. Herbst for identifying this "therapeutic" time bomb, but we should be aware of the awesome medical-legal implications of their endeavors.

The first mention in the professional literature of concern over the embryonic DES litigation then being initiated around the country made the sympathies of some sections of the medical profession painfully clear. Isaacs went on:

> . . . of the 200 to 400 manufacturers of DES in the U.S. most of them are currently involved in DES litigation. With 48 suits on file, five class actions, the problems are just beginning resulting from these publications. . . . Plaintiffs ask the court to order the defendants to establish funds to be used to identify members of the class, provide them with medical examinations and treatment, and to create research programs to determine the cause, prevention and cure of physical injuries, to publicize alleged dangers of these products. . . .
>
> Although these demands seem somewhat overwhelming, it is also overwhelming that thus far the total damages claimed against various manufacturers and other defendants in all DES suits come to a staggering total of over two billion dollars. . . .

The attempt here to discredit DES research and the DES litigation in one step, by representing the research as the cause for the subsequent action, was misleading to say the least. To begin with, in an attempt to obscure and evade being targeted as defendants in lawsuits, DES manufacturers had begun to assert that DES was manufactured by literally hundreds of companies, and that to single out one or several would be unfair to the selected companies. In fact, only a dozen companies had been originally licensed by the Food and Drug Administration to sell DES for the prevention of miscarriage. Some did resell it to other companies for remarketing, but only original manufacturers were made defendants in most DES suits.

To characterize these suits as stemming from "these publications," implicating Herbst's various reports, was to disguise the fact that the suits were caused by the drug, not by the research. To characterize the demands made by the plaintiffs of the drug companies as "overwhelming" only evaded the issue of final responsibility. The lawsuits were initiated largely on the premise that if the government, and the medical profession, both of which were indirectly linked to the DES disaster, were unwilling and unable to identify, locate, inform, and treat the affected young women, then the logical parties legally responsible for compensating victims injured by consumer products were the manufacturers themselves. Isaacs' attempt to put the blame for this "scare" on Herbst and other DES researchers ignored the crucial role played by the drug companies in the creation of the problem in the first place.

It was at this time that Herbst was able to effectively respond to these insinuations that the entire DES problem was somehow fabricated by releasing previously unobtainable sales data firmly implicating DES as the primary factor in the epidemic of vaginal cancer. Herbst produced a chart, which had not been ready by the time of publication of his registry report, indicating the levels of DES sales for the crucial years of 1947 to 1960. With a clear peak at the years immediately preceding 1955, and a calculated latency period of twenty years, Herbst was able to finally demonstrate a precise temporal link between DES sales and the eventual production of vaginal cancer. For those for whom causation was somehow still a vital issue, the matter was neatly put to rest. DES use in the mid-1950s had clearly produced a significant vaginal cancer epidemic in the mid-1970s.

The only question, raised not by Dr. Herbst but by Dr. Isaacs, was that of who would pay for it. Not the government, and not the doctors, even if both had been involved. Whether the manufacturers would eventually bear the brunt of compensation was a matter to be decided by the courts, and by various juries of citizens around the country who would sit and consider the evidence.

16

The first DES lawsuit was a class-action suit filed by a New York lawyer, Paul Rhinegold, in 1974. Filed on behalf of Rhinegold's daughter, it named as defendants twenty drug companies which had manufactured DES. The complaint asked for the establishment of a national DES fund to identify members of the class of DES daughters, to set up research and treatment programs for the class, and to publicize the issue of DES so that the class as a whole would be made aware of their plight.

Rhinegold, who had been instrumental in creating plaintiff's cases out of both the Dalkon shield intrauterine device (IUD) and Mer/29 pharmaceutical disasters, had been remarkably successful in those cases in confronting the pharmaceutical industry with powerful plaintiff's briefs. But this innovative approach to the DES problem foundered on the uncertain grounds that Rhinegold was not claiming that his daughter had been injured, but that she had been exposed before birth to the potential of an injury that could become manifest at some point in the future. The judge ruled that if there was no current injury the suit could not proceed.

The following year a larger DES suit was filed by the firm of Charfoos and Charfoos in Detroit, on behalf of sixteen DES daughters. The major difference between this suit and Rhinegold's was that this was not a class-action suit but a multiple-plaintiff suit in which each of the plaintiffs was individually identified. What was not so clearly identified, in several cases, was the manufacturer of the mother's pill.

The greatest legal obstacle facing most DES daughters was their inability to identify the manufacturer of the drug their mothers had taken decades before. Without the ability of a plaintiff to point a finger at the person or group who committed the injury, the legal system was thought to be powerless to compensate victims for injuries apparently committed by anonymous parties. Aside from the complex issues of causation, and allegations of drug company negligence, any legal solution to the DES problem would have to confront that obstacle and somehow overcome it.

The firm of Charfoos and Charfoos had at the time primarily a referral practice, which meant that lawyers, mostly from the Michigan area, would refer cases to the firm involving relatively complex issues of medical malpractice and products liability. Throughout the early '70s, with the publication of the Herbst reports and publicity surrounding Congressman Fountain's DES hearings in November of '71, calls had continually come in from lawyers inquiring about the possibility of lawsuits involving exposure to DES.

Most of these cases seemed to have little likelihood of success unless this stubborn issue of identification could be resolved. But in several DES cases referred to the firm, the young women in question could in fact identify the manufacturer of their mothers' pills. This inequity, in which the injury and the circumstances were often identical but for the factor of identification, raised the obvious question: Why should some women fortunate enough to have on record a brand name apparently possess a valid claim while other women similarly injured were disqualified?

In order for this question to be answered, and for the additional issues of causation of the cancer or adenosis and possible negligence to be resolved, Charfoos asked a new member of the firm with drug company experience and medical training, Tom Bleakely, to research this medical question: was there sufficient evidence in the medical literature to show that prior to 1947, the year the drug was approved for accidents of pregnancy, to put the drug companies on notice of carcinogenic potential? Not only a clear-cut link would have to be shown between DES ingestion and the daughter's cancer, but a picture of the state of the pharmaceutical art at the time would have to show that there was sufficient basis for the manufacturers to be cautious, and that such reasonable caution was not exercised.

Bleakely returned from the medical library with nearly one hundred separate articles, a collection which would eventually grow to several hundred, all predating 1947, which through animal research, clinical research, and other methods of scientific analysis, warned of the danger of cancer specifically, and warned the drug companies and the clinicians that they were dealing with a dangerous product. Also, from examinations of several New Drug Applications by various DES manufacturers it was clear that no significant animal or human testing had been done involving pregnancy and possible effects on offspring at the crucial time when the drug was being marketed for a new use to pregnant women.

With this pattern of irresponsibility clearly indicated by the medical literature, the possibility of a lawsuit succeeding on the grounds of negligence and failure to warn of danger seemed dramatically improved. The initial hurdle of identifying the manufacturer still loomed large, but a new theory had emerged in plaintiff's law which seemed to provide a promising route around this barrier. Extensive research by plaintiff's lawyers had unearthed a relatively arcane legal theory, up to then confined mostly to legal journals, which seemed to go directly to this question. "Joint liability theory," also known as "enterprise," or "industry" liability, has been intermittently resuscitated in recent times to aid in the solution of various environmental pollution cases.

Though corporations charged with compensating injured parties on the basis of this theory steadfastly maintained that it was some radical and potentially seditious departure from established law, it was actually grounded in a classic, textbook legal case of 1948 known to students of the law as *Tice* v. *Summers.* Two hunters out one day in the country had fired their rifles simultaneously and found they had injured a man. Since it proved impossible to verify whether one man's bullet or the other had actually caused the injury, the court had ruled that in such cases the burden of proof should be shifted from the plaintiff to the defendant: the two hunters were held "jointly liable," and were ordered to share the burden of compensation between them.

In more recent years, in situations where different companies were jointly discharging pollutants into the atmosphere or into a common stream, property owners had successfully sued for damages, employing joint liability theory to force the companies to share in paying compensation. In DES cases, plaintiffs' lawyers, on seeing that the manufacturers had acted "in concert" by filing joint clinical applications, and by standardizing their product to meet FDA standards, maintained that these companies had acted jointly in polluting a "common stream," in this case the stream of commerce, by releasing a faulty and injurious product into the marketplace.

On this basis, Charfoos drew up an initial pleading on behalf of sixteen women, some of whom could identify a manufacturer, and some of whom could not. The pleading confirmed that in some cases the product's manufacturer could not be named. But it went on to plead that this matter was in fact irrelevant to the issue: that the drug companies in creating a uniform product had been legally equivalent to those two unfortunate hunters out in the woods; that the burden of proof should therefore be shifted to the defendants, who would have to show that they had not injured these women.

This first case, known as "Abel," for Gail Abel, the first plaintiff, soon grew to 148 plaintiffs. At about the same time, a Harvard Law School professor, David Rosenberg, filed a class-action suit in Massachusetts on behalf of 28 women. Another suit with 19 women was filed in New Jersey with Paul Rhinegold as co-counsel, and a lawyer in New York filed a suit on behalf of 3 plaintiffs with cancer, 2 of whom later died.

It wasn't long before the drug industry faced DES cases in nearly every state of the country. The suits soon escalated to forty-eight in number, many class-actions, involving more than forty drug companies and totaling over two billion dollars sought in damages. This was by far the greatest legal challenge ever faced by the American pharmaceutical industry and was quite possibly the largest products liability case ever brought against any American industry.

Faced with this awesome threat from thousands of indignant consumers, the pharmaceutical industry moved quickly to fight back. The various DES manufacturers found themselves corralled into a precarious grouping, based on the fact that so many companies were being sued jointly for alleged concerted action in marketing and promotion of DES. The need for cooperation became at once an advantage and a hindrance, carrying the potential for a high level of coordination of the DES defense, but also a great deal of disruptive infighting.

The proportions of this defense were certainly unprecedented in American civil litigation history. Eli Lilly, which found itself involved in more cases than other companies because it was the acknowledged leader in the preparation and marketing of DES, was forced to set up an intricate network of interlocking defense teams, with three different prestigious legal firms managing cases in each of three regions of the country, the East, the West, and the Midwest. E. R. Squibb followed closely in volume of cases, and other companies, such as Abbott and Rexall, faced a smaller (yet still ominous) number of claims.

Further complicating the issue of the drug companies' forced interdependence in the DES defense was the fact that if the enterprise liability theory should prevail across the country, the different companies would be left to sue one another on the question of who pays what to which plaintiffs. Though the accepted hypothesis ran that a defendant should pay compensation based on market share, that notion had yet to see a legal test, while the absolute secrecy or unavailability of accurate sales figures made even the question of market share a tremendous uncertainty. The possibility of fighting over dividing up the amount of a jury verdict between a number of plaintiffs and a number of companies was certainly not pleasing to the pharmaceutical industry, but they were taking the eventuality seriously enough to be silent on the subject of sales figures.

With all these multiple filings for vast amounts in so many states and with so many plaintiffs, years went by before the filings went into court because there were so many legal and medical questions to be hashed out: How dangerous is adenosis? At what risk is a DES daughter? Did DES really cause a DES daughter's vaginal cancer, or were there other, more crucial factors involved?

All these questions were paramount in the mind of a young lawyer named Jeffrey Sussman in 1977, soon after he joined the law firm of Lurie and Cahan and was put in charge of the Needham case. Sussman had picked up the Needham file and was scrutinizing it with a view toward reviving the case and finally getting it moving. It seemed to him that the case had been hovering in legal limbo for some months and that it had received remarkably little attention in the period after the taking of the depositions. He was struck while reading by how little participation the plaintiff herself had had, and it seemed to him that that situation should be rectified.

Sussman finally got hold of Anne at her house in Champaign. She was working in an artist's frame shop at the time and was difficult to reach at home. They arranged a meeting. Anne came to Chicago. She showed up at the office a little early, clearly anxious and agitated. Sussman had the impression that Anne was uninformed so far as the progress of the case was concerned. She seemed remarkably distanced from the fact that it could conceivably go into court within less than two years. It was obvious she felt insecure about her ignorance of what was going on.

Sussman had drawn up an abstract of everything that was going on with the case, its various filings and motions and pleadings. He showed it to Anne to demonstrate that some work had been done for her, that such work had an actual purpose, that it wasn't just fooling around with complex paper in some strange, artificial language. As they began to discuss the case and she looked over the more recent material, the suit she had entered into almost two years before seemed to become real to her, to take on an identity of its own.

A case is far more than piles of research in files. Sussman considered part of his job, as Anne's lawyer in Chicago, to create what he considered a viable plaintiff. It was his feeling that for someone to sue someone else, they should literally as well as legally be the person "complaining"; that the legal language which states "the plaintiff asserts" this or that should not just be an empty formality. A viable plaintiff, even if he or she does little in the case but observe in the courtroom, must appear to the jury to be actively involved, comprehending, not simply the trained creature of her attorneys. As Anne began to take interest in her own case right there in the office, Sussman had the sense that a viable plaintiff was creating herself before his eyes.

This was the first DES case Sussman had ever seen. He had done some medical research at the American Medical Association in Chicago, and through reading legal publications and medical journals he was aware of the DES litigation. But the Charfoos and Charfoos firm had been clearly the leaders, at least in the Midwest, on preparing the plaintiffs' cases on the subject, and he knew that his predecessor at Lurie and Cahan had gone up to Detroit seeking information for the Needham case and had been so impressed with the extent of the research already gathered there that he had ended up by requesting the aid of Charfoos and Charfoos as co-counsel for Anne.

By that time the firm of Charfoos and Charfoos was managing over 250 different cases in more than 30 states. The original suit, "Abel" had been limited by the judge after the first 148 cases, so a second case, "Belz" had begun with another 45 plaintiffs. With publicity and with the painstaking work of numerous DES Watch and DES Action groups in various states, American women were being slowly educated about the dangers of DES. Still, it was clearly only the tip of the iceberg, with only a fraction of DES daughters informed or aware of the problem, and with a great deal of ignorance and misinformation circulating about the extent of the risk, further complicated by varying newspaper reports with contradictory information being supplied by drug industry spokesmen, physicians, or DES citizens' groups.

In March of 1977, the opening skirmishes of "Abel" were held in the enormous Civic Center auditorium in Detroit. The request, made by Charfoos because of the number of plaintiffs and interested parties eager to attend, resulted in some of the first arguments on DES in open court going forward with an appropriately large number of spectators. The defendants had filed a motion for summary judgment on the issue of industry-wide liability, which requested that Judge Thomas Roumell rule on the viability of this group of plaintiffs suing a number of manufacturers.

The result was a preliminary legal test of the enterprise liability theory, with the plaintiffs, represented by Charfoos, alleging that the DES manufacturers had conducted testing, marketing, and promoting of DES along parallel lines. This was the first encounter after two years of research and pretrial maneuvering of a group of plaintiffs with the barrier of identification. And at that early stage, in the lower court, the case was lost. Judge Roumell ruled for the defendants, the drug companies, maintaining that a manufacturer must be clearly identified by a plaintiff as the source of an injury for a suit to proceed. The case was sent to the Michigan Court of Appeals, which would hand down its decision in the summer of 1979, more than two years later.

The atmosphere surrounding the Needham case was thus not terribly encouraging throughout 1977 and 1978, with not a single DES daughter in the country yet awarded a dollar in damages, though the number of cancer cases soon reached almost four hundred, and the number of adenosis cases, comprising the great majority of DES daughters, swelled into the thousands. Litigation had been dragging on for nearly half a decade with not even preliminary issues of identification and liability resolved. But with the government and its agencies retaining an unhurried complacency on the issue, the legal framework began to appear the only structure within which the actual lives of the injured might at least be paid some attention.

Charfoos and Charfoos had over eighty individual cases against White Laboratories, which had made the Dienestrol Mary Needham had taken. White was required to allow its employees at the time of the alleged wrong-doing to be deposed and to open itself up to the close inspection of the party suing it. In this process of discovery, the firm began to put together a portrait of White Labs which included some fascinating revelations about the customs and manners of a rather small but profitable member of the pharmaceutical industry in the forties and fifties.

White Labs throughout its history had produced mostly vitamins. Feen-a-mint, Aspergum, and an iron supplement called Mol-Iron were all White products. These were not prescription products but over-the-counter preparations. In charge of the business throughout the 1940s and '50s was a man named Decesar, who was called behind his back at the company, "Little Caesar." Little Caesar was certainly not a scientist, nor an expert in the manufacturing of complex chemical preparations, but a businessman out to make a profit by getting doctors to recommend vitamins by prescription, which could be purchased as easily without one.

"It was really the damndest organization," recalled Dr. Charles Sondern in an interview with Tom Bleakely prior to his official deposition. "I always said I learned how not to run a pharmaceutical house from that place." Sondern had been hired by White in the '40s because he had developed a very powerful and inexpensive DES preparation called Dienestrol, a minor molecular modification of the original stilbestrol discovered by Dodds, for a company called Breon. Sondern had developed it originally as a poultry preparation, as a hormone to make chickens fatter. What was eventually sold by White to pregnant women to prevent miscarriage began as chicken feed.

Mr. Decesar, according to Sondern, "bought tanks and tanks of cod liver oil during the time of the great shortage, and the company was very wealthy as a result of his shrewd dealings. He spent most of his mornings with his broker and staff. The guy was a wonderful poker-player, put it that way." One of the most unusual aspects of the White organization was its paltry medical staff. "We had the most unusual management there," Sondern remembered, "Neary and I being the only scientists." Edward Neary, who had been medical director at White during the bulk of its DES years, would later testify in its defense at Anne's trial. As for Neary, Sondern spoke plainly: "Now Neary's background, well he put out the shingle after he got his M.D., and waited six, eight months. He had to take it down, he wasn't making any money. So he went to White as medical director. There wasn't much to do, it was all vitamins, Feen-a-mint, and Aspergum. . . ." When it comes to taking responsibility for marketing of DES to pregnant women in the '50s, Sondern explained, "Neary tells everyone I was the DES man, but I was only involved from the poultry standpoint."

"My work was done with chickens," Sondern recalled. "I was really into that up to my neck. Dienestrol was the cheapest estrogen of its day. If it was added to a bag of feed, it wouldn't add to the price more than five cents." Dienestrol became a profitable shelf item for White, a relatively small company, and a particularly potent means of entering the ethical drug field.

Whoever was responsible for the original decision to market Dienestrol to humans, Sondern made it quite clear that all decisions were not made by men of science: "They had what they called the Green Room, we called it that for obvious reasons. We sat in there every Tuesday afternoon after lunch, it was the only day they'd buy us lunch. In there was a banker who was chairman of the board. . . . The Green Room brought out all the decisions. You were told what to do in the Green Room. No written documents, no bulletin boards, no copies to so and so in the organization. It was a crazy administration by a man, well, brilliant in his way, but crazy, also, in his way of administering. . . ."

If Mr. Decesar made decisions according to scientific and rational therapeutic grounds, Dr. Sondern never saw evidence of it. "The boss never cracked the whip," Sondern explained. "He just wanted the chairman to understand it was a good investment." One of the more creative investments Decesar initiated was the development of Dienestrol as an ostensibly less nauseating form of DES than stilbestrol. In fact, the nausea associated with DES was limited to nonpregnant women. Nevertheless, Mr. Decesar further invested smartly in a legion of detail men, who so far outnumbered his tiny medical department as to make the latter only a necessary adjunct to the former. Dienestrol was promoted intensively by these White detail men, one of whom sounded particularly plausible to Dr. Walter Abrams, the only gynecologist in Park Forest, Illinois, in 1952.

In the '60s, little White Laboratories was bought by the giant chemical and drug organization Schering-Plough, which in the '70s found itself saddled with a number of court cases on behalf of White, which had become simply a division of the larger corporation. Schering had retained a number of skilled attorneys to represent its interests in DES litigation all over the country. It participated fully in the gigantic legal ballet, involving immense expenditures of funds and energy, time and travel, known as the national DES defense. Lawyers representing DES manufacturers found themselves enmeshed in a vast web of alliances and conflicting interests with co-defendants in numbers of cases, an effort directed to a great extent by the great drug houses Lilly and Squibb, but cooperated in by equally interested companies like Schering.

In the case of *Needham* v. *White Laboratories,* Schering retained Henry Simon of New York as national DES counsel. In Chicago, Schering retained as its local co-counsel the trial firm of Phelan and Pope, which unlike many of the corporate firms defending industry interests, was used to fighting cases before juries involving life and death issues of personal injury. In hiring these lawyers, after releasing Baker and McKenzie, which had initially deposed the Needhams, Schering was gambling on the importance of emotions and high-pressure personal interaction as well as research in its own defense. Many drug companies that retained skilled corporate attorneys to fight their DES suits had found themselves with superbly prepared paper cases, full of pretrial maneuverings and intricate procedural struggles, which might well fall flat once they reached a courtroom with an injured plaintiff and had to be presented before flesh and blood juries.

The greatest single obstacle to the effective presentation of Anne's case was carefully set in place long before the trial began. In a pretrial motion, Phelan and Pope for White Labs had requested the trial to be "bifurcated," or split into two parts, the first to decide the question of statute of limitations and the evidence of liability, the second to examine the question of personal damages, if the first was won by Anne.

Anne's side argued, unsuccessfully, that Anne's injuries were the only appropriate context within which to view her state of mind at the time of her operation; that her state of mind went right to the statute question of "whether she knew or reasonably should have known" that DES caused her cancer at the time of her confinement to Mayo's. Judge Decker's decision to disregard that point, and to enhance the defense request for a divided trial, resulted in a situation where the lawyers for White could credibly argue at one trial that the DES cancer link was so well known and so accepted by science that Anne either knew or reasonably should have known about it, presumably through her doctors, her parents, or the media. Yet if they lost that first argument, the selection of an entirely new jury permitted them to argue the opposing side, that the DES cancer link was a theory accepted only by some authorities.

PART III

17

At ten in the morning on Monday, March 12, 1979, Anne Needham was sitting in United States District Court, surrounded by lawyers. The courtroom was a modern, windowless box set high in a blunt shaft of black steel and glass that rises squarely out of the Chicago Loop: The Everett McKinley Dirksen Federal Office Building. Lawrence Charfoos and Richard Phelan had just approached the judge's bench and were discussing a series of "housekeeping matters" with Judge Decker. Phelan was fair-haired and lanky, with wandering eyes; beside him stood Charfoos, with darker hair and a broader build. Both men leaned up toward the judge's bench, brandishing conflicting briefs.

The lawyers were discussing two key issues in this case: whether the jury should be advised of the details of Anne's injuries, and whether they should know that the result of their verdict on the statute question would be to deny Anne's suit or let it proceed. From the defendant's point of view, the intention of the motion to split the trial in several parts was to prevent the jury from being aware of the consequences of their actions, so as not to have them unduly moved by emotion or sympathy for Anne.

Judge Decker, a stout, white-haired man of sixty or so, with a florid face, listened patiently to the arguments of counsel and now and then interjected gruff commentary. The matter appeared of questionable significance to Anne, but she admittedly had been drifting somewhat. The entire experience was unsettling for her. The last few weeks had been tough: her relationship with her boyfriend had recently broken down, largely because of the strain put on her, and indirectly on him, by the approaching trial. Her most recent visit to the Mayo Clinic hadn't done much to help the situation. When she was back in January, they had found something.

She had developed a strange, yellowish tint in her eyes. Though she usually only stayed a day and a half, she ended up having to stay an entire week for tests. Her red blood bilirubin count had been dangerously high: apparently, her body didn't digest its old red blood cells properly. The conditions turned out to be unrelated to her cancer, but it was an awful scare. That, with the trial coming, made her anxious that finally after five full years the sickness was catching up with her.

Now, in the courtroom, they were arguing over whether Charfoos could mention her surgery:

Charfoos: I see no way, your Honor, in life to have an appropriate trial without having some discussion of the condition of Anne Needham in the hospital when she was going through surgery, actually two surgeries. . . . This young lady went through a total radical hysterectomy, removing all her female organs during the time they will be alleging she should have been cognizant of some relationship, of her cancer being caused by a pill instead of nature.

The Court: . . . Well, I am certainly not going to permit that evidence to go in as part of your opening statement . . . you certainly would be able to put her on the stand and at least have her testify.

At the word "testify," Anne glanced anxiously at a slender chair set in a wooden box. The box was to the right of the judge's bench, a plain, stark wooden cube marked with a brass plaque, which read simply WITNESS. Above the chair, a sleek aluminum eagle glowered down from a disk mounted high on the wall at a limp American flag balancing out of a bucket which resembled a tall, rather elegant wastepaper basket.

Charfoos wore a cream-colored suit with brown boots. Phelan and Pope wore identical gray pinstripe suits in a classic cut, pants with cuffs, button-down collars. Charfoos and Bleakely wore trousers that flared; the drug company men wore pants that fell straight to their shoes. Behind them, Anne could make out a stout, blond man smoking a short cigar: Henry Simon, national DES counsel for Schering-Plough, which owned White. In the gallery, Anne had seen numerous men in suits: lawyers, you could tell, drug company lawyers.

Charfoos: My memory is not perfect and that is why I am bringing it out, but it is that there would be at least a minimal conversation about what has happened to this young lady, without going into details.

Phelan: No.

The Court: What do you mean?

Charfoos: That she has lost her female—

The Court: Oh, no, no.

Charfoos: Then we can't defend the statute of limitations, your Honor. That's the horns of the dilemma you put me on.

The Court: I am going to say in my statement to the jury that she had radical surgery, period. That should take care of it.

A few weeks before, Anne had moved out of her boyfriend's house in Champaign and into a friend's apartment for a month. She had been moving constantly back and forth on the train between Champaign and Chicago. Tom Bleakely had come down from Detroit to Chicago to spend a day with her, going over every aspect of the case. They had met at the Hyatt and discussed everything, her thoughts, her feelings, her memories of events; they'd gone over what kind of clothes she should wear, what she might have to do and say. It all brought back distressing memories that she'd spent the past five years trying to excise. With the recent scare at Mayo's, and her love affair apparently over, she felt as if the structure of her life was caving in: she didn't feel much in shape for a trial.

Now they were picking a jury; the six people to decide her case. The marshal was reading off the names of certain jurors; they were taking their place in the jury box, in the first six seats in the first row. Judge Decker was telling them:

It is a civil case. It is brought by a plaintiff, Anne Need-ham. She is a twenty-five year old woman born July 30, 1953. . . .

It felt good to know that her case was the first suit to reach trial. It felt good that something was finally being done, after all this time. She wanted this thing to finally start hitting the papers, and the national television, if necessary. Nobody is interested in statistics. She knew the story would have more impact if expressed in terms of a single life. She had been caught up in the momentum of the case, and the publicity was part of that energy. Let Mr. Phelan argue against it up there with the judge. He had nice curly fair hair that covered a good deal of his ears, and a handsome Irish face, but Anne would have liked to fix him with her eyes and stare him down.

It was time for the opening statement by Charfoos. He stood at a small podium behind the jury box, so the jurors were between him and the judge. Looking down at a few scratched notes, he began:

This is the story of a prescription drug. . . . The drug was promoted by its manufacturer, White Laboratories, as being effective in the prevention of unwanted or accidental miscarriages. . . . In fact, the drug was useless for that purpose. . . . Not only was the drug useless . . . but even more devastating we believe the evidence will overwhelm-ingly show that it caused cancer not in the women who took the pill, but in the female offspring. . . .

This, then, is the story of that pill. One of these young women, Anne Needham . . . has had cancer of the female organs. We believe the proofs will show it is because of the pill.

For Anne, this wasn't easy to listen to. It made her acutely self-conscious. She felt as if every person in the room, the jury, the audience, the lawyers, were all staring right at her, seeing a woman with cancer. She hated being the woman marked, the one who had been chosen for the awful fate. But here in this court would be the proof that it was in that pill that the source of the trouble could be located—not in her. She suddenly wondered if her clothes were appropriate, if her hair was all right, if her facial expression was too solemn and serious, whether she should be looking sad, or frightened.

The jury would first deliver a verdict on the statute of limitations question. Only if they found for the plaintiff would the trial proceed to the subject of liability. Charfoos moved directly to the story of Anne Needham and the events of that unbearable week from the time she found out she had cancer to the day she was operated on at the Mayo Clinic.

Charfoos lead the jury through that period: the phone call from Dr. Warren on Friday night, the discussions with the family over the weekend. "Sunday," Charfoos intoned:

Sunday it is just, obviously, a nightmare. Nobody is together. The whole thing is in an uproar, with this young lady having this obviously serious disease.

He went on to describe the first expedition to the Mayo Clinic, concluding with this sad recital:

Thursday a battery of tests for this young lady. And by Thursday night they get the terrible news that it is worse than anybody thought. It means the entire removal of her uterus, the entire removal of both tubes, the entire removal of 80 percent of the vagina, an artificial vagina, and then when all is done, reconstruction in a second operation of the artificial vagina, all to be done in this one stay at Mayo.

Anne looked slowly around the room, wondering why there was a sudden silence. Mr. Phelan had slowly gotten to his feet and after something of a pause, he said quietly, "Your Honor, may I approach the bench?" For some reason Anne couldn't fathom, Phelan had a slow, grim tone in his voice. Judge Decker said, with a shake of his head, "Well, I understand why you are asking to approach the bench. We will take it up later after counsel finishes his statement." For a moment the court seemed frozen, with the jury looking somewhat puzzled, with Mr. Charfoos somewhat taken aback. But he went on to stridently conclude that at no time while at Mayo's or before was Anne made aware of any link between her cancer and DES.

Mr. Phelan approached the bench, and said with considerable gravity:

> Your Honor. I would like to make a motion for a mistrial on the basis of information communicated to this jury concerning the detail of this operation, what was done. . . .

Judge Decker added:

> I said that he could comment on the fact that she had surgery but as to the details of the matter . . . I clearly indicated to you that you could make the comment that she had surgery but to go into the details that you went into now—

Charfoos: No, I don't think so, your Honor.

The Court: . . . There is no question about it, that you were not following my instructions. And the record will show that you were not.

Charfoos: But I don't—

The Court: But it is in the record. I have got your motion. I will consider it during the noon hour.

Charfoos: May I respond briefly for the record?

The Court: Yes, you may.

Charfoos: The Court indicated at the minimum we would be able to show the material that was in the operative report. I did not exceed that.

There ensued a debate between Charfoos, Phelan, and Decker over the stipulations made in the pretrial. Charfoos insisted that he had rendered not "details" but facts, that the operative report, the plain, objective events of Anne's surgery, were admissible under the rules. Phelan maintained that this was contrary to the whole procedure of splitting up the trial; Charfoos countered that in the pretrial record the operative record had been the criterion for admission of factual evidence. Anne looked on at these cold proceedings with slowly gathering dismay. Could it be it would end at this? That the trial wouldn't go on? The disappointment would be unbearable, after all the years. And how much time would there be to wait again? Weeks, months, years?

The argument went on, each citing different parts of the record. Decker shook his head in irritation and resignation:

> The bifurcation, we've wasted all this time, all this time, and perhaps your intention was to waste it.

Charfoos: No, sir, not at all.

The Court: Well, we will see. It is your wasted time, not mine.

Anne watched helplessly as the judge led the jury in, and addressed them solemnly:

> Ladies and gentlemen of the jury, I am sorry to advise you that some unfortunate events have taken place which will make it necessary for me to declare a mistrial in this case. It is unfortunate. I am not going to go into any explanations as to the reasons for it. . . . I am sorry that this event happened. . . . The case will be tried before another jury at another date. So the jury will be excused. . . .

Two months later: May 15, 1979. Anne was back in the courtroom, the scene was identical, the room the same, the characters the same. It was like seeing a movie for the second time. Only small things had changed, the clothes were lighter, the air was heavier, an air-conditioner hummed softly in the background. It was again ten in the morning, and Phelan and Charfoos were right back up at the judge's bench, going over another "housekeeping matter."

They were talking about her mental condition—her mental condition five years earlier, at the time she was going up to Mayo's. This time the statute of limitations was all they were about to discuss, only evidence on the theme of her own awareness would be admitted. A motion had just been made by Phelan that he would produce no evidence after March 8, 1974. In other words, he intended to prove that she knew about DES before her first operation.

They also went over the issue which had caused the last mistrial. Phelan warned the court, "I don't know if we made it clear

. . . as to what part of this injury will be described to the jury by Mr. Charfoos."

The Court: None.

Charfoos: . . . None.

The Court: None at all. I am simply going to say that in March of that year she underwent surgery for the treatment of that condition.

Charfoos wondered whether Decker would "be giving the jury a general view that there is a principal lawsuit"; in other words, if the jury would know the effect of its actions. Decker replied:

> Well, I am going to be very short on that. I am going to say it is a civil suit, that it is brought by her . . . that the gist of her complaint is that her cancer was caused by ingestion of Dienestrol by her mother. . . .

Charfoos: Okay, you have answered the question. You will give some frame of reference to the jury so the jury won't be in a vacuum.

The opening arguments were confined to the issue of Anne, nothing about liability, no history of DES. Phelan creatively reviewed Anne's story during the period in question. He maintained that in Dr. Warren's phone call of Friday night on March the 1st, that "Anne's mother raised the question of whether it was something that she might or might not have taken while she was pregnant." At this, Anne was quite surprised; it was the first time she had ever heard of it.

He claimed that Anne and her mother had gone to Dr. Warren's office on Saturday, the day after his call. Phelan insisted: "They discussed with Anne present in the room the cancer that she had and the relationship of this DES or Dienestrol that her mother had taken." Phelan claimed that Dr. Warren, during that supposed visit, had gone back into Mary Needham's records he'd received from Dr. Abrams, and had discussed those with her. He maintained that Victor "of course, called Dr. Warren, and . . .

went to see Dr. Warren and they discussed the problem. They discussed the association with DES." He assured the jury Victor had gone back home and discussed this with Mary and Anne.

"Naturally, the first thing that they were concerned about," Phelan continued, "was what caused this, what was it that would create a condition like this in a very young woman. . . . And again, the association came up. A discussion of the drug and a discussion of the fact that the mother had taken the drug during pregnancy with Anne back in 1953."

Charfoos began his opening by discussing the background of the statute case. He brought up the principal lawsuit, which concerned Anne claiming that her cancer was the result of a pill her mother had taken, that "certain testimony seemed to indicate that the drug company might be able to defend this case on what is called—" Phelan leapt up, "Excuse me, your Honor, I think this is pure argument." Charfoos went on to say, "The reason that we are here, then, is because the drug company has raised a defense that Anne filed her lawsuit too late, that in fact—" Phelan leapt up again to object. Decker sustained the objection.

The jury was promptly excused so Decker and the two attorneys could discuss the matter. Phelan said in an undertone, "Your Honor, I don't have the words but this is not—the jury is not to be told what the effect of this verdict is to be." Charfoos assured them, "Not a word." Decker warned Charfoos: "Not a word? You are getting as close as you can to it without going over the precipice." Charfoos protested: "Not a word was discussed at the pretrial." Phelan broke in: "Well, I would simply like the Court to admonish the jury. Mr. Charfoos has now told them that they are raising this defense because Miss Needham had filed the suit too late." Decker brooded for a moment, and muttered: "Had filed the suit too late, yes."

Phelan, after conferring with Henry Simon and other counsel at his table delivered their private verdict: "I have been instructed, your Honor, to insist on the motion for mistrial. If the Court is inclined to grant it, I will accept it." At this point Anne was going crazy. She could not believe her ears. Another mistrial? For what? She wanted to stand up and scream, scream at all these men, to figure it out, make some sense of it. She felt suddenly tired, defeated, it was all out of her hands. Her desperate attempt to have some control over her life seemed to have failed. After some deliberation, Decker granted the mistrial.

The following Monday, May 21: Anne was back in place at the plaintiff's table, waiting for her third attempt at a trial. The familiarity of the scene by this point was somewhat disconcerting, but any feeling of routineness was alleviated by an opposing atmosphere of relief, as if all conflicting parties had agreed to go forward and would try heroically to vault the hurdle of the statute question. Judge Decker himself seemed to share this new tenor of agreement:

> Well, gentlemen, here we are again after two juries and some time has passed. I am preparing today to go ahead and at least make my third attempt in this case to get to a jury. There should be no problem in that connection, if we all understand before the trial begins what the ground rules are. . . .

Charfoos compromised this atmosphere of good will by challenging those immutable ground rules. It was unprecedented, he maintained, for a court to deny a jury knowledge of its basic reason for being there. "What we are doing here," he insisted, "is almost Kafka-like."

With that procedural rejection lodged for the record, the plaintiffs begrudgingly conceded the point, and a new jury was selected. As if to compensate for the delays encountered so far, this third mirror-image version of the same trial seemed to progress with accelerated motion; points were resolved with a minimum of debate, the case moved smoothly forward from step to step as if lubricated by a sense of familiarity. Without more than routine discussion, Phelan swung into his opening argument.

He made a point of Dr. Warren's close relationship to the Needhams, of his immediate knowledge of the nature of the cancer he found, and of its novel cause. Phelan was certain Warren had told Anne and her mother the night he called their house about a connection to DES, and that Anne's mother, from her experience as a pharmacist, was doubtless aware of the connection regardless of any such warning. He reiterated the claim that a Saturday morning meeting had taken place in Warren's office with both Needhams present, where they presumably had discussed DES.

He also insisted there had been a second meeting, at the Needham home, on the third or fourth of March, before Mary and Anne left for Rochester, where Anne, Mary, and Victor had discussed Anne's condition, and where Victor, being a pharmacist, had talked about DES. "In fact," Phelan claimed, "he [Victor] was the very one who gave her the drug . . . he discussed it knowing there might be a possible association." Phelan concluded:

> I think at the conclusion of the case you will come to the conclusion that Anne knew or reasonably should have known that there might be a possible connection between the cancer . . . and the drug that her mother had taken in 1953.

Charfoos offered a notably different version of the events of that period. He denied that any meeting had taken place in Dr. Warren's office other than when Anne's cancer was discovered. She heard nothing from him from that Monday until Friday evening, when Dr. Warren called and asked first for Mary Needham. When Anne finally got on the line, Charfoos continued, Dr. Warren was unable to use the word "cancer" let alone speak of a cause; "Anne Needham and her mother categorically, unequivocally deny being in Dr. Warren's office that Saturday, March 2," he further claimed, "and there will be a witness to corroborate that." Furthermore, at the time she entered Mayo Clinic she was unaware of any cause; the hospital record would confirm her ignorance. And there would be proof, written, recorded proof, that the first time Anne knew of any such drug was in May, when the first questionnaire arrived from Mayo's.

With both sides of the dispute virtually holding their breath, the trial of *Anne Needham* v. *White Labs* proceeded as planned into its second day. The defense was to present its main witness, Dr. Jerome Warren, who would testify, according to Phelan's opening argument, that Anne was familiar with DES at the time she left for the Mayo Clinic. In the corridor outside the court, a sterile pale space tiled with white linoleum and harshly flooded with fluorescent light, Anne and Mary Needham waited patiently before ten for court to begin.

Just before ten, Dr. Warren appeared, accompanied by the defense lawyers Phelan, Pope, and Simon. He glanced quickly at the Needhams, and smiled neatly, adjusting his dark tie between the lapels of his suit. At one point he broke away from the defense brigade and walked over to Anne and Mary. Timidly, he reached out to grasp Mary's hands and said beneath his breath, "Mary, I hope after all this we can still be friends." Anne wasn't able to say anything, she simply looked away. Mary, who had known Jerry Warren for twenty-five years, turned on her heel after fixing him with her eyes, and also walked away. Shaking his head, Dr. Warren reluctantly retreated and rejoined his parley with the members of the defense.

When Anne walked in to take her accustomed place at the plaintiff's table, Dr. Warren was sitting quietly in the witness box. Mary Needham, because of a defense motion to exclude witnesses, was bound to wait outside. The gallery, as usual, was packed with lawyers, observers, seasoned court buffs in their traditional baggy suits, reporters, and a miscellaneous sample of the general public. Dr. Warren eyed this large body of spectators with evident dismay, and looked now and then to the defense table for a hint of support.

Richard Phelan approached the box with a friendly air and gently asked Dr. Warren to state his full name. Dr. Warren sat tensely forward on the chair, and haltingly whispered, "My full name is—" Judge Decker glanced down at the anxious witness and said sharply, "Doctor, that doesn't help you a bit, you will have to sit back and relax and speak up." Dr. Warren did what he was told.

Anne sat there and listened as Dr. Warren emphasized his long-standing closeness to the Needham family, a sentiment both accurate and barbed, because she was well aware the defense would twist that intimacy into a weapon: how could Dr. Warren, as such a friend of the family, not have advised the Needhams about an association he so clearly understood? Anne herself doubted that Dr. Warren had been quite so aware of the DES cancer link as he now claimed. He had certainly not mentioned it at the time of the biopsy, nor during the brief phone conversations afterwards. But, Anne was willing to admit, he might well have been aware of the DES link; the point was, he had never transmitted any such knowledge to her.

Dr. Warren, meanwhile, was telling the court:

My relationship with the Needhams was more than just a casual relationship; my relationship with the Needhams was very close. In fact, it was the type of relationship where if we would meet each other in the hallway we would hug one another, especially Mary and I, and subsequent to her pregnancy she became a patient of mine. I operated on her. We had an extremely close relationship, both with her, her children, and Mr. Needham.

Well, Anne reflected, that certainly had been true. Unfortunately, with recent events, since her cancer and the lawsuit, there hadn't been much hugging and kissing in the hallways of the medical building lately. Dr. Warren was describing now their close physical and professional proximity:

. . . Their original drugstore was on the first floor of a two story building, as I recall, but I am not too sure of it, and then they had another drugstore in another medical center to which I moved and we were approximately twenty to thirty yards apart. . . .

He went on to testify to his extensive familiarity with the DES situation from the very first publication of the Herbst report in 1971. That report, he emphasized, was a "blockbuster." "We were well aware of it," he recalled, "we were well aware of the fact that the DES was markedly implicated as far as causality was concerned, and of course, the drug was no longer prescribed."

The courtroom was absolutely still as Dr. Warren recalled that day in February of 1974 when he discovered Anne's cancer:

I examined Anne Needham and at that time I found a possibly one-inch sized ulcer in the vagina, in back, a very punched-out ulcer, which had been bleeding. It looked very suspicious to me. I did a biopsy, which is taking pieces of the ulcer, and sending it to the laboratory.

Phelan: Were you concerned?

Warren: I was very concerned.

Anne was moved by this; everything that had seemed so far away, because she had so strenuously put it away, was now forcing itself back into the present in this extremely bizarre setting: the enormous room, with the crowd of people, the oppressive silences all around except for the witness's voice. Dr. Warren seemed far away on his platform, vividly remembering that awful object he had found in her. It was almost too much; Anne stared at her lap, biting her lip, eyes closed momentarily. Dr. Warren continued, gravely, recalling the return of the biopsy report at St. James Hospital, where he'd opened his box and seen the words on the page: clear-cell adenocarcinoma.

When they got up to the subject of the phone call that evening, where Phelan had been so certain they had discussed DES, Dr. Warren began to slow down, to hesitate and qualify, and his memory seemed to falter, and at points fail: "I believe she [Anne] might have gotten on the other phone . . . my memory is a little hazy right now. . . ."

> When I placed the call, Mary answered the phone. I knew it was Mary and I said, "Mary, we've got a problem." . . . I said, "Mary, I just got the biopsy report from the hospital. Anne has a malignancy of the vagina. It has to be taken care of immediately, immediately. . . . And Anne got on the—or Mary must have said something, because Anne got on the line and I said, "Anne, we've got a serious problem here. It has to be dealt with immediately."

Phelan: Doctor, do you remember at that time whether you specifically used the term "cancer"?

Warren: I don't recall.

Phelan: Do you recall whether at that time Mrs. Needham, Anne's mother, spoke to you about anything other than just the report that there was cancer?

Warren: No.

Phelan retreated then, shaking his head. This was not how it was supposed to be going: he had said in his opening that Warren would testify that he had discussed DES with Mary and Anne during that phone conversation. Phelan tried one more time: "Is that your best recollection of the entire content of that conversation?" Warren hesitated, then offered meekly: "I recall that I wanted to meet with the Needhams on the following day."

That brought them to the supposed March 2 meeting, on Saturday morning. Warren was sure there had indeed been such a meeting, and that Mary and Anne had been there. When asked if Anne was present at all times, Warren seemed to hedge:

> It was my recollection that she was. . . . As best as I can recall, I told the Needhams that their daughter had a malignancy and I told them that I would make an appointment with a doctor at the University of Chicago. . . .

Phelan allowed that information to sink in, then asked the crucial question:

> Did you have any conversations at that time as to the cause of the problem that had been found in Anne?

Warren, astonishingly, in light of Phelan's stated assertion that he would testify precisely to the contrary, said: "I don't think we did." Phelan appeared somewhat perplexed by this, and rephrased the question:

> Did you have any conversations with the mother and Anne about the possibility of any association between the DES and the condition that was found in Anne?

Warren slowly shook his head, and admitted, "We may have discussed it then. I just don't recall." On a final tack to prove the crucial point, Phelan yet again asked:

> Now in your conversation with Anne and her mother on that Saturday morning, March 2nd, 1974, did you or Mrs. Needham have an occasion to raise the subject of the possible association between this finding that you made . . . and this rare condition that you found in Anne Needham?

Warren replied weakly but resisted the temptation toward certainty:

I don't recall how deeply we discussed it. We may have alluded to it. However, I was so concerned about getting her to call [the specialist] that my primary motive was to get her to see him, get her scheduled to see him, and have treatment instituted as soon as possible. We may have discussed again the possibility of DES, I just don't recall.

This was a far cry from the claims Phelan made in his opening, about elaborate, detailed, intimate conversations between the doctor and his patient about the cause of her condition. But Phelan could not allow the interrogation to founder there, in the murky reaches of Warren's limited memory. He raised his voice and asked again, more pointedly:

As you look back at it, Doctor, and you reflect on this conversation, is it your best recollection now that the subject of her mother's ingestion of this drug . . . was discussed however briefly with Miss Needham, and her mother, on March 2nd, 1974?

Despite Phelan's evident qualification, from detailed discussion to a modified "discussed however briefly," his reference to "best recollection," and his limitation of the question to that one alleged incident, Charfoos objected, "Leading suggests the answer. Too, the doctor has just testified that he does not recall having this conversation one way or another." Decker overruled Charfoos: "You may answer, Doctor." Warren looked directly down at his lap, as if examining his hands; in a marked undertone, he murmured, "To the best of my knowledge, I believe we discussed it." Anne looked at him, silently indicating her disappointment. It was what had been expected; still, he had vacillated, obviously and extensively. The only hope for her position swaying the jury would be if it registered negatively. If those recurrent "To the best of my knowledge," "I believe," "as I recall," and all those slight demurrals were seen to reflect a hazy memory prompted by skilled and recent coaching.

Charfoos took over Phelan's position to begin his cross-examination. That morning, Sussman and Charfoos had overheard Dr. Warren in conversation with the defense lawyers, referring to them by their first names. If this indicated a relatively close association, that could be employed to impeach the witness. Charfoos began: "You indicated that you have spent some time with Mr. —, I am sorry, the defense lawyer, Mr. Phelan?" Warren admitted, "Yes, sir."

Charfoos went on:

Q: And what do you call him?

A: Mr. Phelan.

Q: And the other gentleman next to him?

A: Mr. Simon.

Q: All right. Have you gotten on a first name basis with them?

A: On occasion, yes.

Q: That is not the only people that you have spent time with from the defense side of this lawsuit?

Charfoos plodded with Warren through the details of his intimacy with the defense in the case, a more recent but possibly more determining acquaintance than with the Needham family. He then reestablished Warren's essential vagueness about the events of that period, and the revealing fact that for the alleged meeting at his office, there was no office record of the visit. Warren had suggested that the lack of record was because, "I don't call them in as patients. I called them in as friends."

With the failure of Warren's testimony to convincingly demonstrate that Anne had been advised of the DES association, the defense had been severely compromised in its claims. To solidify that uncertainty, the plaintiff called to the stand Anne's childhood friend, Denny Rauen, who testified in convincing detail to Anne's presence with him on that disputed Saturday morning at Saumanac Park, when Anne had come to his house where he and his band had been practicing, to how they had spent the morning and most of the afternoon in the park together.

With that testimony completed, the statute of limitations portion of the trial was essentially over. The testimony of Anne Needham, Victor Needham, and Mary Needham effectively corroborated the plaintiff's position. The jury retired after two and a half days of testimony to weigh these varying points of view. The verdict was returned in considerably less than an hour: for Anne. On the plaintiff's side, there was encouragement, but certainly no jubilation. A major obstacle to the case had been overcome, but it had always been a tangential barrier to the real question: Would White Laboratories be held responsible for making the pill that caused Anne's cancer?

18

Between the middle of May, when Anne Needham finally won her case on the statute of limitations, and the middle of August, when she went to court to prove the liability of White for her cancer, the legal atmosphere for the plaintiff's side in DES litigation distinctly began to improve. In July 1979, two decisions were made in DES cases which strongly indicated that the tide was turning, and that after five years of research and maneuvering a good deal of the work done by plaintiff's lawyers around the country was beginning to pay off for DES daughters.

In July, Judge Walter Skinner of the United States District Court in Boston certified a large class-action on behalf of all DES daughters in Massachusetts. The suit, filed by Harvard Law School professor David Rosenberg, employed the enterprise liability theory in selecting six drug companies as defendants. By granting that legal grounds for such a new breed of action did exist, Judge Skinner confirmed that at least in one state enterprise liability would provide a legitimate means of resolving the issue of identification, still by far the major legal problem facing most DES daughters.

Meanwhile, in New York City, Joyce Bichler, a twenty-five-year-old social worker who had suffered cancer, followed by radical hysterectomy and vaginectomy, became the first DES daughter in America to be awarded monetary damages in a DES cancer case. The only two previous cases, other than Anne's, had been inconclusive, because one had been settled for an undisclosed amount on the eve of the verdict, and the other had been lost on the identification question. Joyce Bichler's attorney, Leonard Finz of New York, successfully argued the enterprise liability thesis before a jury of three men and two women. After eight weeks of evidence and a prolonged five-day deliberation, Joyce Bichler was awarded $500,000 in damages against Eli Lilly and Company.

In the Bichler case a single company, Lilly, had been selected as the sole defendant because of its reportedly large share of the market. Enterprise liability provided that "the burden of proof" must be shifted from the plaintiff to the defendant; the theory also shifted the burden of compensation onto any reasonable defendant, that is, one that might reasonably have manufactured the pill in question. The result was that Eli Lilly bore the brunt of the defense, with the option of suing other drug companies who also made and distributed DES to share in paying the damages.

Neither the Bichler decision nor the ruling in Boston provided any legal precedent for Needham, because only if a decision is affirmed at the appellate level is precedent created. But the large and visible presence of drug company lawyers as the Needham trial began in Chicago indicated that a watershed of sorts for DES litigation was certainly imminent.

For Anne Needham, this would be the heart of her trial, but the part in which she would not participate. Both the statute section and the portion following, to ascertain damages, required her intensive involvement. But the liability issue was an abstract matter, a question really of public concern, not of private interest. Whether DES had caused Anne's cancer would be decided by the conflicting testimony of expert witnesses; whether a prudent drug manufacturer should have known DES would cause cancer, whether its failure to warn and failure to adequately test for safety constituted negligence and not merely a historical shortcoming in the state of the medical art, would not have much to do with Anne personally. But Anne as the victim, sitting silently in her plaintiff's chair, would remain the focus of the trial, even if she was only able to watch.

Monday, August 13 was taken up by a selection of the jury in the morning and opening arguments of counsel in the afternoon. Both opening arguments were essentially refinements of the openings in the first mistrial, back in March. But there was time for a witness. Anne, as the plaintiff, was bound to bring evidence to bear showing that White should pay her damages. White, as the defendant, was bound simply to refute that evidence with its own expert testimony. As Anne's side had the burden of bringing proof in the case, it was Charfoos' task to present the first witness in her favor, Dr. Michael Shimkin of the National Cancer Institute in Bethesda, Maryland.

Shimkin was a specialist in oncology, the study of "neoplastic diseases," or cancer. He had been a consultant to the FDA on various drugs and their carcinogenesis, had testified before congressional committees on the use of tobacco and, more recently, against the use of DES as a feed additive.

"Early in life," Shimkin recalled, "I became interested in estrogenic compounds and got, among others, a very early sample of what was called stilbestrol in those days—now it is called diethylstilbestrol, or DES—and injected that into animals and fed it into animals and got a galaxy of tumors, in breasts, testes, and other organs. . . ."

Judge Decker halted the questioning there, and the court recessed until the next day. Tuesday morning was consumed by Shimkin's recitation of the history of cancer research, particularly the study of cancers caused by agents external to the body.

In the early days, Shimkin continued, other animal researchers were using these newly isolated estrogens to induce cancer in laboratory animals. In France, Antoine Lacassagne injected estrogens into male mice and they developed cancer of the breast, while William Murray in Bar Harbor, Maine, was implanting ovaries in male mice and creating cancer of the breast. In 1938, Leo Loeb was the first to get some DES and inject that into the male mice, and they too got cancer of the breast, at just about the time Shimkin was beginning his research at the National Cancer Institute.

Charfoos asked, "In your opinion, Doctor, how reliable a bellwether, or forerunner, are animal studies in predicting whether products will or will not cause cancer in humans?" Shimkin cleared his throat, took a long sip from a glass of water, and said distinctly, "I think that they are extremely reliable. There are a few exceptions, but in general, we don't differ that much from animals to ignore such data. They certainly are red lights to indicate when we are in areas of possible danger."

In reviewing his own work in the field, Shimkin produced a paper published in the *Journal of the National Cancer Institute* in 1941, in which he showed that estrone, a natural estrogen, and stilbestrol, the synthetic, were both reasonably similar in their cancer-producing activity. Shimkin estimated that he had published in various easily accessible journals prior to 1950 between a dozen and fifteen articles on the general subject of estrogen-induced cancer in laboratory animals. Charfoos concluded this review with the question:

Q: Doctor, by 1950 was there any question in any reputable scientific research group in this area but that estrogen could cause cancer in the animal species?

A: Certainly not in my mind.

Q: Did you know of any reputable researcher—

A: No, sir, I did not.

Q: —that had any opinion to the contrary?

A: No.

On the subject of extrapolating such information to the human species, Shimkin replied, "We compiled a monograph in 1945 . . . in which I wrote the concluding chapter on the possible relationship to man. I certainly indicated that . . . these were potent carcinogenic agents which should be used very cautiously." Charfoos asked, "Were you the only person at that time or up to 1950 that was warning about the potential of cancer being caused in humans if these estrogens were given to them?" Shimkin cleared his throat and answered evenly, "Oh, no. It was quite a common type of statement."

In the case of stilbestrol, Shimkin testified to the significant difference between prescribing estrogen in small doses to nonpregnant women, either menopausal or postpartal, and to pregnant women; that clinical experience on nonpregnant women provided no basis for shifting the indication for use during pregnancy, especially when the dosage increase could not be computed in percentage terms, but could more accurately be expressed in terms of orders of magnitude.

Q: Doctor, in your opinion if a researcher . . . was proposing to increase their dosage a hundred times over what had been used up to that point and they were going to use it on pregnant women, would animal tests be a reasonable thing to do to start to see what would happen?

A: I don't think that is reasonable. I think that is essential.

Q: Doctor, assume a researcher or some other group was planning to market this drug to humans, in your opinion as of 1950 was there sufficient information to allow them to be on notice that cancer was a potential from this drug?

A: Definitely, yes sir.

Q: And if they still elected to market this drug in your opinion was some form of warning of the cancer potential required?

A: I would think so, yes.

Shimkin was presented with the 1950 New Drug Application submitted by White Laboratories for the use of Dienestrol for accidents of pregnancy. The application included, as examples of clinical testing, several papers by George and Olive Smith, and two tests by their own contracted researchers, a doctor named Goldcamp and a doctor named Rakoff. Shimkin first examined the papers by Smith and Smith and was asked to comment on them. After a brief inspection, he concluded:

A: Well, these were—I don't know whether these are even really historical controls. These are compilations of previous experiments which they did do, and they said, this was our experience before and with this new procedure our experience is better. But these are what you would class as historical controls, and in my opinion are inadequate to demonstrate an effect.

Q: In your opinion, would a reasonable and prudent person wishing to market that drug for pregnant women have needed more testing before actually doing the marketing?

A: I would have so recommended.

Q: Why?

A: Well, because I don't think that it was enough on these anecdotal interesting observations to prove the point that this was a useful procedure and also by that time it was known that these were carcinogenic agents.

Of the two clinical reports submitted by White, Shimkin was equally critical as to their scientific worth. The first, by Dr. Abraham Rakoff, Shimkin characterized as a report of rather limited clinical experience, "Total number of cases, twenty-two patients, twelve have delivered, so actually it is just twelve patient experiences; of the twelve patients who have delivered, four have aborted, eight presumably delivered at term." He examined the paper at a respectable distance, "Eight presumably delivered at term, I don't know whether they were alive. I presume they were." He regarded the document with one eyebrow raised, rather skeptically.

Q: Doctor, by any scientific standard existent as of 1949–1950, would any reputable scientific person in medicine call that a scientific study that can be relied on for marketing this drug for pregnant women in the United States?

Shimkin gingerly took up the Rakoff report and held it up to the light at his side, an incongruously old-fashioned brass lamp with a green glass shade, the only old object in the room, complete with a crooked shade. "No sir," Shimkin growled, "this was a series of clinical observations." Charfoos: "Why is it not scientific?" Shimkin: "Well, it doesn't purport to be. It is an observation on twelve patients, no controls, no follow-up. It is just a statement," he said, his tone betraying his contempt, "of *what was done.*"

Q: Could you as a physician, scientist, and researcher have made any conclusion whatsoever as to whether or not Dienestrol would help prevent miscarriages from that document?

Mr. Pope: Objection, your Honor. It is outside the area of his competence.

The Court: Overruled.

A (by the witness): I don't think so. It has no basis one way or another.

Shimkin quickly delivered his critique of the other White report, a short, two-page "private communication" by a man named Goldcamp. Charfoos asked, "Do you have any belief that that was ever published?" Shimkin shook his head. "Oh, it could not be."

Q: Why?

A: Because it is incomplete and trivial.

Charfoos asked, "Would this be considered a scientific report as to the effect or usefulness of that drug?" Shimkin pursed his lips. "Well, at least it didn't kill the patients." The jurors glanced significantly at each other; Judge Decker frowned visibly; Phelan and Pope stared squarely at their legal pads.

Charfoos turned then to the Herbst reports:

Q: Doctor, starting sometime in early 1970, did you eventually read or hear or become familiar with reports of young women having clear-cell adenocarcinoma as a result of their mother taking a drug called DES?

A: My first awareness of it were the reports by Dr. Herbst in Boston in 1970–71.

Q: Doctor, assuming a young woman is diagnosed to have clear-cell carcinoma, and that as a history her mother had taken DES or Dienestrol, do you have any opinion within reasonable medical certainty whether there was an association or a cause and effect?

A: Yes. The chances of a causal relationship are extremely high.

Q: Doctor, when you say "very high," what do you mean by that?

A: In biology, a hundred percent is an impossibility. Already there may be rare, rare cases in which this factor was not identifiable. Maybe the estrogen came from some other source in dogs, and others. . . . But the chances biologically are up to what I think in common parlance would be known as pretty certain. Now, I am not going to go for a hundred percent, but make it, you know, ninety-nine-point-five or something of that sort.

Then, finally, the question of efficacy. After causation, this was a major issue in proving negligence. (After the failure to warn of danger, the complementary issue was failure to warn of uselessness.)

Q: Doctor, did there appear certain articles including but not past 1952 which raised questions as to whether these DES drugs even prevented miscarriages?

A: One was Crowder from Long Beach. The other one was Robinson from Columbia University. These were both published in the *American Journal of Obstetrics and Gynecology.*

Q: Doctor, did there come out after 1952 additional articles which clearly show that Smith and Smith were not correct on this point?

A: Well, the classical ones which I think are to the point are Ferguson in 1953 and then Dieckmann here in Chicago, also published in 1953. . . .

Q: Doctor, are those two articles in your mind authoritative on this subject?

A: I think particularly Ferguson is a lead-pipe cinch.

As a fitting conclusion to his testimony, Charfoos asked Shimkin to go through a large stack of scientific papers, published in reputable journals prior to 1952, dealing with the general subject of estrogens and cancer. Shimkin began to read a long list of titles of papers, while Judge Decker shifted impatiently in his chair. At one point he stared glumly down at the giant stack of paper, and commanded in exasperation, "We're not going through that entire stack; there is nothing which will make me go through that entire stack. . . ." He shifted and leaned his round head on his hand, flipped his black robes across his shoulders, as the list continued, his head began gently to incline, and he glanced frequently at the clock. He took off his glasses, rubbed his eyes, and glanced gloomily to the back of the room, as if haunted by phantom cases.

Shimkin's cross-examination was conducted by Phelan's co-counsel, Michael Pope. Pope was short and squat where Phelan was tall and lanky, with a square, beard-shadowed jaw, tough black eyes, and a habit of hunching over to give himself a predatory look. Pope swaggered up to Shimkin and began his questioning right at the top of his voice:

Q: Do I correctly understand that you have testified synthetic estrogen and natural estrogen produce basically the same results? Is that right?

A: Right.

Q: You have also testified during the '30s and '40s and '50s many people in the animal research area were injecting estrogens into mice and getting tumors? Is that right?

A: Right.

Q: This was a well-known fact, wasn't it, Doctor?

A: It was to me, yes.

Q: Well, now—

A: I presume.

Q: —let's not quibble.

Charfoos: I will object to the form so that we have some ground rules right now. Remarks like "let's not quibble" really don't belong in the question.

Pope: Well, Mr. Charfoos—

The Court: Just a moment. I will agree that no one is going to quibble here so far as I am running this trial.

Pope: All right. Fair enough.

Pope continued to shout his questions while Shimkin grew quieter and quieter. Pope's questioning clearly attempted to impeach the witness on the grounds not of scientific competence, but of limitation of experience. That is, that Shimkin's research, confined to the ostensibly artificial world of animal research had little relation to the real world of clinical experience. In rapid fire succession, Pope asked:

Q: You don't have any formal training in the area of obstetrics, do you?

A: No, I do not.

Q: Okay. How about gynecology?

A: No, I do not.

Q: Okay. How about surgery, Doctor?

A: No, I am not a surgeon.

Q: Okay. As a matter of fact, a pregnant woman who had some concern about her pregnancy, she wouldn't go to you, would she?

A: No, and I wouldn't accept her, either.

Pope further challenged Shimkin to produce any specific warnings he had made to practicing physicians about the clinical use of estrogens. Shimkin produced his monograph for the American Association for the Advancement of Science, published in 1945, in which he wrote:

The appearance of mammary and other neoplasms in mice injected with chemically isolated estrogens has created an interesting and important question. Can the clinical use of such preparations, particularly in large doses and for extended periods of time, lead to the development of mammary and other neoplasms in man? . . . It has been less than a decade since potent estrogenic compounds have come into excessive clinical use, and it is too early to draw conclusions that such therapy is innocuous. . . .

Pope redirected himself to questioning the relevance of Shimkin's animal work to hormone use by humans. He asked, "Well, I take it there is a great deal of difference between a man and a mouse, right?" Shimkin responded wryly, "I think most of us can tell the difference, yes."

He elaborated:

There are, of course, differences. . . . In rodents the pituitary is much more involved in the production of [certain] hormones . . . the rat and the mouse do not need vitamin C. . . . These are all true. Also mice have tails, and we don't. But these differences . . . are not as striking as the similarities. Most of the time when you encounter toxicity . . . we have learned that these represent potential signs of something to watch for in man.

The following morning, Pope wrapped up his cross-exam by taking the large stack of scientific articles supplied by the plaintiff and loudly asking Shimkin if he had read each and every one of them. Shimkin replied that he had not read each one recently but that he was generally familiar with them. Pope responded:

> Okay. Would it be a fair summary of what these documents contain to say that they basically show that estrogens, synthetic or natural, given to animals, most of them mice, produced some tumors?

Shimkin mulled that one over a bit, and replied simply, "Yes." Pope turned smartly on his heel and advised Judge Decker, "I think that's all, your Honor." Charfoos, on redirect examination, asked Shimkin about the relationship of his animal work to human beings. Shimkin replied, "Well, I was interested in cancer in man. The animals are only a model in order to conquer the disease in man. It is no particular pleasure to cause tumors in animals. . . ."

Pope, on redirect, asked Shimkin, "The Herbst report, which came out in 1971, you have characterized that as a 'bullet out of the blue,' haven't you." Shimkin replied that he had. Pope smiled with satisfaction, leaving the impression that if Shimkin had been surprised by the Herbst report in 1971, how could he claim that manufacturers had been sufficiently warned?

Charfoos, on redirect, asked Shimkin to clarify the statement:

Q: What did you mean by a "bullet out of the blue"?

A: Bolt out of the blue, I believe I said. I try to avoid bullets. This was a sudden, dramatic demonstration of what we had been predicting would occur, but the circumstances of the phenomena. . . . The site, and the fact that it happened as an effect upon the fetus, these were the bolts out of the blue. The fact that estrogenic compounds were finally, absolutely, lead-pipe cinch demonstrated to be carcinogens in man had been anticipated ever since the early '40s, and really the surprise of it was that it took so long to do so. . . .

Dr. Shimkin was excused. Mary Needham took the stand.

Mary wore a black dress, with a pink scarf round her neck. Her straight blond hair was piled loosely on top of her head; she held her chin with one hand, pursed her lips, and with her head cocked at a slight angle, gave her full name and full address, while winking wryly at Anne. The purpose of Mary's testimony was to establish the identity of the pill as a White product, and to certify that indeed Mary Needham took the pill on prescription from her doctor, Walter Abrams.

"I work at Marshall Field's . . . ," she said softly. "I also work at a jewelry store as a certified diamond expert. . . . I was married on August 6, 1946, in Des Moines, Iowa. . . . We were both students at Drake University, studying pharmacy. . . . I did not finish, I went on to become a mother. . . ."

The trial had finally made Mary feel like a human being. For so long she had been forced to deal with the fact that her child was sick and suffering because of something she'd done. But on the eve of that trial and that morning, before she took the stand, Mary thought to herself, "By God, there isn't anybody that's going to beat me again." Defiantly she raised her voice as Mr. Charfoos asked her about the circumstances surrounding her taking DES back in 1952.

"I went to see Dr. Abrams," she recalled, "and he prescribed Dienestrol. After Anne was delivered, he told me I needed some 'repair work,' and Victor was very indignant." Phelan jumped up at that point and objected as to relevancy. Mary looked right at Phelan and thought, "He's got that nice Irish grin that would charm the pants off you. But watch out." She went on, "And then in 1974 Anne went to see Jerry Warren, who did a biopsy. . . ."

Judge Decker leaned over his bench and said quietly to the quiet room, "It is stipulated that the plaintiff had cancer, surgery, I've said all that. . . ." Mary looked up at him wonderingly, and ran her finger lightly across her cheek, her eyes drifting frequently to Anne, who smiled encouragingly back. She tilted her head and tucked one hand into the narrow black belt around her waist, and she waited to see if she needed to go on. Phelan stood up at that point and halted Mary's testimony by conceding what had been disputed since the start of the lawsuit. "It is stipulated," he said slowly, "that there is no contest about the identity of the drug." Charfoos shrugged, "Then there are no further questions."

Mary stood and stepped down from the witness box. Tom

Bleakely stood up from the plaintiff's table and led her slowly back to the gallery in the rear, where, now that she was no longer a witness, she would be allowed to sit and watch the trial. She took a seat in the second row and stared fondly at Anne, who wore barrettes in her hair that day, and a plain brown skirt reaching below the knee, with pleats. Her fair hair had been lightened by the summer sun, and her freckles deepened by a recent tan.

Anne was proud to see her mom up there on that stand. She thought to herself how about a week ago she had felt like pulling out of the trial. It was the coward in her; she got so wrought up, but she finally pulled herself together and took comfort that for the most part she'd just have to sit and watch. That wasn't easy though, because all the science and law and testimony, even though it didn't mention her, was still about her. She could feel the jury's eyes constantly upon her, and the eyes of the watchers in the rear; she had allowed herself to get all worked up over the subject of her clothes: all her things were winter stuff. So today, in spite of the heat, she wore a brown velvet jacket and a heavy blue open-collared shirt. She wore no jewelry but a simple watch on her left wrist.

The court adjourned until the next morning. Anne walked out into the corridor to smoke a cigarette. She'd stopped smoking at the Mayo Clinic five years before. It had been Saint Patrick's Day: the doctors had told her mother to take her somewhere out of the hospital, because they were worried she was getting too depressed. Anne was still smoking, and she would drag her IV on that rolling pole behind her, slowly creeping with all the pain down to a lounge at the end of the corridor where the patients were allowed to smoke.

Her mother had come to visit that Saint Patrick's Day. Anne said she'd go anywhere, just to any old bar. They wheeled her down the tunnel to the Kahler Hotel, and they went to the bar where there were patients watching TV in wheelchairs. There was a nice guy from Kansas, also in a wheelchair, with blond hair and blue eyes, and Anne and he got to talking. Anne took out her pack of cigarettes, pulled one out, and sat there with the cigarette in her lap, just toying with it in her hands. Finally, this guy looked down at it and said, "Hey, aren't you going to light that?" Anne looked down at the cigarette in her hands and thought to herself that she knew what it caused. She lit the cigarette, took a puff, and it tasted terrible. She threw the pack away.

When the trial started, Anne started smoking again. She couldn't help it, it was the only thing that helped her nervousness. Anne stood there as the lawyers filed out of the court, there seemed to be a good deal of forced camaraderie between lawyers on opposing sides, back slapping and friendly remarks, and "give my love to your wife." It seemed strange that they were able to separate their jobs and their lives.

Day four, Thursday morning, a new witness was called to the stand. But the witness would testify by means of a recorded video-tape. Some months before the trial, Phelan and Bleakely had flown to Bergen, Norway, to tape a deposition that would be used in this and several other DES trials. Now, at the center of the courtroom floor, a scaffolding of steel dollies and a frame held three large television monitors, with one screen facing the jury, another facing the judge, and the third facing the tables of counsel. At 10:10 the jury filed in and noted the video monitors with evident interest. Judge Decker leaned sternly forward and admonished them, "Let's make sure everyone stays awake through this." A technician played with some switches, and a color image sprang to life on all three screens, depicting a fair-haired young man in a dark blue suit, with hair parted straight down the middle, and bright blue eyes. This was John Gunnar Forsberg, professor of anatomy and reproductive physiology in Bergen, Norway.

Forsberg's testimony would link the work of Michael Shimkin to that of the next witness, a prominent clinician. Forsberg had designed a brilliant series of experiments in which he had created a model for the human fetus using the neonatal (newborn) mouse. He had subsequently defined a precise correspondence between the female mouse shortly after birth and the human fetus before birth, in terms of the development of the reproductive organs. In short, Forsberg's testimony would demonstrate what happened to the fetal organs of the offspring female when bathed in a powerful solution of DES while still in the womb.

Tom Bleakely, also on videotape, began his questioning with a simple request: He asked Forsberg if he would care to define "science." Forsberg hesitated, tugged at the elastic band holding up his glasses, and then politely complied. He spoke in a strong Norwegian accent, with long vowels and a springy rhythm: "The essence of science," he replied, holding both hands flat out on the conference table, "is a critical attitude toward reality. That you can't say anything is true until you have tested all the possibilities. Because the ways of God are unpredictable under nature. . . . You must have control experiments, for instance, so the experimental situation isn't intervening. . . ." Bleakely asked how long the concept of controls had existed, and Forsberg replied, "For as long as science has existed."

Forsberg went on to describe his research. "It is primarily," he said, "on the effect of the sex hormones on the rat vagina." The jury squirmed somewhat at this, but all their expressions remained solemn. "I have found that certain hormones," he went on, "pass through the placental barrier, and exert an effect on the fetus." This, he explained, is known as the "transplacental effect."

Forsberg briefly described that he was able to set up a model of human development using the neonatal mouse, that the neonatal period, in the week immediately following the birth of the mouse, is equivalent to the eighteenth week of the human fetal development during pregnancy; that is, the first trimester, when the Smiths and others were recommending massive doses of DES.

Bleakely and Forsberg reviewed a series of papers published in the *American Journal of Obstetrics and Gynecology,* where Forsberg had clearly demonstrated the permanent effects of DES on the vaginal epithelium of the female mouse. Dienestrol, he explained, had the same effect as DES, and "DES produced abnormalities in this test system," he said, pronouncing each word distinctly. "Other steroids did not." Forsberg held up to the camera a series of photographs showing magnified images of the changes produced.

Charfoos, meanwhile, passed copies of these same photographs to the judge and jury.

The jurors examined each photo with evident interest, showing them to one another and pointing out various changes evident to the naked eye. For many of the jurors, it seemed that Dr. Forsberg's photographs were the first concrete evidence that DES did indeed cause permanent changes in the genitalia. Even Judge Decker, as he inspected the enlargements, seemed to watch the

214

video screen with new interest. A subtle change seemed to come over him, as if until that time he had not really believed that DES did what it was said to do, in man or mouse.

Bleakely asked Forsberg if he had an opinion on the subject of causation. "Yes, I have an opinion," Forsberg scrupulously replied.

> My opinion is that today we cannot prove that there is a cause and effect relationship. That is, there is no scientific proof, but we do have indications of an association. That is ingestion of estrogens provides a basis for the development of clear-cell adenocarcinoma.

In order to describe that association, Forsberg employed the following analogy:

> If someone fires a gun into my heart I will die. That is cause and effect. If someone fires a gun into my leg, and I go to the hospital, and get an infection that results in my death, there was an association between the gunshot and my death. . . .

Bleakely asked if Forsberg's research held out any consequences for the future. Forsberg replied:

> Our lab work had relevance for the future situation . . . we have found changes in the genital tract of the mouse, which turned out to be similar to human patients. . . . We have changes in the incidence of mammary tumors, the lymph system, perhaps changes in the prostatic gland. . . .

On his video-taped cross-exam, Phelan inquired what the attitude on the part of clinicians was to work such as his in the 1930s, '40s, and '50s. Forsberg responded, frowning:

> There was an attitude, well, the clinical doctors had an attitude that the animal work was not relevant to the clinical situation. What we did in my opinion was of essential value for clinical study, but I was aware that doctors had a different opinion of our work. . . .

In the courtroom, the scene was quiet, subdued by the vivid transmission. The jury seemed to perceive the significance of this deposition as heightened by the technology used to display it. The jury was wide awake and alert, clearly impressed by this televised lecture; Decker flipped quietly through a transcript, following closely Forsberg's words; Phelan slid along a legal pad gently with the tip of his pen; Pope constantly scratched with his pen on yellow paper, studying the screen intently; Anne touched one finger to the corner of one eye, her long hair loose and halfway down her back.

Phelan asked Forsberg, "What was the knowledge of any connection between ingestion of DES by the mother and cancer in the offspring in the 1930s, '40s, and '50s? Isn't it true that there was no reason to believe there would be danger to the offspring?" Forsberg politely asked the court reporter to read the question back to him, and he sat pensively, biting his lower lip, one hand hovering near his mouth: "I can't give an opinion . . . at that time I had no contact with other people . . . but the general consensus," he admitted reluctantly, "was that they didn't think these substances were harmful to the fetus."

Phelan pressed on: "If you had been practicing back in those days . . . you would have prescribed synthetic estrogen for habitual abortion, wouldn't you?" Forsberg sighed audibly and said, "I haven't the standpoint, all who are listening to this should realize this is speculation," he looked around the little room helplessly, and gave in. "I think that I would have prescribed synthetic estrogen as a doctor in practice. . . ." Bleakely, on redirect, moved quickly to redress this point. He asked, "What would you do to test the drug, let's say, we haven't done any animal testing of our own."

Forsberg replied carefully, critically, but with a kind of relief:

> I can say that I hope that if I had been a good doctor, if you can't prove that this drug is effective, it is of no value to me. If you can't prove it has no serious adverse effects, I would not use this drug.

With this final testimony, the three colorful screens abruptly faded, and went blank.

Friday morning. The fifth day of Anne's trial was dedicated to the testimony of Dr. Albrecht Schmitt, a prominent clinician at the Medical College of Pennsylvania and a visiting professor at the Chicago Lying-In Hospital. A native of Marburg, Germany, Dr. Schmitt had come to the United States in 1956 on a Fulbright scholarship, had studied at the Massachusetts General Hospital, and then under a Damon Runyon Fellowship continued studies in clinical cancer research at the Cancer Institute in Buffalo.

Schmitt would testify on the clinical aspects of the DES question, to supplement the testimony of Dr. Shimkin, who was more of an animal research man. Schmitt was a leading specialist in the field of colposcopy, a pioneer in the introduction of the use of the colposcope into clinical practice in the United States. Because of his background in using this sophisticated magnifying instrument in making the kind of directed biopsies which aid in the detection of DES-related changes, Schmitt had seen over three hundred DES daughters in his own office, three with advanced cancer.

Charfoos asked Schmitt how many young women were currently reported in the Registry of Clear-Cell Adenocarcinoma with a history of maternal DES ingestion. Schmitt gravely replied, in a thick German accent, "There are close to four hundred." When asked if after reviewing the medical records and slides of Anne Needham he had an opinion of the cause of her cancer, he sternly concluded, "The patient's mother was exposed to Dienestrol when she was pregnant with her daughter, and the daughter developed clear-cell adenocarcinoma." Charfoos asked for a clarification of the issue of cause: "In your opinion, within a reasonable medical certainty, does this young woman have that disease because of this drug?" Schmitt replied firmly, "That is corect."

Schmitt justified this unusual certainty by citing what to him was conclusive evidence on cause: the report released by Dr. Herbst in 1976 at Hot Springs, Virginia, and later published in the *American Journal of Obstetrics and Gynecology,* that DES sales figures indicated a precise nineteen-year gap between 1953, the highest year of DES sales, and 1972, the highest incidence of clear-cell cancer. This evidence evidently permitted him to employ that hard and simple word "cause" when discussing the circumstances surrounding Anne's cancer.

Schmitt was asked to describe for the benefit of the jury Anne's condition just prior to surgery in February of 1974. Stepping up to the drawing board, and making vague lines with a felt-tip marker, he began to explain the nature of adenosis and clear-cell cancer. "Now adenosis," he explained, "means that glands, which you normally don't find in the vagina, are found in the vagina. They are what we call displaced glands. . . . Now in the case of Anne Needham," he turned gently toward Anne and then began drawing delicately on the board, "the tumor in this patient was in the posterior aspect of the vagina and was surrounded by adenosis. The same tissue we found here we find in ninety percent of all patients exposed to stilbestrol during pregnancy. . . ." With a gentle shrug, Schmitt sat down back in the stand.

Through this demonstration Anne remained outwardly calm, but her face flushed noticeably at several points, and she seemed to be holding herself unusually rigid. Her arms fell stiffly to her sides, her expression was impassive but interested, as if attending a lecture in some academic suject, entirely outside herself.

Charfoos stood before the jury and addressed the witness with a rather long, hypothetical question: "Assume, sir, that around 1949 a company is interested in marketing a DES-like drug. . . ." Schmitt nodded.

"Assume further that as part of their testing, this company retains . . . some friends of friends that work in the drug company, and these investigators take certain pregnant women and give them this drug . . . and by the time they are ready to go to the Food and Drug Administration, one of their investigators had twelve babies born." Charfoos advanced on the witness, and stressed each word: "Eight were living, four were dead. Do you think that this is enough, in your opinion, to justify marketing this drug to women in America?"

Phelan leapt immediately to his feet, shouting indignantly, "Number one, the doctor does not have before him all the information! He does not have all the articles that have been written, he does not have fifteen years' experience that was given to the FDA!" Charfoos, ignoring him, continued, "Doctor, I want you to assume further that this company had never worked with pregnant women before, had never sold this pill to pregnant women, and that when they do sell it to pregnant women they are going to increase the dosage a hundredfold—"

Phelan again leapt up to object, stuttering, "Your Honor, this, this is virtual . . . that is inaccurate! I have made my objections to the basis in fact of this hypothetical!" Judge Decker gestured Phelan down, and said sharply, "You have made your objection. And if counsel is mistaken, you may point it out." Phelan sat down and Decker gestured to the witness to answer.

A small balding man with a charcoal gray moustache and a charcoal gray suit, Schmitt was busy studying the two reports submitted by White. He glanced at them almost in astonishment, rifling the pages and squinting fiercely, resembling a stern German professor going over the homework of some outrageously bad student. Leaning forward from the waist, his eyes peering defiantly out at the room from under bushy eyebrows, he snapped, "This certainly was not adequate testing!" Charfoos asked quietly, "Why not?"

Schmitt clutched the two reports and brandished them furiously at the jury. "Number one! What I have here, twelve babies, eight living and four dead!" He glanced around the room indignantly, as if dressing down unruly students. He shook his head in dismay, voice lowered. "This is certainly not an impressive result for a drug which should do something good for habitual aborters. . . ." He went on with a kind of furious sadness, "This is in no way impressive, this is certainly in no way any statistical number you can build anything on. . . ." He sat up in his chair, held out the report, displaying it on the counter of the witness box, his voice rising in volume. "To go ahead and to increase the dosage one hundred times is absolutely irresponsible!"

Continuing in a darker mood, he said, "And at this time it was already known that stilbene," he paused to spell out the word, beating time on the counter with each letter of the word, "stilbene was a carcinogen! Let's make this clear to the ladies and gentlemen of the jury since they should know it!" Eyes wide, he stood up and glared at a jury collectively astonished at this outburst. "Stilbene was known in the '30s as a cancer-making drug, and to have the *guts*"—he rose out of his chair and his voice shook. "I am getting angry, I am sorry, I am getting angry now. . . ."

Phelan was already advancing on the witness, "Doctor, if you will—" Charfoos nodding in his direction, somewhat shaken, offered, "I will withdraw the question." But the witness would not withdraw but stood in the stand waving the two White reports and shouting, "To increase the dose one hundred times! It is irresponsible!" Charfoos approached the box and said quietly, "Doctor, please let me ask you the question—" Schmitt glared at Char-foos as if he'd never seen him before; then, slowly calming, shook his head and closed his eyes as he sat down, muttering, "I am sorry, I am a clinician, and I have my feelings."

Phelan by this time was rapidly approaching the bench, red in the face. Standing directly in front of Judge Decker he demanded with barely suppressed rage, "I would move that those remarks made as they were, be stricken and I would also make a motion for a *mistrial,* on the basis of those remarks, your Honor!" Decker stared back at Phelan and said after a moment, "The motion for mistrial is denied. But," and here he turned to admonish Dr. Schmitt, "you are here for the purpose of answering questions, and not to express your personal feelings." Schmitt, now relatively subdued and calm in his chair, nodded solemnly, somewhat chastised.

Phelan began his cross-exam pacing slowly around the room, glancing now and then at a pad of notes. He started out with a beguiling friendliness, at low volume. "Good morning, Dr. Schmitt," he said, nodding politely to the witness in a simulation of old-world courtliness. Schmitt nodded sternly, eyes narrowed; Phelan continued to circle around his prey, and spoke softly, almost with concern: "Doctor, I noted your answer here that you have some strong feelings about diethylstilbestrol. Is that true, Doctor?" Schmitt glared back at Phelan from beneath bushy eyebrows and answered suspiciously, "What do you mean, this 'strong feeling,' Mr. Phelan?" Phelan slowed down even further and continued to gently probe, like a doctor inquiring as to the state of a patient's health:

Well, I gathered from your answer . . . that you have these strong feelings. I am wondering if you consider yourself biased, if you feel that your feelings are so strong that you can possibly be fair in giving your opinions. . . .

Phelan looked significantly at the jury, as Schmitt snapped, "No. I am fair." Phelan drawled, almost casually, "Pardon." Schmitt: "I am fair. I am objective." Phelan, nodding skeptically, "I see . . ."

"The Herbst articles," Phelan continued, voice darkening, ". . . when he found the six persons, the six women in the hospital in Massachusetts . . . that was an *unusual* finding that he made, wasn't it?" Phelan eyed the witness ingenuously. "Unusual," Schmitt shrugged, "that was an unusual finding to have so many young girls in one institution in such a short time, this is correct. . . ." Phelan continued to build volume, "In fact, it was a *startling* discovery, wasn't it?" Schmitt stared back at Phelan, suspecting a trap: "I don't know to call this a *startling* discovery. It was a startling discovery for me, as I had never heard. . . ." Phelan moved to quickly cut him off, "Excuse me, Doctor. It is a very simple question.

"In *fact*, Doctor, you believed that not only was it startling but it was probably the most *revolutionary* finding that occurred at the time!" Phelan was shouting; he swung around, and regarded the jury with a triumphant gleam. Schmitt hesitated: "I don't know what you are going to do and what you want me to say, Mr. Phelan." Phelan interjected sharply, "Excuse me, Doctor. I just want you to tell the *truth,* that is all!"

Charfoos stood: "Objection, repetitious." Decker overruled, Phelan ignored it. "I am referring, Doctor, to a deposition that you gave February 22, 1978. . . ."

One of the defenses used by the drug companies in DES cases was the fact that doctors tended to characterize Herbst's brilliant discovery of the DES to cancer link as "startling," "stunning," "revolutionary," etc. Which was all very well, but for the fact that the drug companies were able to raise the question: "If it was so startling, how could you expect us to have predicted such a thing?"

Plaintiffs argued that they were not claiming that the drug companies should have been able to necessarily warn of the transplacental effect specifically; they maintained that if the drug companies had done the appropriate reproductive testing, some effects would have been produced, as they had later by such men as Forsberg. Forsberg's tests were important because they represented the testing the companies should have done and could have done, but didn't. Clinicians like Schmitt had regarded the Herbst report as "startling" mostly because of the special and horrifying circumstances; but in Schmitt's case, it was even more startling, for him personally.

Phelan glanced down at some notes in his hand quoted from the year-old deposition by Schmitt, in which he described the

Herbst reports as "important and revolutionary discoveries in the field of obstetrics and gynecology." Phelan stood perfectly still and asked softly: "Do you still feel that way today? . . ." Schmitt, after a long silence, suddenly shouted, "For *me!* Because I did not know that DES was being given at all!"

That produced something of a stunned silence. Phelan quickly shouted back, "Doctor, are you telling us today, here in Chicago, Illinois, that it wasn't until 1971 that you knew that DES was being given to pregnant mothers for accidents of pregnancy?" He swung around to the jury, greeting them with a look of pure incredulity. "Yes!" Schmitt shouted back just as loudly, "Sir!"

It took some time for Charfoos to clear up this issue on redirect but it seemed that soon after Schmitt had come to the United States, he had attended a meeting of the American Society of Obstetrics and Gynecology at Lake Placid, New York, in 1953, where the famous Dieckmann report denouncing the use of DES was read. Schmitt, upon hearing this, assumed for some time that this report had effectively put DES use in America to a halt. It wasn't until much later that the Herbst reports in 1971 alerted him to the unsavory fact that the Dieckmann report had only somewhat slowed American DES enthusiasm but had not entirely curtailed it.

Phelan temporarily shifted tacks. "Doctor," he asked, glancing down at notes, "the Smiths . . . were in the 1940s and the 1950s some of the leading endocrinologists in the world, were they not?" Schmitt scrupulously replied, "Certainly, sir, you cannot say the leading. How do you know who is the leading. They were *among* the leading, let's put it that way." Phelan nodded and went on: "In fact, Doctor, those doctors that gave Dienestrol or natural estrogens in the '40s for accidents of—for threatened habitual miscarriage, that was a *reasonable* thing to do at the time for a doctor, wasn't it?"

Charfoos leapt up. "I am sorry. There is no issue on that. There has never been a claim that medical doctors . . . were wrong in prescribing this drug." Decker overruled. Schmitt qualified:

Yes, it was given by doctors. . . . Not all have given it. That is why I never heard, sir, about it, because my col-

lege never gave it. . . . If you say customary, then I
agree.

He ended in a long shrug, his hands outspread. Phelan went
on: "Isn't it a fact that the only person who has ever written in
any journal, with the exception of some person who wrote in a
case study, that DES causes cancer, is yourself, isn't that a fact?"

"No," Schmitt replied. That was not a fact. In fact, he explained, Dr. Keith Raher, former president of the American College of Obstetricians and Gynecologists, had been asked during a
panel discussion what course he would recommend to a physician
asked by a lawyer to testify in court that DES did not cause cancer. That, Schmitt maintained Raher had said, "would be difficult
to defend." "In other words," Schmitt concluded emphatically,
"he said the same: cause and effect. . . ."

Phelan brought up a similar colloquy in which Dr. Herbst
had said, "It is inaccurate to state that we have claimed that there
is cause and effect between DES and these clear-cell carcinomas."
Schmitt responded, "Your Honor, it is true, but I should have a
right to say—" But Phelan abruptly cut him off: "That is all I
have."

It was left for Charfoos, on redirect, to let Schmitt complete
his answer. Charfoos: "What else did Dr. Herbst say in that same
meeting?"

Schmitt eagerly swiveled in his chair to face the jury and
exhorted them: "Ladies and gentlemen of the jury, I know this article so well. . . ." The ladies and gentlemen gazed back at him
with a perplexed mixture of astonishment and interest. "Herbst
has stated clearly, absolutely clearly, that DES is what he calls an
'incomplete' carcinogen." He formed his arms into a giant cradle
and gently rocked his arms back and forth, as if rocking a child:
"Carcinogen . . . Genesis in the Bible means the making of the
world. . . . Herbst stated very clearly . . . and he did use the
word 'carcinogen,' or cancer making. . . ."

Schmitt's testimony was over, as was the plaintiff's case. An
animal researcher on Monday, Tuesday, and Wednesday had
testified that he and his kind knew all about estrogens and cancer,
that he himself had caused cancer in animals with DES, and that
such work was widely published; an animal researcher from Norway had testified on Thursday to the fact that he had caused can-

cer in offspring rats and mice with DES, which showed that such testing was available, and that such results would have occurred; on Friday, a prominent clinician testified that DES did cause cancer, and that it had caused Anne's cancer. All three witnesses testified to the fact that DES was woefully inadequate to prevent miscarriage and that the testing done by White Labs was similarly inadequate to determine either the safety or the efficacy of the preparation.

It rained all that Friday, August 17, 1979. The week ended in a confusion of raincoats and umbrellas. Anne stood up wearily from her hard swivel chair, which rolled on steel casters across the brown-nylon-carpeted floor. She went off to find the raincoat she'd left in the witness room. Phelan had slipped into his khaki trench coat and was busily searching for a lost umbrella between the high cardboard stacks of evidence boxes. Anne stood at the back of the room wondering if she could go.

"Can I go now?" she asked Tom Bleakely, who winked and said she certainly could. As the lawyers and observers bustled out of the room in a flurry of coats and hats and rubber boots, Anne walked out into the corridor and stared out the tall plate-glass window at the rain coming down. She saw Mr. Phelan go back into court, open the door, and ask, "Did anybody take an umbrella I left in this room?" She heard Bleakely shout, "I sold it." Through the door, she could make out the modern room and all those empty chairs.

19

Monday, August 20, just before 10 A.M. On the twenty-seventh floor of the Everett McKinley Dirksen Office Building, lawyers, witnesses, observers, and clerks milled around the corridors, sipping coffee, chatting, planning strategy. Some brief, strained fraternizing went on between the two sides, but most of the neat clusters of men in ties were strictly clusters of interest.

At the defense table Michael Pope sat quietly in last Tuesday's gray pinstripe suit. The only defense lawyer yet at the table, he scratched away intently on a legal pad, while scratching his scalp with great concentration through brown hair lightly streaked with gray. In the far right corner, as two lawyers from some other case argued a motion before Decker, the court reporter sat tapping away at his tiny keyboard and staring dreamily off into space like a blind man reading braille.

Richard Phelan soon joined Pope at the table. Lounging back in his swivel chair flat against the wall, one leg flung across the other, he brushed a stray particle from his right eye as he conferred with a female associate.

He wore a now familiar beige poplin suit, which he continually brushed off with one hand as if it were constantly acquiring an invisible layer of dirt. The two opposing lawyers before the bench continued to haggle over some interminable motion with Decker, requesting more time, extensions, continuances, delays, in some case involving the CIA. At once both lawyers turned, each in identical gray flannel suits, simultaneously clutched their briefcases, and like Tweedledee and Tweedledum mumbled gratefully in unison, "Thank you, your Honor." Swinging smartly on their heels together they paraded in mirror image down the aisle.

Charfoos came in with Anne Needham. She stood briefly in the doorway, examining the room with a startled expression, as if having forgotten what it looked like. She disappeared momentarily into the witness room to drop off a coat. Charfoos strolled casually around the room, conferring now with Bleakely, now with Sussman, stopping finally at the plaintiff's table, that overworked length of wood scattered with significant paper, all clipped and bound and filed away in manila, plastic, and cardboard.

At the rear, the visitor's gallery filled slowly with an audience largely comprised of various drug company counsel, with their leader presiding coolly at the center: Lane Bauer, leading counsel for Eli Lilly in the Midwest, in the same blue knit suit he wore for three days last week. Two ancient court buffs, both sporting floppy bow ties and old gray suits that hung loosely on their narrow frames, took the two best seats in the gallery. It was the middle of August, but they were dressed for the middle of winter.

"Who's the girl?" the one on the right whispered into his companion's hearing aid. He pointed directly at Anne. "She's a nice-looking one, ain't she?" Anne, with her light-colored hair falling loosely across her shoulders, her large dark eyes and clear, even-featured face, glanced curiously at them. The other man shrugged and whispered back, "It's a horrible case, dragging on and on. Two mistrials." He leaned forward and whispered louder, "She's suing some drug company. I've seen a lot of these cases. She hasn't got a *chance*." He smiled knowingly to himself, as both old men bobbed with an acquired reflex out of their seats as the bailiff sang: "The Court will rise." The first court-fly pointed directly to Charfoos, muttering, "Hell, he's not from Chicago. Don't think Decker likes him much."

Judge Decker trudged wearily toward his high-backed leather chair, shrugging his black robes impatiently into place around his shoulders while glancing automatically at the clock. He dropped heavily into his chair and weighed his white-haired head on one propped-up hand. In the witness box sat a distinguished man in a dark blue blazer, black-rimmed glasses, a snowy white shirt, and a very quiet plaid tie, all quite tastefully topped with a formidable fringe of white hair. He held his head up with a patient air and eyed the scene before and beneath him with a strangely placid smile. This was Dr. Edward Neary, the former medical director for White Labs.

Richard Phelan approached the stand, introduced the witness, and began running him through a string of credentials, experience, and other matters pertaining to the objective record of his life. Neary was a graduate of Jefferson Medical College in Philadelphia, class of '33, a graduate of Seton Hall College in South Orange, New Jersey, and a private practitioner for approximately four months before going to White as director of professional services. He was put in charge of advertising copy for the product line and the medical training of detail men, until 1943 when he became medical director at White. As medical director he was in charge of all medical oversight of new drug development.

Under Neary, White introduced several new products to supplement its extensive inventory of vitamin preparations. They came out with a chewable sulfa pill for mouth and throat infections, a powdered penicillin mix which when added to water formed a liquid that could be kept refrigerated for up to ten days; a preparation for iron deficiency anemia called Mol-Iron, and finally a kind of chewing gum containing aspirin which eventually became Aspergum. The first two products represented a significant departure for White, because they signaled its entry into the ethical, prescription drug field. The next such product that came along was a new form of DES which the British scientists who invented it called *Dienestrol*.

This drug, Neary explained, seemed from all available literature to be identical to DES in all respects but one: it didn't cause the nausea in nonpregnant women commonly associated with stilbestrol. Dienestrol came along a bit later than the original stilbestrol, becoming available in England and Canada at about the same time the first DES hit the United States in the early '40s. Around 1944, White Labs first began to consider marketing this different DES to women in America. Everything seemed propitious for the move: DES was selling well, despite the nausea problem. And but for some unusual animal studies, it was apparently entirely safe.

Neary summarized those animal studies quite neatly, as follows:

Well, first of all, with respect to the work that had been

published on studies of estrogens in experimental animals, we learned that in certain species of animals, notably rats and mice, and especially in those strains of these animals that had been inbred to be unduly susceptible to cancer, that estrogens could induce tumor formation.

In order to begin to market the drug, White had to do some clinical testing. So Dr. Neary went out in search of "clinicians who were expert in the area of endocrinology, expert obstetricians and gynecologists who had experience with investigation of estrogens specifically." The two principal investigators who ended up being retained by White were a Dr. Abraham Rakoff, a professor of obstetrics and gynecology at Jefferson Medical, a classmate of Dr. Neary's, and Dr. Joseph Goldcamp from Cincinnati, affiliated with the University of Cincinnati Medical School.

Neary asked both of these physicians to carry out clinical investigations of Dienestrol for use in menopausal syndrome. A Dr. Teage from the University of Alabama was subsequently hired to do some animal toxicity studies. All these reports eventually demonstrated to Dr. Neary's satisfaction that Dienestrol in all aspects but one, the nausea, was identical to DES.

They filed their first New Drug Application (NDA) with the FDA in the middle of 1946, for two indications only: menopausal syndrome and suppression of breast lactation after delivery. The only contraindication included in the labeling was the routine warning about use of the drug by women with a personal or family history of cancer of the reproductive organs or the breast. In the early part of 1948, White management decided to seek FDA approval for a new indication: threatened and habitual miscarriages. That permission was received from FDA in November of 1950.

Neary reviewed all the literature, he explained, relating to DES safety and efficacy before application for marketing. He read all the relevant articles by the Smiths and by Priscilla White at the Joslin Clinic for Diabetes in Boston, who claimed that DES was helpful in preventing miscarriage in diabetics. These were all the best of studies, Neary explained, done with the best controls, the finest methods. These were all fine people, top people, with the highest reputations, publishing results in the most highly respected journals in their field. And in not one of these studies was there any warning of toxicity, certainly not in the recipients of the drug, let alone in their offspring.

On the subject of those animal studies, Phelan asked Neary:

Q: Was White Laboratories or yourself aware of any literature in which pregnant animals were given amounts of synthetic estrogens, and then the offspring of these pregnant animals was examined?

A: Yes. At White Laboratories we were familiar with published work by Dr. Greene, Dr. Burrill, and Dr. Ivy from Northwestern.

Q: . . . Doctor, in connection with that standard—examination of these [offspring] rats . . . did Drs. Greene, Burrill, and Ivy discover any tumors or cancer?

A: They discovered no tumor formation.

With that, Phelan's direct exam was over. Charfoos' cross began.

Q: You would concede, sir, that when you joined White Laboratories, you had in effect no expertise in any field whatsoever other than a medical degree?

A: I considered myself a qualified physician.

Q: You certainly did not hold yourself out as an expert in pharmacology?

A: No.

Q: An expert in developing, testing, and workups of new drugs as required, scientific knowledge as to how to design tests, perform them, the laboratory work, all that?

A: When I joined White Laboratories?

Q: Exactly.

A: No, no.

Q: Who was the person who had that expertise at White Laboratories, say, as of 1945, 1947?

A: Insofar as clinical work was concerned—I was principally responsible for it.

Charfoos then went on to ask about Neary's qualifications to develop and test such a product:

Q: Who in your company in 1947, 1948, 1949 was the expert on estrogens and their use in the human being?

A: That would have been either I or one of my associates.

Q: Are you claiming Dr. Daley [the other half of the medical department] was an expert in estrogens?

A: No. His training was equivalent to my training.

Q: So, it was two general practitioners that were working together at that particular time?

Neary shook his head as if the question was slightly silly. He said, in a deep, rich voice, "Well, by the time that 1946 rolled around, I had acquired, I think, a good deal of on-the-job training, Mr. Charfoos."

Q: With estrogens?

A: With therapeutics in general.

Q: What research did you personally do in the field of estrogens in human beings to see what effect they had?

A: I did no personal research.

Q: . . . Did you participate in the original decision to engage in research regarding Dienestrol?

A: The actual decision to do research was a management decision.

On the subject of animal tests, Neary appealed to the ancient tradition of "years of experience" and elected to dismiss the animal data.

Q: Doctor, is there any question whatsoever that you . . . were aware that there was laboratory proof . . . before 1950 that these drugs were causing cancers in certain animals?

A: We were aware of it. . . .

Q: Now will you tell me the name of the person or persons that you consulted with and hired to prove that that was not a worry that had to be imposed on the people you were going to sell this drug to?

A: We hired no one to consult in that respect. . . . We did not consider these studies as being absolutely applicable to what would occur in the human.

Q: Now who at White was actually making those crucial decisions?

A: The decision was made [to market Dienestrol] to the best of my knowledge on my recommendation to management. And the decision, therefore, was made by management.

Q: Would you name each physician in management, other than yourself.

A: Management didn't consist of any physicians.

Q: Each scientist in animal studies in management?

A: Management was composed of business people.

Neary was then asked about basing the entire New Drug Application on the Smith and Smith articles:

Q: You understood the articles were at that time recognized as theoretical?

A: The work of the Smiths . . . was somewhat controversial.

Q: So you were marketing a drug whose use at that time was considered controversial as to efficacy?

• *A:* Yes.

Charfoos handed Neary a file of exhibits representing that 1950 NDA. "In your direct testimony," he began, "there were introduced some articles, by Smith and Smith, Priscilla White . . . and some others. . . ." Charfoos was speaking quietly, respectfully, which induced a certain suspicious befuddlement in Neary. "And it was your testimony, sir, that those articles"—he moved back to the furthest point away from the witness, leaving the jury directly in between—"affected or influenced White Laboratories' decision to go into the business activity of selling Dienestrol for the prevention of accidents of pregnancy?" Neary nodded solemnly and gazed out through thick lenses at the court with owl eyes: "That is correct."

He was handed an article by Smith and Smith, the key article in the series, where the Smiths concluded with the claim that "stilbestrol renders normal pregnancy . . . more normal. . . ." In the study the drug was given to first pregnancy patients, and it was claimed to prevent what might have been an expected rate of miscarriage when compared with an abstract and hypothetical rate of "fetal salvage" published previously by a man named Hertig. Charfoos:

Q: This was . . . use of diethylstilbestrol in women who had not had a miscarriage by history, who had not aborted in history, and who were of normal pregnancy history, and these normal women were given DES, is that correct?

A: That is essentially correct. . . .

Charfoos approached the stand and stood above the witness, asking abruptly, "What kind of method was being used?" Neary hesitated, meticulously removed his glasses, and studied the paper with great attention. "They treated all the patients with the drug. . . ." Charfoos, leaning over him, prodded him gently: "Well, I think if you read the article, sir. . . ." Neary recanted: "Allegedly it was alternate controls. . . ." Charfoos asked:

Q: If you were to start with a group of, say four hundred, and you gave every other patient this drug, how many patients would you expect to get the drug?

Neary, glancing up, offered shyly: "Roughly half of them. . . ." Charfoos, drawing audible breath, raised his voice somewhat:

Q: Could you explain why over three hundred got the drug?

A: No, I cannot.

Q: My final question to you, sir, given a paper that works with perfectly healthy women . . . and whose basic scientific numbers are seriously questioned . . . wouldn't you agree that that would be a poor basis to rely on for marketing this drug to women who were going to threaten to miscarry?

Neary, leaning forward with a solemn, professorial air, said gently, "No, I would not agree. . . . The Smiths selected women who were pregnant for the first time, so that their group of treated and controlled patient . . . groups would be homogenous, because," he hesitated, pursing his lips and seeming to search his memory, "because, one would expect threatened abortion to occur in perhaps fifteen, maybe twenty-five percent. . . . So all these so called *primigravidas,*" he pronounced the word with great attention, "would statistically have included a fair percentage of patients who would be expected to threaten to abort. . . ."

"So," Charfoos asked incredulously, "you still think this paper is defensible?"

Neary, spreading out his hands, rumbled, "Yes, I do."

"Are you aware," Charfoos went on, "that Drs. Smith and Smith themselves in writing acknowledged the paper was in error?"

A look of sincere confusion passed across Neary's eyes. Phelan, leaping up, objected: "No foundation. . . ." Neary charmingly conceded: "I don't recall that. . . ." For the record, Charfoos read a quote from the discussion following the reading of the Dieckmann report criticizing the Smiths' methods, where George Smith admitted, "We wish . . . we had given placebo to our controls."

Charfoos, standing at the center of the room, glanced through his notes, crossing off each question with a stroke of his pen. "Would you agree, Doctor, with the following proposition: that estrogen stimulation, on a continuous basis . . . may carry endometrial hyperplasia on to cancer?"

Neary, after a long search for words, found some: "I would agree with the proposition . . . on the basis of very recently reported experience . . . recognized in the past few years. . . ." Neary helpfully defined "endometrial hyperplasia" as "an excessive production of the . . . lining of the uterus."

Charfoos mused, "And you said in answer to my question, 'Yes, but that's only recent information.' Doctor, that statement was made by Smith and Smith in October of 1941!" Neary cleared his throat: "I have no recollection of that."

Charfoos, withdrawing to his favorite corner, called out from the back, "Doctor, would you agree with the following proposition: 'There is not a shred of evidence to document the belief that endocrine treatment of diabetes offers any advantage to either mother or child'?" This was in reference to a common claim for DES, that it aided diabetic women to carry their pregnancies to term. Neary replied, "I would not agree with that statement."

Charfoos advanced and asked softly, "Doctor, were you familiar with the physician, writer, author . . . Dr. Nicholson Eastman?" Neary did recall him. "Would it not be important, Doctor," Charfoos pursued, "since he did write his book in May of 1950, and did publish it, that at least if you were going to make a fair presentation to the FDA, that you put in the negative as well as the positive?" Phelan objected to the form of the question. Charfoos looked directly to the judge, saying, "It goes to the very heart of the lawsuit, your Honor."

The Court: Well, you are asking him—

Charfoos: It is most relevant. . . .

The Court: You may answer the question.

Neary, who had been observing that exchange in something of a daze, blinked and looked up sharply, as if startled. He asked for the question to be repeated, drew a deep breath, and began to speak:

A: I would feel, Mr. Charfoos, that the Food and Drug Administration was well aware of the somewhat controversial aspects of this form of therapy for accidents of pregnancy. There were certainly a number of well trained obstetricians who didn't agree with the findings of the Smiths, Priscilla White, and so on. There were many other equally well trained obstetricians and gynecologists who did believe it.

"So," Charfoos gravely asked, "you were assuming that the Food and Drug Administration would put in the negative aspect?" Neary just as gravely replied, "I think that this was a natural assumption."

Dienestrol was marketed as superior to regular DES because it allegedly prevented nausea. Neary readily admitted that this was only a problem in nonpregnant women. Charfoos:

Q: So, if Dienestrol had no advantage over DES in pregnancy would you explain to us, please, why you were going to market it when there were already a number of other companies with DES in the field?

A: . . . DES had already been marketed for the prevention of accidents of pregnancy. As a consequence, management in order to be competitive decided that this was an area that Dienestrol should also be marketed in.

Q: The answer then is, in order to be competitive?

Neary nodded complacently and slid softly into the trap: "That was primarily the reason, yes." Charfoos followed up by holding up the Goldcamp and Rakoff studies and asking, ". . . Was it really your intention, as a physician and a representative of the medical community, to represent to the FDA that those two preliminary results in any way, form, or manner demonstrated either safety or efficacy in the use of Dienestrol in pregnancy?"

Neary neatly prevaricated: "At that point in time, Mr. Charfoos, the federal regulations did not require a demonstration . . . of efficacy. . . ." He put one hand to his forehead, as if strenuously remembering that time: "And, in point of fact, the application that was submitted, including the preliminary reports of Goldcamp and Rakoff, did satisfy the FDA. The application was approved. We were permitted to market the drug." Neary sat triumphantly back in his chair.

Charfoos regarded him with one raised brow: "It satisfied you as a physician? That met your quality of care?"

Neary nodded affably. "If the FDA was satisfied with it, I was satisfied with it."

Charfoos handed Neary the Crowder report, which concluded that DES did not prevent anything, let alone miscarriage. This represented the school of thought previously mentioned by Neary, which did not agree with Smith and Smith and White in Boston. He read Crowder's rather blunt conclusion: "We have therefore concluded that Stilbestrol is of no value in the treatment of threatened abortion." He looked up at Neary, challenging him to disagree.

Neary looked down at his lap, demurring: "I had some serious reservations about the reliability of that report. . . ."

"Do you mean he used controls that you didn't like?"

"No, no, Mr. Charfoos. This was a controlled study in the sense that he compared the use of stilbestrol . . . with, as I remember, just bed rest and sedation. . . ."

"Got better results than DES, didn't it," Charfoos cut in. Decker snapped, "Let him finish his answer." Neary rumbled on: "Crowder stated that they had something like two hundred thirty-odd patients in the control group . . . and thirty-five were eliminated because of improper diagnosis. . . . All of the patients eliminated were in the control group. . . . It doesn't seem quite reasonable."

Charfoos moved in: "Once you read it, did you bring it to the attention of management?"

A: To the best of my knowledge, I did.

Q: Did anybody instruct you, request you, or ask you, to carry out any tests of the . . . article to determine [its] accuracy or inaccuracy?

A: No one so instructed me.

Charfoos was handed the Robinson and Shettles report. He read its even blunter conclusion: "The present study indicates that diethylstilbestrol is a dismal failure for threatened abortion." Charfoos asked, "Did you bring that to the attention of management?" Neary answered, "I am sure I did." He then stared around the room, not at Charfoos or his lawyers or the judge or the jury; he looked right between everyone there, as if staring directly at nothing. He began slowly to speak, as if directly from memory:

A: Our feeling on the basis of available evidence was that the drug was not ineffective, and that the data we had to support the effectiveness . . . more than outweighed the data reported by Crowder . . . and by Robinson and Shettles. . . .

Charfoos produced a piece of paper from a file and asked: "Doctor, as a matter of fact, in 1950, in August, you were told in writing: 'Use of estrogens in the treatment of threatened and habitual abortions is far from proven.'" He was reading from a letter sent to White from the AMA in response to a request for AMA Council approval for Dienestrol in pregnancy, which would have allowed White to advertise it in the *AMA Journal*. The letter went on:

> And the data submitted by White Laboratories does not strengthen the case for estrogens. The series of cases is completely uncontrolled, and the criteria for the use of estrogens are obscure.

Charfoos asked, "Once you were told that from the AMA . . . that there was no basis from the papers you submitted for accepting this theory, did you bring that to the attention of management?"

A: Management was well aware of that, yes.

Q: Did they order any additional tests to prove the AMA's council wrong?

A: No, they did not.

They moved from the question of efficacy to the question of danger. Charfoos consulted his pad, made some rapid slashes with his pen, and fired out, "Doctor, by 1945 was animal testing generally accepted . . . as a method of testing pharmacological products?" Neary agreed that it was.

Charfoos asked, "Doctor, would you agree with the following proposition, that before marketing Dienestrol for use . . . in the state of pregnancy, it would at least appear prudent to have examined the literature available . . . for any effects on second generation offspring? . . ." Neary responded that that had been done with animals, by Greene, Burrill, and Ivy. Charfoos asked, "Would you agree . . . that there was sufficient research . . . to indicate that embryonic tissue may be more susceptible to carcinogenic transformation than adult tissue?" Neary agreed that that was accepted generally. And finally, Charfoos wondered if Neary would agree it was known "before 1950 that if you gave the mother rat certain drugs, the female and male offspring would have certain changes, if you gave them estrogens." Neary concurred with that statement, shrugging, as if unimpressed by this line of thought.

"Well," Charfoos said, raising his voice to nearly a boom,

"do you know of any reputable tests that were done by 1950 on offspring . . . that resulted in proof to your company that these young girls"—he turned quickly to indicate Anne Needham; the jury shifted as a body to face her momentarily, as if they had forgotten that she was still there—"that the young girls weren't going to be affected . . . one way or the other?"

"As of 1950," Neary offered hesitantly, searching again through his file of memories, "I recall a paper by Drs. Davis and Potter . . ." Charfoos closed in: ". . . In Dr. Potter's article . . . she only looked at one dead female!" Neary nodded wearily, "I recall that." Charfoos said, "She said no conclusions could be drawn from looking at one dead fetus. Do you remember that?" Neary responded weakly, "She found no abnormalities . . ." Finally, Charfoos turned to the Goldcamp and Rakoff reports as evidence of safety. "Are you aware," Charfoos asked, "that Dr. Rakoff and Dr. Goldcamp's preliminary data were submitted to you in the last two or three months of 1949? . . ." Neary responded that such was indeed his recollection. "And that," Charfoos pressed on, "as of January of 1950, the company's application was stamped as received and being processed by the Food and Drug Administration?" Neary replied softly: "Yes."

"My question to you, sir," Charfoos expanded his voice to fit the room, "is very limited. What was the *rush* that you couldn't even wait for Rakoff and Goldcamp's final reports?" Phelan strenuously objected to the form of that question. Decker sustained the objection.

Charfoos concluded with this series of questions: "Do you recall an editorial, quote: 'Synthetic estrogen's chemical relationship to coal-tar justified a warning on purely theoretical grounds . . . results obtained in hormone experiments make it imperative that clinicians should know the potential dangers of the substances they are using in practice'?"

Neary: I believe that appeared in, I think, the *Canadian Medical Journal?*

Charfoos: That's exactly right.

Neary: That was the editor's opinion, that was an opinion not necessarily shared by the expert medical community. . . .

Charfoos produced a paper, submitted by White, by a man named Karnaky, which noted a distinctive darkening of the nipples in the newborn children of mothers given DES. He asked, "Was anybody able to explain why the newborns' nipples were being affected during the fetal period?"

Neary: This is a typical manifestation of estrogen therapy. The fetus was certainly being exposed to relatively high levels of estrogen.

Charfoos: So as of 1950 you knew in human beings that by giving the mother estrogens the offspring female child was going to have some changes?

Neary: Yes.

Charfoos: This would be a good time to stop.

Phelan, on redirect, had just one question.

Q: Did you write a letter in response to those letters that you had received from the AMA that Mr. Charfoos referred to, in connection with the Council on Pharmacy and Chemistry?

A: As I recall, I did.

Neary for a moment didn't realize it was over, but sat languidly on the stand waiting for another question. Phelan strolled up to the stand, as Neary stepped gratefully down from the box and slipped discreetly out the back. Phelan disappeared for a moment with him, and reappeared immediately in the doorway with an old man at his side.

The old man walked with an erect and solid carriage up the aisle toward the bench, another distinguished, handsome man with a finely groomed fall of white hair. He wore the classic, careful, conservative schoolboy uniform adopted by all the defense witnesses: navy blue blazer, gray flannels, white shirt, black shoes. The only singular divergence permitted was a rather large bow tie which appeared to hold up his chin.

Dr. Abraham Rakoff took the stand as Phelan quickly began his routine questioning. Rakoff was a classmate of Neary's at Jefferson Medical College in 1933, where he returned after his internship to work in the gynecological clinic and continue his research in endocrinology.

Phelan stood close to the witness and spoke casually with him, as if conferring with an old friend.

"Endocrinology," Rakoff recalled nostalgically, "was just beginning. I was lucky to get in on the ground floor. . . . Pregnancy tests were just coming into vogue, hormones were being discovered that were being secreted by the ovaries and the placenta. . . . At that time, there was nobody in the city of Philadelphia devoting themselves entirely to that field. . . .

"Between 1938 and 1940," Rakoff recalled, "I was interested in seeing whether we could take the blood of pregnant women and see how much estrogen there was in different phases of pregnancy. . . . We found that the amount of estrogen during pregnancy was enormous, and that it increased as pregnancy went along . . . several hundred fold. . . . We became very much interested in many of the new estrogens that were beginning to appear. Dr. Dodds in England had synthesized recently several synthetic estrogens, stilbestrol, Dienestrol, et cetera. In Canada, they were beginning to make estrogens from the urine of pregnant mares. . . ."

The head of Rakoff's department had patients sent to him from all over the country because of repeated miscarriages:

> We were able to demonstrate that some of these patients who lost repeated pregnancies . . . had estrogen levels lower than normal women at the same period of pregnancy. We argued that if we could restore the normal levels that perhaps this would help the patients carry the pregnancy. . . . We decided to use natural estrogens and we gave them injections two or three times a week.

Phelan finally asked, "In 1950, 1951, and 1952, was the drug Dienestrol, which you are familiar with, safe for use by women who were pregnant?" Rakoff stared directly back at Phelan.

"Yes. Dienestrol is an estrogen which in its biologic actions is . . . quite similar to the natural estrogens and to diethylstilbes-trol. DES had already been used in hundreds, probably thousands of pregnant women by that time without any reported untoward effects. Therefore, it appeared to us that Dienestrol would be just as safe as diethylstilbestrol."

Rakoff glanced blandly around the room, and went on: "Furthermore in our experience with Dienestrol in nonpregnant women we found that it was better tolerated than diethylstilbes-trol, and as a matter of fact, that's why we liked it." He looked up at Phelan and smiled brightly. "And as a matter of fact, that's why I *still* like it." The smile did not leave until Phelan asked:

Q: I asked you, Doctor, if it was safe for use for the mother . . . do you have an opinion as to whether it was safe not only for the mother but for the offspring as well?

A: Yes. . . . Our fetal salvage was the same as for normal women or better, and we did not notice any increased inci-dence of any abnormalities in these babies.

Charfoos went directly into his cross-exam:

Q: Dr. Rakoff, are you the man who recommended to Ameri-can obstetricians and gynecologists that they should use Dienestrol by itself in these dosages for the prevention of miscarriage?

He pointed to a large chart at the center of the floor, repre-senting the dosage schedule recommended by White. Rakoff an-swered, "Yes. I recommended they could use these, either alone or in conjunction with progesterone."

Charfoos walked back to the table and shuffled through some papers. "Did you give White Laboratories permission to state that that was scientifically valid for clinical use in the United States without anything but estrogen?"

Rakoff shrugged. "White Laboratories could do what they pleased. I simply provided the information. . . ." Charfoos picked up a document from the table and was now approaching the stand. He deposited the paper on the counter in front of Rakoff with a distinct grimace. "That," he said rather grimly, "is the so-called eight-living, four-dead report." Phelan loudly objected to that characterization, an objection Decker sustained.

"Now, Doctor," Charfoos was speaking softly, "was it your intention that that document, showing eight live births and four mortalities, should be the basis for White Laboratories going to the FDA and getting clinical approval for that dosage?"

Rakoff shrugged again. "I had nothing to do with what White Laboratories would do with this data. I just provided the data."

Charfoos planted himself in front of the witness table, and spoke intimately, man to man: "In fairness to you, you wouldn't want this published, would you, Doctor?" Phelan objected; Charfoos continued, "Doctor, this isn't publishable, is it?" He leaned even closer: "Is it, Doctor?"

Rakoff regarded him with a jaundiced eye: "I would disagree with you."

"Are you the man," Charfoos asked, "who made this statement?"

The use of estrogens alone in patients for accidents of pregnancy is neither physiologically sound nor rationally indicated.

Rakoff hesitated, and then admitted: "Yes." He hastily elaborated:

Dr. Vaux and I made that statement in one of the first papers we wrote. . . . However, as time went on and the work of the Harvard people began to appear, the question arose in our mind, was it possible that the estrogen alone might be helpful . . . in other words, was it true as Priscilla White said, that estrogen was "the poor woman's progesterone."

Charfoos seized quickly upon the phrase: "Are you the individual who said that . . . if a person was poor you would give them just the estrogen because progesterone was more expensive?" Rakoff waited a half-second and let his chin drop toward his tie. "Right."

After Rakoff's testimony, Phelan hauled out an enormous blow-up of a document he maintained was distributed to White detail men. It was a large piece of foam board, with type set in gigantic letters. It said that the use of Dienestrol was only investigational; that there were two schools of thought on the subject, one, represented by Vaux, Rakoff, the Smiths, and Priscilla White, who had found estrogen therapy effective for prevention of habitual abortion; Crowder, on the other hand, had failed to observe any connection.

With the introduction of that last large but not entirely earth-shattering piece of evidence, Phelan dropped his bombshell. With two more witnesses announced as coming, with every expectation of his case running three more days, he turned to Decker and grimly shrugged. "The defense rests, your Honor."

Wednesday, August 29, was a particularly warm morning: a thick haze drifted in off the lake, shrouding the matte-black upper stories of the towers surrounding the twenty-seventh floor courtroom. In the Federal Court Building, compliance with the Federal temperature standards had all the lawyers wilting. The rule held the air at a steady 78 degrees, but the lack of air conditioning boosted the humidity, and all the elevators with heat-sensitive buttons kept stopping all morning at all the wrong floors, flashing warning signals, generally acting as confused, unpredictable, and irritable as their passengers. Above the judge's bench the chrome bald eagle hung on its metal platter, in its right talon a bundle of arrows, in its left an olive branch; the modern, stylized bird head merged into a chromium scroll: *"E Pluribus Unum";* an angular message surmounted by a sleek medallion of thirteen stars.

The various contestants sent for sodas from the second floor cafeteria and paced the corridors with perspiring faces, ties and jackets loosened, fanning themselves with legal pads. "It's like a Mississippi courthouse in here," one drug company lawyer said to his companion, with a face redder than Clarence Darrow's. It could have been a sultry, sleepy Southern court in the matter of temperature, but in here the windows were all sealed shut, without a hope of breeze.

Charfoos paced up and down the outside corridor, tie loosened, jacket off, face filmed with perspiration, discussing with co-counsels Sussman and Bleakely the other side's surprising move of the day before. "They rolled right over," Charfoos was saying. "I can't understand. They folded like in a poker game." He looked up with puzzled suspicion as Dick Phelan stepped out of the elevator, smiling genially in their direction. Cool and confident in a crisp cord suit, he moved briskly off in the direction of the courtroom, as Anne Needham appeared on the floor from out of the opposite elevator. Anne smiled shyly at all three of her lawyers and made a faint, visible sigh in reference to the heat. "Frankly," Charfoos was telling Sussman in an undertone, "I don't see what Phelan got by closing up so fast. I'm kind of disappointed."

At 2:00 P.M., the jury filed in, all dressed neatly in ties and jackets, shirts and skirts. They seemed to be collectively wilting in the still air, the foreman holding up one hand as if trying to catch a loose draft.

Decker arrived a moment later and hauled himself into his high leather chair. Wincing visibly at the close atmosphere, he began his remarks to the jury in a gloomy tone, as if every word were sweating: "You've heard the evidence," he advised the jury. "What you are now about to hear are the closing remarks of counsel. These are not evidence but are intended to help you understand what you heard over the last week. You will now hear from Mr. Charfoos." Decker gestured wearily, like a TV host welcoming a guest performer onto his show, as Charfoos took the floor. Charfoos planted himself directly in front of the jury and sighed with an air of sympathetic exasperation. "Good afternoon, ladies and gentlemen of the jury," he said. "The first piece of evidence I have is that it's hot in here." He unbuttoned his jacket and held it open by one lapel. "And if this jacket starts slipping off, I can't help it."

He had been leaning over, looking toward the jurors' eyes, but he straightened and went on: "What I do have some control over is the evidence in this case. . . . What you've heard in eleven days is the culmination of four years, building up for this final presentation. . . . We've made every effort to compress those four years into seven days. . . ." He put down a pad of notes on the plaintiff's table, not far from Anne, and turned slowly to face the jury: "What are the specific charges against White Laboratories?"

We charge they did knowingly and willfully . . . send out a drug into the marketplace that was both useless for what it was being sold for . . . and that unreasonably harmed the receiver, in this case the baby in the womb.

"What," he went on, "is the legal responsibility of a drug company in a case like this?"

A manufacturer of a prescription drug is held to the skill of an expert's knowledge . . . and is held to possess whatever expert knowledge is available at the time of the sale.

"Think of it"—his tone softened—"as food. . . . . It is the same with a drug. That drug is expected to be *safe* for the purpose it was intended, and *useful* for the purpose it was intended. . . . They must know as much about that subject as anybody in the country. They must be the experts!" Pause; the jury seemed to nod together.

The narration of the cycle of error began again: "These people did the following things wrong":

They had ample evidence . . . that their drug was useless. Very eminent people in the field, much more skilled and qualified than they, were telling them: Your drug is useless in pregnancy.

"It was wrong," he went on, "to keep marketing it without testing. . . . It was wrong to perform no animal tests . . . on pregnant animals knowing that they were increasing the dosage one hundred fold, knowing that they had never given it to pregnant women before. . . . It was wrong to have no information about what was going to happen to that fetus. . . . It was wrong to know, as they have admitted, that it was a carcinogen; that it could cause cancer, at least in animals. . . .

"This," Charfoos insisted, "was not the Middle Ages! Science was advanced. We were past the Atomic Age, and into a new age!" He stood beside the first row of jurors, and the tone of voice implored them to believe this crucial point. "How important," he asked, "were the animal studies?" He reminded them of Shimkin's statement:

I was interested in cancer in man. The animals are only a model. . . . It is no particular pleasure to cause tumors in animals. . . .

He spoke of Dr. Forsberg: "DES, Forsberg told us, induced permanent changes in female offspring where the mother had taken the pill." On Dr. Schmitt, he said, "I won't pretend that Schmitt wasn't a little different. . . . His enthusiasm floored me a little. . . . But what did he tell us?"

He told us that currently in the Herbst registry there are close to four hundred women with DES-related adenocarcinoma. . . . He told us about adenosis. . . . He told us about latency . . . that it was known at the time of testing that stilbene was a carcinogenic compound. . . .

"And to have the guts"—Charfoos' voice became Schmitt's—"I am sorry, I am getting angry now—to increase the dose one hundred times! It is irresponsible!" The voice became his own: "Then he concluded to explain his anger: I am a clinician, and I have my feelings!"

Charfoos stressed the tragically unused capabilities of Charles Sondern, the poultry expert at White Laboratories, whose deposition was briefly read at the trial. "The only man in White Laboratories that had any real experience with estrogens was never consulted once! . . . How sincere were these people when they tell us about their great thinking . . . when they didn't even consult Sondern in their own company?" Charfoos recalled his questioning of Neary: "Didn't White Laboratories carry out through any doctor, pharmacologist, scientist, or any other person any studies whatsoever to determine the effects of this drug on the fetus? Answer: 'There were no studies as such performed, to my recollection.'"

He continued to reiterate the testimony: "Did your company undertake any independent studies in house? No. Did your company commission anyone to do animal studies externally when you increased the dose? No.

"Later, on the stand . . . he tried to talk us into the idea that those studies done in 1946 were for the purpose of determining whether there would be cancer," Charfoos said. "I submit to you that that later answer was outright fabrication! They never did a thing about cancer or . . . the change of the female organs. . . . I suggest to you that this is symptomatic of their attempt to create a defense of an indefensible position."

Arms spread wide, voice higher and compressed, tone imploring, he said, "They were about to move into unknown territory!" Eyes wider, body crouched: "They were about to move into a new world! They were about to influence and affect all the people who would take their drug!" The court was still; no voices. Then, in a lower register: "Not a single study.

"It was negligence," he went on, "to continue to market that drug after receiving notice in writing, in writing, would you believe it, from the Drug Review Committee of the American Medical Association, saying, Your drug does not work as far as we can tell and we don't believe your information. At the minimum, at the minimum there was an obligation to get back into their laboratories and see if they were right or wrong, and not to use people out in this country . . . as a gamble that they were right or wrong!

"You could walk from one end of the hall to the other at White Laboratories in 1948–49 and you wouldn't find a single person qualified to undertake what they were about to undertake! They didn't bring a single person from the outside to do one reputable set of animal tests for pregnancy. . . . They didn't consult with anybody whatsoever, they just unilaterally put it out of their minds that they were going to worry about those things.

"I will tell you what happened." Charfoos picked up copies of the Goldcamp and Rakoff reports. "Somebody was sitting in that building . . . and read an article saying that they were now using it in pregnant women. He rushed out and got Rakoff and Goldcamp and said, Quick, give us a couple of studies so that we can get word to the FDA. Within ninety days of those quickie studies being submitted, they are on the doorsteps of the FDA saying, Knock, knock, we want in; please don't object to our marketing this drug! . . . Given that information, it was unconscionable. . . . It was an invitation to disaster. . . . There is no excuse for White Laboratories in this lawsuit. . . . There is no doubt . . . that the defendant White is totally liable in this case."

Thursday morning, Phelan's turn. In the corridor as he arrived, he was all smiles, greeting the opposition with a cordial air. Sunny and warm this morning; thunderstorms arrived just after dawn. The air had cooled and the lake haze dissipated, but the humidity inside the court building was still high, the elevators still out of whack.

Today the plaintiff's side was all in gray: Charfoos in gray tweed, Bleakely and Sussman in dark gray wool; the defense was brown, with specks and strips of plaintiff's gray subtly wavering through. Just after ten Anne Needham walked through the door, entering shyly and quietly in a dark gray blazer, with a scarf of brown and yellow stripes fastened at her throat.

At 10:15, Phelan strolled up to the wooden lectern set up before the jury. He stood there smiling, leaning with both hands on the lectern like a preacher at his pulpit. He began with an air of homey, casual intimacy:

> I think we ought to try to focus on what I believe are the
> . . . real issues in this case. Whether a drug manufacturer
> in 1952, armed with the skill of experts, knew or should
> have known that ingestion by the mother of a drug like
> Dienestrol, or DES, would cause cancer in the female
> offspring.

Charfoos: Objection, your Honor.

The Court: Could cause cancer.

Phelan: I am sorry, your Honor. . . . Could cause cancer
in the female offspring.

"What would"—Phelan paused and let his eyes roam across the jury ranged before him—"a reasonable, prudent manufacturer know in 1952? How would that reasonable, prudent manufacturer find out information? What papers, what tests, what research, what persons would they rely on?

"Let's take Dr. Shimkin and let's substitute the information in [his] head and put it over in Dr. Neary's head. Was it reasonable in 1952 that the taking of this drug could cause cancer in the female offspring? What warnings did he give? What did he say in 1968 and 1970? Let's examine what Dr. Shimkin *really* said.

"In 1945, Dr. Shimkin wrote and presided over part of a symposium . . . on cancer and estrogens and its possible implications in the human being. . . . I asked, 'Doctor, would you look at that article, and would you tell us where it says . . . in there that if a mother, a pregnant mother, takes this drug, that this could cause cancer in the female offspring?' He leafed through it, and began to read: '. . . Can the clinical use of such preparations, particularly in large doses and for extended periods of time, lead to the development of mammary and other neoplasias in the human being?' " Phelan looked sharply up and slapped his lectern with a resounding whack: "This was the conclusion of his work given to scientists! That is what he said in 1945!

"Three hundred articles," Phelan mused, crouched low, and suddenly sent out both hands, fingers out, straight toward the jury: "So even Dr. Shimkin, who was supposedly the authority, gave no indication! . . . In 1946, [he said] 'any but the most tentative extrapolations to man must be regarded as unwarranted'! Who had more animals? Who had more backing, more staff, more time to decide . . . than Dr. Michael Boris Shimkin?" He came around from behind the lectern, and stood inches from the jury: "This isn't a game of smoke! This is a game of science!"

His voice lower, more resonant and calm, he said, "But what was going on in the real world? Doctors were . . . taking care of women, pregnant women, pregnant women who had miscarriages, pregnant women who could not carry to term, women generally who were *suffering*." He leaned forward and caressed the word. "What did we know? What did a reasonable, prudent, manufacturer know?" He shook his head sadly, as if dispelling ancient, absurd superstition: "Members of the jury, this substance wasn't something that was brewed in the cauldrons of England! This is a natural substance. . . . This is in every one of us. . . . It is generated in the ovaries of women. . . . It was in our own bodies. . . .

"White Laboratories," he said with a touch of pride, "wasn't galloping off into the market. . . . We were a small company, we were doing what we did best. We were able to put it in a different form that was less expensive, and more easily tolerated. . . . White Laboratories was not trying to foist something off on the public. White Laboratories was able to design and formulate a product that had less side effects so that it could help women in these important times. White Laboratories did not rush to the market. White Laboratories relied on persons who had dedicated their lives to the treatment of people who were unable to bear children, to find a way to help these persons! That"—and he paused dramatically—"was what this drug was about.

"You have," Phelan fervently reminded the jurors, "that great function that American juries have and that I believe is reserved for us here in America, in this great system. To make up your own mind . . . to decide . . . what a reasonable, prudent, manufacturer in 1952 should know. . . . I believe you had the opportunity to hear one of the most knowledgeable persons in the . . . endocrine field: Dr. Rakoff, who has spent forty years in the field of treating women, women who have had problems of pregnancy. . . . Dr. Rakoff, who has taught every single day of the calendar academic year since 1939 . . . said unequivocally, without any question, any reservations, any problems, that this drug was not only safe for use by the mother, but for the children!"

After Phelan's last, dramatic pause, a brief recess was called at 11:40. During the lull, morale at the plaintiff's table was low:

Charfoos: He's good. He's damned good.

Sussman: He's a plaintiff's lawyer, really. . . . That's where he gets the emotion.

Needham: I hate him. I really hate him. I was getting hot under the collar in there. I just glare at him; he won't even *look* at me.

At 11:50, when proceedings resumed, Phelan strode right back to his pulpit and sailed right back into his defense, homey, enthusiastic, articulate.

"Charges have been made here that in some way or another, White misrepresented this product, the product that Dr. Rakoff tested twice, investigated, spent his whole life on prior to that time. So I would like to spend a few minutes with you on the publication we gave to doctors. . . ."

He hauled out the big piece of foam board with the gigantic type.

"Here within this brochure, we talked exactly about the suggestions that had been made to us about the use of . . . Dienestrol."

> . . . Published reports have suggested that treatment with female sex hormones may be a benefit in cases of threatened and habitual abortions. . . . However, very little is known of the causes of spontaneous and habitual abortion. The problem isn't simple, nor is therapy a cure-all. . . . At the present time there are chiefly two schools of thought concerning sex hormonal therapy . . . Vaux and Rakoff . . . and Crowder . . .

"Right here!" Phelan gestured to the jury, and pointed to the board triumphantly, "the Crowder article. . . . We did not think it was applicable," he shrugged as he said this, "but there it is."

"Ladies and gentlemen," Phelan concluded, becoming suddenly sober, "I began by indicating that the burden in a civil suit is upon the plaintiff on all the issues. I submit to you that by any measure of the evidence submitted by the plaintiff herself through her lawyers, they have not reached the level, they have not been able to submit to you any information that a reasonable, prudent manufacturer in 1952 knew or should have known that this natural estrogen, synthesized, could cause cancer in the female offspring. They have not offered any credible evidence that this natural estrogen . . . produced the injury complained of in this young woman. . . . I believe under the law and the evidence submitted in this case that White Laboratories is not liable to the plaintiff, Anne Needham."

Charfoos jumped right into his rebuttal. "If White Laboratories had really been smart, they would have had Dr. Neary as well briefed in the handling of this drug back when it was done as they apparently briefed this fine gentleman in his closing argument. But"—he raised one hand in moderation—"what is the underlying question . . . that has to be discussed here? That is really twofold:"

> Item one: if the manufacturer sells a product and that product is unreasonably dangerous, and harms somebody, that manufacturer will be liable if the product is defective . . . either because it didn't work or because it had inadequate warnings.

"The second issue"—Charfoos held up a second finger—"is

the negligence of failure to test. Not one word. Silence for two hours on why they didn't run a single reputable test inside or outside that lab. Silence on Dr. Neary. Almost a day and a half of testimony, and they had not one word to say in favor of their own Dr. Neary. Silence on the realities of latency. . . . They had two years. What is two years in cancer or the potential of cancer in human beings?"

Charfoos offered an analogy: "What they are really saying is, Hey, we saw some folks across the street that were starting to run after a truck that had turned over and some valuables were falling out. I suggest they ran right through a red light and joined the people who were running through that red light. . . ." Phelan leapt up, wide-eyed and shouting, "That is a suggestion that there is some kind of criminal intent here. There has never been a scintilla of evidence!"

Decker said, "Well, I haven't heard anything about criminal intent." Phelan, still standing, red in the face, shouted, "He's talking about looting some kind of a truck! I think we ought to talk about facts in this case, and not some bizarre fantasy!" Decker leaned forward and admonished Charfoos, "Well, let's stay out of red lights here and let's talk about Dienestrol." Charfoos, bowing, murmured, "Well, and a few other things, your Honor."

Charfoos' rebuttal continued. "You know, in the first place, he started off with this business that Dr. Shimkin . . . found no evidence of breast carcinomas in women . . . that follows because it was in the mice. . . . He wants to have Shimkin be something that he never stood for. It is a complete misstatement as to what Shimkin said.

"But"—he walked around the lectern and leaned on the counter of the jury box—"there is more. Another half truth: This drug was out for eleven years with no problems." He dismissed that claim with a frown. "What is the significance of eleven years? Zero. First of all, there were problems. . . . But the first nine years were for point-one and point-five milligrams in nonpregnant women. . . ." He drew himself up and looked directly at Phelan: "Don't give me eleven years, sir! You had warnings in the literature . . . that increased doses would cause problems in people or animals. Don't give me eleven years. You had two years and you didn't examine a single dead fetus . . . and ran no tests yourself!"

The pace slowed and the spaces between the words grew

longer. ". . . I am asking you to place over there"—Charfoos gestured toward the defense position—"what they haven't accepted. Responsibility. To this moment, with overwhelming proof that that drug of theirs put cancer in my client's body . . . based on the facts and the evidence and the truth, the drug company was wrong."

Decker returned after lunch to give his final instructions to the jury. "You've been an attentive jury," he began in gruff appreciation. "Counsel for the plaintiff and for the defendant have both paid you a compliment on that basis and now I'm going to get into the act and say that I have been observing you while this case went on, and I had some sympathy for you at times . . . listening to a case involving the type of testimony we had here day after day . . . listening to the reading of depositions is not the most exciting process I can think of . . . but I am sure you tried to absorb what you heard, and when you go back into the jury room you will attempt to . . . reconstruct the evidence as you heard it.

"As you know," Decker charged them, "the defendant in this case is a corporation. The corporate defendant is entitled to the same fair and unprejudiced treatment as an individual would receive under like circumstances. . . . You should decide the case with the same impartiality as if it were a case between two individuals. . . . "

The jury would retire to consider two separate counts, on each of which the drug company could be held liable.

"On the first count, the plaintiff alleges that she was injured as a result of the use by her mother of a drug known as Dienestrol. . . . She claims that in 1952 . . . the defendant knew, or should have known, that the drug could cause cancer in the female offspring of a woman who used the drug to prevent miscarriage. Additionally, the plaintiff claims that the drug was not apparently useful . . . for prevention of miscarriage, and that it was unreasonably dangerous for that purpose. And the plaintiff claims that the taking of the drug was the proximate cause of her injuries.

". . . Now, in the second count the plaintiff claims that she was injured and that the defendant was negligent in failing to warn her mother's physician that the defendant's drug could cause cancer . . . and claims that the defendant did not properly test the drug Dienestrol. . . . The plaintiff further claims that the defendant's failure in these areas proximately caused her injuries. . . ."

Decker further instructed the jury that unlike a criminal case, a civil suit did not have to be proven beyond the shadow of a doubt. The proofs simply had to be more probably true than not true. And the burden was not so much that the drug was the absolute "cause," that is in the scientific sense, but rather "proximate cause," defined as "that cause which in natural or probable sequence produced the injury complained of."

In order for Anne to win, she had to prove only one of the counts. If she proved any of the following, she could win her case. On the liability aspects: That it was unreasonably dangerous because it didn't work, or that it was unreasonably dangerous because it failed to warn of the cancer potential, or because the defendant was negligent in failing to adequately test the drug. She also had to prove that the drug was a cause of her condition.

"Now let me say this as a final word," Decker commanded them. "You are not partisans in this case . . . what you are is judges; you are judges of the facts."

At just before 4 P.M. the jury went into seclusion. During their deliberations, all the actors in the case waited tensely in the corridors. Charfoos sat quietly in a black vinyl chair beside an aluminum ashtray against the wall, puffing on a cigar, telling Anne, "This is what we call the pits." Anne said quietly, "I'm really nervous, but I'm still pretty confident." She puffed on her fifth cigarette of the day and sighed, "I just wish it was over."

The jury was out for forty-five minutes. During that time, the plaintiff's party huddled on the plastic benches in the corridor. Charfoos, pacing up and down, smoked his way through several cigars; Sussman, visibly nervous, smiled ruefully after taking his third or fourth drink of water; Bleakely outwardly calm, relaxed in his chair, only a shoe tapping insistently across his knee indicating any tension.

The clock on the courtroom wall read 4:30. By then, the defense attorneys had left. Anne Needham sat with her mother in the visitors' gallery at the back of the courtroom; the waiting parties had moved in from the corridors, as the moment seemed close to arrival. At 4:45 the bailiff appeared in the doorway to announce that the verdict was in.

Henry Simon, head counsel for Schering-Plough, was the only member of the defense still around. He made a hurried call to the offices of Phelan and Pope to retrieve his errant attorneys. The bailiff decided to wait for either Phelan or Pope before the reading of the verdict. Judge Decker rushed in from his private entrance behind his bench and flounced stiffly into his chair, his robe slightly askew on his broad shoulders. He barked, with routine irritation, waving one hand with a choppy gesture, "Simon's here. That's enough. Let's get this over with." The jury was sent for, and just as they began to file in, Pope and Phelan appeared together at the courtroom door, with brief slapstick confusion in the doorway as both struggled anxiously to get in past each other.

The jury foreman, a dark-haired young man with square gold-rimmed glasses and a round face, appeared at the front of the room with the crucial paper in his hand. Resplendent in a crimson blazer with a large seal on the breast pocket, filled with all the weighty pomp of his privileged position, he held proudly for a moment to the decision resting in his palm. Judge Decker announced to the jury as they filed in, "Please be seated. Everyone be seated except the foreman." He asked, "Mr. Foreman, does the jury have a verdict?"

The Foreman: Yes sir, we have.

The Court: Will you please hand the verdict to the clerk, and the clerk will read the verdict.

The Clerk: On the issue of liability, we, the jury, find for the plaintiff, Anne Needham.

Before the outburst, Decker raised his hand and said, "Just a moment, just a moment, please." The room was silent. "Anything else, gentlemen, so far as—" he glanced at Phelan, who shook his head and said in a low tone, "No." Decker went on, "Well, the jury will return to the jury room and we will let you know when we will need you again."

Anne continued to sit for a few beats in her swivel chair, as if momentarily stunned. She stood up finally between the chair and the table, holding herself very straight, her hands resting on its top. One hand traveled anxiously to her hair and ran its fingers through the light mass like a lively comb. She seemed concerned not to let the waves of feeling bowl her over right then. Sussman reached her first and hugged her, and Anne gasped and said, "I've got awful knots in my back." She cricked her shoulders and laughed finally, as if releasing an enormous load. "It's just the tension."

Mary Needham came up next and wrapped her arms around her. "I can't believe it's over," Mary whispered, knowing that it really wasn't. Tom Bleakely reached her next and for a brief moment laid an arm across her shoulder, and they smiled at each other without saying anything. Anne laughed almost uncontrollably again, and reached down to pick up someone's lost umbrella: it sat alone on the brown nylon carpet at the center of the floor.

With a sheepish smile, Richard Phelan crossed the floor to congratulate Charfoos. He genially shook hands with Bleakely and with Sussman, and finally turned to Anne. With visible difficulty she held out one hand for him to shake. He took it for a moment and formed a brief smile. She stared silently back at him, her lips perfectly straight, and he dropped the hand and turned away. Restrained celebration: Mary Needham and Anne Needham embracing, their heads rested for a long time on each other's shoulders. Charfoos stood off in one corner, shaking various hands, lighting a final cigar. A small dark man in jeans with dark hair and a small moustache, holding a small pad, approached him and they exchanged a few words. The reporter scribbled silently and quietly disappeared.

20

Friday morning. At ten o'clock sharp the courtroom was crowded with press, visitors, and various attorneys who flocked here after news of yesterday's verdict was released. The second DES daughter to win a jury verdict in the country, Anne had suddenly become national news. Wire services, television crews, newspaper reporters, women's health care activists, all were visibly present in the packed visitors' gallery.

Just after ten, with the milling crowd not yet in their seats, Richard Phelan came striding down the aisle, red in the face, brandishing a folded newspaper in the face of Judge Decker. Phelan, in a voice only a deaf court-fly in the furthest corner couldn't hear, orated with trembling, nearly convincing indignation, "This morning on page six of the Chicago *Daily Tribune* appears the article 'Drug Maker Held Liable in Vaginal Cancer Case!'"

Phelan waved the offending gazette around some more as Decker nodded glumly. "I know," he said, shrugging. "I am a constant reader of the *Tribune* along with the *Sun-Times*." He shook his head and added gloomily, "I've got nothing else to do particularly on the train in the morning. . . ."

"My problem is, your Honor," Phelan went on loudly, "on the eve of the damage trial, the representation is made, and it is in quotes, Mr. Charfoos says, 'These four hundred women represent America's equivalent to thalidomide'!" His voice cracked in exasperation and he held his hands high as if to consider the proposition ridiculous. Decker nodded and sighed: "I read that."

"Your Honor," Phelan protested, "this jury was home. I don't know whether they've read the newspaper and been infected with it. . . . This lawyer"—he indicated Charfoos, sitting at the plaintiff's table, with a folded copy of the *Tribune*—"goes right ahead . . . and compares this drug with thalidomide!" Decker shrugged one more time and noted, "Well, I read the article." Phelan advanced on the bench shouting, "The infection, Judge, is incurable!" After a brief, mock conference with his co-counsels Pope and Simon, Phelan thundered, "Your Honor, I would ask the Court to grant a *mistrial* on the basis of this gratuitous statement . . . published in the Chicago *Daily Tribune!*"

Decker asked Charfoos to come forward and had him sworn in. "Did you make any statement," he asked testily, "to any reporter yesterday?"

Charfoos nodded. "Yes, your Honor."

"And were you correctly quoted in this article?"

"No," Charfoos answered.

Decker asked him what he did say, and he said, "The man was sitting here, your Honor, he was taking notes and he asked me a question: How many are there? There are four hundred. . . . Your Honor, I was walking out, I did not give an interview, I did not seek a reporter."

Decker snapped, "Why did you say anything to the reporter at all?"

Charfoos shrugged and said, "The verdict was in. People were excited. Questions were being asked. I really did not mean to give an interview. . . . It took place right in this court as the gentleman was writing up his notes. . . . I am sorry. With the verdict in, I really did not mean to do anything, I don't believe I did. . . . Questions were asked. I made an answer."

Decker had the reporter sent for and had him sworn in directly. Today, Robert Enstad wore a blue blazer, a tie, and a pad in his back pocket. He stood calmly with both hands clasped behind his back as Decker told him, "We are having some discussion here, Mr. Enstad . . . as to exactly what was stated to you yesterday at the conclusion of the liability trial. . . ."

Enstad mentioned that he thought the *Tribune* might want a lawyer present. Decker barked, "Are you unwilling to tell me at this time what your conversation was here?" Enstad shrugged, "We did confer, yes." He went on to maintain that he did not independently bring up the subject of thalidomide. Charfoos asked, "Did I say the other things in the article that are quoted?"

Enstad: The rest of it is. . . .

Decker: He charged there had been some four hundred documented cases.

Charfoos: That I did say.

Decker nodded irritably. "I know you said that."

Enstad was allowed to go, but Charfoos stood on the spot. He waited patiently before the judge in a position as close to one of supplication as may be achieved in the vertical posture. Decker launched into a protracted scolding.

Mr. Charfoos. This is not only the third time—I have lost count of the problems I have had in connection with what you have done in this case. I granted two mistrials in this case. . . . We have had two juries here to try this case in an attempt to get a fair trial for you. We finally succeeded. We worked nine days. . . . We are not finished. We have a jury here that is supposed to be free of anything like this. . . . You couldn't wait, apparently.

Charfoos shook his head firmly. "No, that is not true," he said. Decker called for a brief recess to consider Phelan's mistrial motion. Tom Bleakely stood up and asked that the motion be viewed "In light of all the circumstances." He asked that the jury might be questioned as to whether they had seen the article. "I would ask particularly," he said, turning and indicating Anne, "that if the court is planning on punishing anybody, it not be our client, Anne Needham." Decker scratched his chin for a moment. Finally he called out to the marshal, "Bring in the jury."

The six jurors filed in. They were asked if they had seen the *Tribune* piece. One juror, a rugged-looking man with long fair hair turning gray and a deep facial tan, raised his hand and nodded. He had not, however, discussed the article with any of the other jurors, none of whom had seen it themselves. The rest of them had all been faithful to the Chicago *Sun-Times*. Decker called the *Tribune* reader, Alexander Supler, back into his chambers.

Decker asked the juror about the article and his reactions to it. "Well," Supler responded, "I felt bad about it . . . and I thought, 'Oh, this is a hot tomato! Better not let anybody know about this,' you know. But I noticed they all bought the *Times*. . . ." Decker asked him what he meant by a "hot tomato."

"The only thing that concerned me," Supler replied, "was that I saw the amount of money that was involved and that they were asking for a million dollars." Decker asked him about the mention of thalidomide. He shrugged, "No . . . it didn't bother me a bit, no. It had nothing to do with it. . . . There are still a lot of questions in my mind as far as this lawsuit is concerned, in regard to monies, I mean. I have not reached any kind of conclusion on that. . . ."

Decker remarked that the amount of money being asked was certainly no secret, that the lawyers would be going over that shortly. "The real question to you is," he asked, "do you feel that you can act fairly on the damages issue?" Supler nodded sincerely. "I really think I can, Judge," he answered. "I don't think that the article did anything, really. My thinking has not changed in the least bit from yesterday." With that Decker seemed to be satisfied. "Well," he said and shrugged, "that's fair enough. Go back there and simply forget that you read the article. . . . We are going to go ahead."

Decker came out of his chambers and announced, "On the basis of my interview with this one juror I have concluded that we are going to proceed with the trial."

A visible relief circled the plaintiff's table, which was practically holding its collective breath. Anne sat back with an audible sigh: She couldn't have borne another mistrial. She suddenly remembered that night in the car, traveling up to Mayo's. She had told her mother, "Maybe God's trying to tell us something. We forgot the slides and the car broke down and maybe He just doesn't want us to get there." Now in the trial they had had two mistrials, and finally they had come this far. Her mother had said on the highway, "We've gotten this close, we've got to keep going."

Mr. Phelan was politely asking, his face registering no obvious disappointment, "Your Honor, is the court going to rule on my motion?" Decker leaned forward and said, "The motion is denied." Sussman approached the bench and made his own motion, to amend the complaint in relation to the damages asked: to $5 million. A palpable rush of low-level noise seemed to circulate in the room.

The day finally began around eleven, with an opening statement by Charfoos. He kept it short and simple. "I am going to say merely two things in regard to her injury. One, that I think you will find it distasteful and substantial. Two, that you will find it is going to affect her permanently, irrevocably, and profoundly, for the rest of her life."

Phelan stood immediately up and he too kept his statement short. "We are gathered here," he said in a low voice, "to decide what will fairly compensate Anne Needham for the injury she sustained. . . . At the end of the evidence . . . I will address you concerning my suggestions with respect to the amount of damages."

Tom Bleakely began to read from the deposition of Richard Symmonds, Anne's surgeon at the Mayo Clinic. For Anne, who had never heard this deposition, it was one of the most trying moments in a very trying day. The detail, the clarity, the objectivity of the record brought the experience back to her far more strongly than her worst and deepest dreams. Each word seemed starkly printed across her field of vision; as she heard the doctor remember, she remembered: It was reenacted for her in her mind like a dark, distasteful play. The drama seemed removed from her as she listened and then couldn't listen.

Bleakely read from Dr. Symmonds' notes taken after his first meeting with her, on March 7, 1974.

Patient has adenocarcinoma and adenosis, involving upper two thirds of vagina and cervix. Discussed options of radiation and primary surgery, as treatment. Radical hysterectomy and vaginectomy, skin graft vagina after a few days . . .

Anne wore a dark blue corduroy jacket and a long beige skirt. She kept perfectly still as the medical history was being read, taking a few long deep breaths at several rough parts. The jury was still and extremely attentive. She kept her hand firmly in her jacket pocket and watched Bleakely closely as he read.

Will attempt to preserve ovaries if nodes are negative. Patient especially prefers to have surgery rather than radiation. I have discussed risks and complications of the procedures: leaks, incontinence, et cetera with patient and mother.

Judge Decker looked down at his hands. His glasses came off. He closed his eyes. He ran one thick hand across the bald top of his head. Phelan stared down at his table, not writing a word, though he held tight to his pen out of habit. It sat motionless on his legal pad, as if unable to move.

We accomplished a radical hysterectomy and partial vaginectomy. . . . A radical hysterectomy is accomplished . . . to insure that one obtains good clearance, wide clearance of the malignancy, one goes further lateral to cervix and uterus, adjacent to bladder, uterus, rectum, and takes out a much bigger block of tissue. . . . In this case, the upper part of the vagina was removed: eighty percent of the female tract.

Anne visibly swallowed and couldn't look up or around the room. She saw herself in the hospital, crawling across the floor; in her wheelchair pulling her IVs on their tall pole down to the lounge for a smoke; the pain and all the drugs after that first operation; the "female tract," the "block of tissue," the "removal of the uterus"; she swallowed, and kept on swallowing.

The cavity that's created by removing the uterus and the eighty percent of Anne Needham's vagina was packed with gauze to maintain the cavity, to prevent its closure. After this had healed for a period of ten days, we then obtained a split-thickness skin graft. We shave a partial thickness of the skin off of one buttock. In this case, the patient's left buttock.

We apply the split-thickness skin over a sponge rubber mold, of the proper size to fit the cavity. And then we insert the skin-covered mold into the cavity and leave it there for about eight to ten days. In this instance it was removed in ten days, on the twenty-eighth of March.

> We obtained a good take of the skin graft, and after we removed the sponge rubber mold, then it's necessary to insert a polyethylene plastic mold to prevent contracture, shrinkage, of the skin-grafted area. And then it's necessary for the patient to wear the mold for usually six months, to a year.

For Anne, listening to her own medical history surrounded by this crowd of people, reporters, lawyers, friends, and family comprised a kind of exposure of her life, her problems, her most private and troubling experiences that she hadn't had to go through since her deposition. She had been nervous and tense throughout the trial, but she had also been lulled by the liability portion into forgetting that the entire action was directly routed in her. Today was damages, and she was being forced to relive those times.

> We have seen Anne Needham on many occasions since that time. The vagina is of normal depth, diameter, and function. . . . There is very little difference from the standpoint of appearance or from the standpoint of function. . . . There is some dryness of the vagina, but this is more secondary to loss of cervix, loss of mucus, loss of normal vaginal secretion than it is to loss of vagina per se. . . .

Anne's hair was held in clips above her ears. She felt her hair now and then, and occasionally her hand would steal toward her face and one finger would run lightly across one cheek. She was holding herself tightly in control, body rigid, trying to send her mind somewhere else while the depositions went on, preparing for her own time on the stand when she would need all her wits about her.

Bleakely began to read from the deposition of Dr. Kenneth Noller, the physician at the Mayo Clinic who had made a specialty of women exposed prenatally to synthetic estrogens.

> Examination was what you would expect in any pelvic surgery: a bit of scarring but in general, good healing and nothing that would suggest recurrent tumor. . . . At that time I thought the graft had taken very well, and the length

and caliber of the vagina was normal. . . . She had stated
there were no problems with sexual intercourse, though at
times the skin graft did tend to constrict down if she did
not wear her mold continuously. . . .

On June 2nd, 1977, Anne was complaining of a problem with urinary incontinence during orgasm. . . .

Anne's face was burning. She couldn't look at anyone. She
stared at her lap. She could feel the tears in her eyes, and the
burning sensation of acute self-consciousness and embarrassment
became a trembling in her limbs and a hardening of her back and
spine. She could feel the muscles in her shoulders, tighter than the
thickest knots, and all she wanted was to run away from there and
never see any of them again. Then with dismay and panic she
heard Mr. Charfoos softly say, "We will now call Anne Needham
to the stand."

Anne seemed to change color, breathing deeply, as she
slowly stood, keeping her right hand safely inside her side jacket
pocket. That hand felt good in there: close and comfortable and
somewhere inside, just where she would have liked to be. Her
mind went abruptly blank and she seemed to see nothing at all,
nothing distinct, no details or edges, everything just merged into
everything else and nothing stood plainly out. The surface of her
mind seemed smooth and unaffected by what was happening
around her. She felt her head go up and her body move forward,
and she moved without any palpable effort automatically toward
the stand. The rush of air all around her felt like a distant
murmuring, and the faces and voices and the shapes of things dissolved into a colorless, undifferentiated mass. At last she found
herself sitting behind the brass WITNESS plaque. Now she was
holding up her hand in the air, solemnly taking the oath.

Tom Bleakely performed the examination. A fair-haired man
in his late thirties, with a wide, open face and a gentle manner,
Tom had specialized in DES cases at Charfoos and Charfoos and
had been in close contact with Anne for about a year before the
trial. He stood close to the stand and spoke to Anne quietly.
When she said her name she whispered hoarsely, and Judge
Decker had to say, "Keep your voice up."

She began speaking clearly, distinctly but without much
volume. She went through her family history, that she lived at

home with her younger sister, Mary, that she had three brothers and three sisters, that her sister Pamela had a son, her nephew, about eight months old, and her sister Cathy had a little daughter, two months old, her niece.

"Are you married now?"

"No, I am not." Her eyes dropped slightly.

"Have you ever been married?"

"No, I have not."

She recited her education: "I grew up in Park Forest, and I went to Rich East Township High School. . . . I was at the College of Saint Teresa in Minnesota for a year. . . . I was trying to get into a nursing program they had. It was a four-year program. It was"—she hesitated—"rather tough. I kind of backed down from it." She glanced down suddenly as if somewhat ashamed. "I came back home. I got a job. I was working evenings in a nursing home. I was going to school at the same time. . . . That was Prairie State College, Chicago Heights. . . . I was trying to keep my eduation going at that point, just to keep taking some classes as long as I was home. I did have some free time in the evenings. . . ."

Bleakely brought her forward with a jerk: "Let's talk about February of 1974. . . . Did you seek medical attention for any specific reasons?"

"Yes." Anne made a frown and jumped in: "I went to see my gynecologist. . . . I had an infection earlier that I had seen a dermatologist about. . . . It was underneath my arms. This was in January." She seemed to be remembering in spurts of images; she went on in short, clipped sentences: "I went to see the dermatologist. He took a scraping. He couldn't decide what it was. He suggested I might possibly have a yeast infection, and to go see my gynecologist."

Anne sat up straight and stared straight forward. There was no motion in her head or her body. "I called to make an appointment with my doctor. He was on vacation. I had to wait a couple of weeks. I finally saw him late in February." Anne ran her hand slowly across her forehead. It was warm in the room, and she seemed to be perspiring. She felt as if she couldn't find any air. She felt like she did nowadays in elevators, she could almost feel the oxygen mask closing in on her face. She wanted to get outside, to breathe; she took her right hand out of her pocket and let it hang limp in the air by her side.

"He was giving me my exam. . . . I complained of the discharge I had had. I complained that I had hemorrhaged and blacked out a short period of time before that. He was . . ." she shook her head and shrugged. "We were just discussing what was going on with my body." She looked up at Bleakely, around the room, almost naïvely. "He proceeded to go ahead and do the exam," she pressed on. "He got extremely excited and ran across the room. He said he had never seen anything like this before."

She stopped again. She took a tissue from her jacket pocket. She held it to her face. Then she looked down at it, as if surprised she was holding it, and put it quickly back in her pocket. "We had a nurse come in. She took a look. He decided I should go to the hospital. I didn't go to the hospital. He took the biopsy right there. I delivered it to the hospital." Anne closed her eyes for a moment and took three deep breaths. The room was still. The people, the room, the judge, the lawyers, had all disappeared. All there was was that gentle voice, calm, insistent, painfully prying her open.

"It was Friday evening when he called and gave me the results. He really didn't give me the results." She touched one hand briefly to her cheek. "He just—he wouldn't say to me that I did have cancer. He just said, 'Don't worry, we will take care of it.'" Her memory was clear, but the tone was of recalling something distant, a long time ago, in some other place. "We received a phone call from a radiologist Dr. Warren recommended us to speak to. We were supposed to go see him. We weren't to see him for about a week and a half to two weeks. It was quite a period of time," she said matter-of-factly, "and I was concerned about that."

Anne started to get back inside the story, to tell it as it unfolded in her mind. "My mother contacted Mayo Clinic. This was on a Monday. This was after the weekend. We went up that next Tuesday. The following day, we made our trip to Mayo.

"We traveled by car," Anne said. Her voice lost some of its hoarseness and became suddenly crisp and sharp. "It was kind of confusing, to get everything organized to go. We weren't sure what we were going to do when we got there. We started out"—she laughed, remembering—"and had car failure for a couple of hours.

We finally made it into Rochester on Tuesday evening, quite late."

"Was there any discussion at Mayo's," Bleakely asked, "whether or not radiation or surgery should be performed?"

Anne drew a breath. "I was frightened . . . of radiology. I had worked for a year and a half in a nursing home. I had seen people suffer after the treatments. Cobalt treatments, and such." Her voice broke: "I didn't want to see myself," she paused, suddenly flustered, "in that kind of shape.

"When we got there we discussed surgery. I was told that there might possibly have to be some radiation treatment. But I was glad that at least they could try and remove it surgically."

"How many operations," Bleakely asked, "did you have during that hospitalization?"

"I had three," Anne replied. "They had explained what they were going to do. I knew when they got in there they weren't sure how much they were going to have to remove. But they explained about the removal of my tubes, my uterus, and my vagina." She closed her eyes a second and said in a muffled voice, "They explained how they were going to build it up." Anne looked up and began to speak faster.

"The first time then, it was removal. Then, as you heard in the deposition, they packed me with materials, to keep an opening. After that, the second surgery is when they put the skin graft in, which did not go in—it should have gone in a little bit earlier than it did, but during the first surgery I was exposed to quite a bit of Merthiolate." She looked quickly down, as if embarrassed. "We did not know at that time I was allergic to it."

"Was it your understanding," Bleakely said softly, "that by consenting to this surgery that you would never be able to have children?"

Anne nodded helplessly. "I realized that they were going to remove quite a bit."

Bleakely looked at the floor. "How did you feel about that, Anne?"

She ran one hand back into her hair. "It was kind of tough," she said slowly. "It was very tough. But at that point I was pretty much in a state of shock as to what was going on with me." She added, "I was putting myself in the hands of the doctors."

Bleakely took out a photograph and showed it to Anne. "Would you identify please, Anne, what that consists of?"

"That," said Anne, not looking at the photo, "is the area where my skin graft was taken from."

"At the time this skin graft was removed," Bleakely asked, "was it your understanding that the skin being removed from this area was, in effect, going to constitute your vagina for the rest of your life?"

Anne closed her eyes for a moment. "Yes. I knew that was the only way they could rebuild what had been removed. The only thing was we were hoping it would take. Sometimes," she added quietly, "they don't take very well.

"At the end of the second procedure when they did the rebuilding, they repacked me but it was with some other kind of material. I just heard from the deposition," she said quickly, "I didn't know this before, that they had sewn the vagina around the mold. They had to remove that mold and give me another one to use. I am pretty sure that is exactly what was involved in the third surgery. I was knocked out for that also."

Bleakely approached the bench holding a piece of tube-shaped white plastic in his palm. Phelan took a very quick look at that, swallowed, and shook his head, murmuring, "No objection." Bleakely carried it on a yellow legal pad slowly past the jury. Then he showed it to Anne. "That," she said in a hollow voice, "is the vaginal mold that they gave me originally to use."

Bleakely asked, "How long did you wear that mold, Anne?"

Anne pondered. "Possibly for—I am pretty sure about the first six months. After that I was allowed to wear it not quite all the time. I would wear it every evening," she recalled reluctantly, "when I was in bed. I would wear it not full, complete days; I would wear it"—she paused—"partially."

"Were there any modifications in your clothing or under-clothing necessary in order—" Bleakely hesitated delicately.

Anne offered, "The mold would not stay in. It was constantly slipping out. I had to rig up some way—I would wear a lot of padding and things in order to be able to function with it in. Otherwise it just wouldn't stay."

"Do you have to wear it presently?"

She looked straight at Tom. Her eyes were wide, calm, but dazed. "I wear it every so often, now." She cocked her head to the side, and regarded the room with a steady gaze. "It is my impression, that since everything is suspended in there," she sighed, "it just relieves it."

"Have there been complications from the surgery?"

Anne responded shyly. "I do have trouble," she stared at her hands, "every now and then, with urinary incontinence. . . . I can't control my bladder all the time. Immediately after surgery, it was very bad for a good year and a half. I could not walk fast at all without losing some urine. It tightened up. . . . I asked my doctors about that. They said it would tighten up. They said it would take about a year and a half, maybe two years. But my entire feeling has never completely come back. I go almost whenever I am guessing it is time to go. Sometimes, I think my bladder is full and it is not. Other times, I can't tell it is, and it is." She sniffed. "Sneezing. Sometimes when I run. If it is full and I don't know that it is.

"It was hard," she went on, "especially the first year after I got home. Sometimes you get ready to go out and get out, and move a little too fast, and you have to run back and change. It was kind of hard not knowing if you are going to make it through, say, a party, or if that last beer is going to run right through."

"Do you think it is going to get any better?"

"No, I don't. . . . They told me it would be a year and a half, two years, and . . . the feeling should come back. According to the doctor I spoke to, the nerve endings would heal over, or something, and readjust, but they haven't."

Bleakely asked about medical costs. "I am still paying off bills," she said. "It is generally a couple hundred dollars every time I go back. This last winter I had some tests done. It jumped up to about six hundred dollars just for that visit alone." She estimated her total medical expenses, with travel, at about "ten thousand, eight thousand . . . I just keep paying bills off."

There was a long silence. Bleakely looked up from his pad and asked, "How did it feel to have cancer?"

Anne shivered. "It was"—she waited—"extremely frightening. It is not the kind of thing you expect to have."

"How do you feel about it now, knowing that you have had cancer?"

"Every now and then . . ." She seemed to be breaking down. "Just one second," she murmured, sitting silently for a moment. She touched her eyes, which were red and puffy. "The whole thing is quite an emotional drain." She stopped again. She looked at the jury. "I have been through quite a bit," she told them. "I still am going through quite a bit. It gets hard when sometimes—just the word 'cancer.' Even though it is not anything to do with me." She shook her head and held both hands together. "It sounds crazy, but even when John Wayne died . . . It sounds corny, I know, but when they made the announcement, just the word 'cancer'. . . was very hard to take."

"How do you feel about the future?"

Anne sighed. "I do have somewhat of one. So, that is a good point. I will just do what everyone else does: work." She said with a trace of defiance, "The things that happened to me aren't going to change. It is just my adjustment to them. That has been hard for me, and there are still more adjustments to go. I will just do what everyone else is going to do when this case is over: go on."

Phelan stood up and said, "Anne, I just have a few questions." He had adopted a fatherly voice. She gazed back at him with sharp eyes. "When you were back at Mayo Clinic last, at that time you saw Dr. Noller again?"

"Yes."

"He found no evidence of any problems at all?"

She said firmly, "No, nothing at all. We were concerned about the blood count. I went there for tests because of that."

Phelan paused, thoughtfully, checked his pad, and asked, "It has been five years and four months since your surgery, Anne?"

"Yes."

Phelan made rapid slashes on his pad with his pen. "You mentioned this incontinence problem," he said. ". . . I am not certain I heard everything, but at the present time the condition has gotten better than it was then?"

"It is definitely better than it was," Anne admitted, but added sharply, "It is not the same as it could be."

"Are you going to go into the health-care business?" Phelan asked.

"No, I won't."

"Are you going into the pharmacy business?"

Anne seemed somewhat puzzled. "No, I don't think so."

"Is that a right estimate of your expenses, eight to ten thousand?"

Anne said, between her teeth, "To tell you the truth, I am sort of blank on that right at the moment."

Phelan sat down.

Bleakely, on redirect, asked, "Anne, even though the cancer has not recurred to date, do you have fears in that regard?"

Anne nodded numbly. "Usually, I am full of quite a bit of apprehension when I go back to the clinic. I am afraid they will find something."

Bleakely asked about physical scars. "I have an incision," she said hesitantly, "they made below my navel, quite low—it is just a long one. Then I have two small openings where they had tubes for drainage. . . ." She stopped and waited. He asked about the pain.

"There was an awful lot of pain." Anne seemed to be struggling for words. She sighed, as if in defeat. "It is kind of hard to describe pain." She tried: "After each surgery, I was very doped up, but the pain kept coming through the drugs. The pain was quite severe and at times it was worse than others." She thought a bit. "When they did a lot of the surgery, they moved around so much. . . . They thought at one point I was having an awful lot of, like a gas pain or something, where I would just be doubled up and it was quite severe.

"I still get them," Anne volunteered. "Every now and then I still get them, but not with the severity that they were." She seemed to be recalling it all with a kind of clarity she had never had before; having to testify before these strangers brought so much to the surface she hadn't wanted to feel. One of the main things she had tried to numb herself against was the memory of that pain. "The pain from the graft was quite extensive," she went on. "You don't sit for quite a while." Her features distorted in a wry smile, but her eyes grew dark and small. "There was just so much removed," she said hoarsely, "and so much moved around. It was bad." She bit her lip. "It definitely was bad."

Anne sat on the chair for a few moments, feeling the pain herself. Each question felt like a stab down low, where most of the feelings had been. Each time she opened her mouth, each word hurt. The sentences she had to pull out of herself, like a long rope where each word marked a snag. She took out a tissue and blew her nose and waited patiently. She was astonished when she heard Tom Bleakely finally say, "Thank you."

Judge Decker pulled himself out of wherever he had been and said with great gentleness to Anne, "That will be all." Anne looked up at the judge, and he was looking right down at her. And his expression seemed to have softened for the first time yet. She said right up at him, "Thank you." Anne stood up and looked once at the jury. She felt like she was on stage. The courtroom stretched out endlessly before her with the audience filling the rear, and a huge heaviness seemed to lift from her, and roll away somewhere. It felt like the departure of stored anxiety she had never felt before, and it drew itself out of the muscles in her back, and out into the room. She felt weak in the legs. She hobbled stiffly down from the platform as if she'd been cooped up in a compact car.

Charfoos cleared his throat and said, "Shall I get our next witness, your Honor?" Decker answered, as if somewhere far away, "Yes. Well, let's see. Who is it?" Charfoos said, "Mrs. Needham, the mother." The judge replied: "All right, put her on."

Mary Needham came slowly up the aisle in a long beige dress. She kept her head up and her back straight as she took the stand. She held one hand up to her chin, cocked her head a bit to the left, and waited. Charfoos asked her to describe Anne's condition immediately before the surgery.

Mary drew a short breath. "Anne," she sighed, "was like a zombie. We just went through living each day until we got to the hospital. . . . She was out of it for quite a few days after the surgery, and not really coherent." She began to cry. She put down her head and covered her face with one hand.

Charfoos said gently, "Do you want me to ask another question? Are you all right?"

Mary nodded and bit her lip. "Yes." Charfoos asked her if Anne felt self-conscious about her scars.

"She doesn't like anyone to see them," she said. "She finds them uncomfortable. When anyone else is around, like in a swimming suit, or sunbathing in the backyard."

"Let me ask you a broader question," Charfoos said. He thought for a moment. "Have you noticed a difference in personality in your daughter since she recovered from surgery? . . . Is Anne the same person, or different in any way?"

"Yes," Mary said, nodding as if admitting something. "She is different. . . . She had an anxiety syndrome, I think. . . ." Mary stopped short and mentioned wonderingly, "She is very sensitive to things. . . .

"Anne and I," she offered suddenly, "have always been very close. Since the surgery, sometimes it is difficult for us to be together . . ." her voice trailed off and cracked. "Because I"—she felt for the word—"I empathize with her too much."

"What was she like," Charfoos asked, "before those differences?"

"She was just a carefree daughter." Mary smiled, remembering. "A young, happy girl, like my other ones."

"How important was it," Charfoos asked, "for the women in your family to eventually be mothers?"

Mary frowned. "Annie," she said finally, "was the middle child. So everyone would turn to Anne. The younger ones would go to Anne, and the older ones would go to Anne. Because I worked, she was the mother in the family. Doing the cooking and corralling people and assigning jobs. That was the way it was.

"With the onset of two grandchildren in the last year," Mary went on, "I have felt Anne's pain." She looked straight at the jury. She stopped and breathed deeply in. "Because she would have been the mother." She was just barely not crying. Charfoos had no more questions. Phelan had no questions. Judge Decker had no questions. Mary was excused

It was just past noon and time for lunch. Phelan sat for a while alone at the defense table while his partners went downstairs. He apparently hadn't been feeling well this morning, and he was having noticeable trouble breathing through his nose. He leaned back in his swivel chair and held his right hand up to his face and let his fingers splay across his eyes. During lunch, he offered Charfoos half a million dollars to settle. The offer was refused.

At two, the court went back into session. Charfoos led a stocky, dark-haired man with gold-rimmed glasses and a dark-complexioned face down the aisle toward the witness stand. This was Dr. Leroy Levitt, vice president for medical affairs at Mount Sinai Hospital in Chicago, president of the Chicago Board of Health, and former dean of the Chicago Medical School. Dr. Levitt was called as a psychiatric expert in the emotional problems of surgical patients.

Charfoos asked Levitt to describe Anne's surgery. Levitt had a wonderfully rich, mellifluous voice, deep, dark, and sympathetic. "Technically," Levitt allowed, ". . . it is spoken of as a gynecologically mutilating procedure. . . . It is a pejorative term, used to describe the magnitude of the surgery. . . ." He gazed back at Charfoos with gentle equanimity.

Levitt employed his large, sturdy hands to illustrate his message; they moved in slow melodic rhythms in the air, as if he were conducting himself in a virtuoso solo performance. Charfoos asked about complications and Levitt responded, telling of ". . . A lack of neurological response for bladder filling. . . . In sexual activity . . . there may be relaxation of the urethra. . . ." He glanced up and gazed out at the room through his square gold glasses. ". . . This was told to me by Miss Needham . . . this did actually happen. . . . From what I know and from what I have read, and from other surgical patients . . . it is not a reversible condition."

He stepped to the drawing board to illustrate the extent of that mutilation. "The surgery removed eighty percent of the vagina, the Fallopian tubes, the uterus, and the lymph node drainage. . . . There is a considerable amount of tissue back of the uterus against the nest of which the uterus rests. . . . There is, in a way of speaking, an eventration," he shrugged. "It is a terrible word, a removal of the total content of the cup of the pelvis." He moved solemnly back to his chair. There he sat placidly as Charfoos asked him the significance of these radical procedures. Levitt paused and stared at his hands. He seemed to be gazing into the depths of her injuries.

"Well," he began, "it is of catastrophic impact. . . . It is massive, sudden, just short of massive trauma. One can't think of any other kind of procedure that would be more annihilating to one's feelings about themselves." He described Anne's mental state at the time he interviewed her as one of "moderate established reactive depression . . . meaning that there is considerable loss not only of the organs that are involved, but in terms of one's future and one's concept of themselves, their body image, their self-concept, that would undoubtedly produce a feeling of profound loss of self-esteem, inability to function . . . anxiety about what is going to happen, what will happen in the future. . . ."

"Did you find," Charfoos asked, "any history of cancer concern, or phobia about cancer?"

Levitt frowned and nodded. "It is not always spoken of, but it is always there. . . . The future is always uncertain . . . as to recurrence or what will happen. . . ."

"Do you have an opinion," Charfoos asked, "as to whether or not this has affected her ability to enter into normal relationships? . . ."

Levitt spread his wide hands out on the counter. "It is very sensitive," he shook his head, "to be in that position, knowing what has transpired since the surgery . . . the urinary difficulty, the artificial vagina . . . the possibility of closure, or shrinkage. . . . My impression is," Levitt said, smiling hopefully, "that Anne is a very honest person . . . but to have to tell somebody about what happened to you, to have to give information about something that ordinarily one doesn't have any particular concern about . . ." he shook his head again, and folded his hands neatly on the counter. "Every young person is concerned in situations like that, but to have to draw it out to that length . . ." he shook his head sadly.

"Based on her history . . . as she was before this trauma, and the history afterwards, do you find a difference in her self-image?"

"A considerable difference," Levitt avowed. "Prior to the surgery, Anne . . . grew up in Park Forest, the third of seven children . . . striving and ambitious . . . a lot of friends, attractive, a suburban life quite to the average, if one can use that term. . . . Very outgoing, well put together, a competent young woman."

"And the difference?"

"Well, the surgery itself, the trauma of the procedure, the many visits to Mayo, the interruption of her work activity, the heightened concern of her brothers and sisters. . . . The difficulty in communicating to friends about it; people—" he looked up suddenly and lifted one hand, as if in solemn warning. "People react very strangely to people who have certain kinds of illnesses. . . ."

"What is the prognosis for her with this condition? . . ."

"Well," Levitt sighed. "It is hard to be prophetic. . . . If somebody has good ego strengths, by which I mean their capacity to meet reality, to weather stresses, to take what comes and make the best of it . . . I think I was impressed by her ability to bounce back . . . I think that . . . the outlook for her development further, in meeting up with whatever life should bring, she has a good reserve. . . ."

Phelan jumped up to begin his cross-exam. He began, as usual, cordially, as if meeting someone at a cocktail party. "I had the opportunity to meet you for the first time this morning, Doctor. . . ." He picked up Anne's medical records. "Prior to your two interviews with Anne . . . you had not reviewed these records?"

"No," Levitt shook his head.

"Doctor . . . you are not a surgeon, are you?"

"No, I am not."

". . . You have not physically examined Anne, have you?"

Levitt seemed shocked. He was a psychiatrist. "No, of course not."

"Now in the case of Anne," Phelan smoothly pursued, "would it be true, Doctor, that pursuing a career . . . would help enormously in the psychological area? . . ."

"Oh." Levitt nodded generously. "I think productive work is always helpful, yes. . . ."

Phelan glanced down at his pad. "Would it be 'enormously' helpful? I want to make sure I have got the word right. . . . This morning when we were in the witness room . . . I believe you said, 'enormously.' . . ."

Levitt stepped neatly out of the trap. "I think work is always very, very helpful."

"Now . . . in respect to Anne's ability to deal with . . . males, as I understood it, sometime prior to the operation until October of '75, she had a close relationship with a friend by the name of John?"

"Yes, sir."

"And then after October of 1975, she had met another young man and had lived with him . . . up to about three weeks prior to . . . February?"

"Yes."

Phelan put down his pad. "Thank you very much, Doctor."

Charfoos, on redirect, asked, "Does Anne have a history of full-time work prior to these events?"

"Yes . . . interspersed with school."

"Always achieving, in other words, one way or another?"

"Yes, that is true."

Charfoos put down his pad. "No further questions." It was time for Charfoos to close. The ante was raised during the break to $750,000 by Phelan. Anne turned it down. Taking up a position at the lectern immediately opposite the jury box, Charfoos began his statement.

"All people come as you find them; Anne Needham, the person that was Anne Needham . . . was an achieving, reasonably ambitious, family-oriented, fun-loving . . . carefree person . . . marriage, children, possibly a secondary career. . . . That's my client"—he paused—"that was.

". . . How much, through the wrongful act of the defendant, was taken away from her? What part of her? What nature of her? What substance was . . . diminished, reduced, destroyed? . . . Her physical appearance, her scarring, her hesitation . . . at a most basic level that interferes with a normal relationship . . . and the next stage that is normal and God-given . . . to every woman in history: She will want children. . . . She will not have her children. She will not have his children.

"In March of 1974, in the words of Dr. Levitt, a catastrophe occurred. A change in her basic existence. . . . What object of self-identity, what feeling about yourself is more crucial? . . . Is it unreasonable to feel an ongoing concern for that which was, and that which may not be again? Is it unreasonable for her to feel . . . pain when she saw her newborn niece and nephew?

". . . That pain was a living, breathing, realization of the denial of her destiny . . . everything that she had been taught, everything that she had looked forward to, everything that she had contemplated. . . ." He turned to face the jury, and then toward Anne. "A catastrophe!

"This . . . is not a matter easily evaluated. . . . But the law has given us certain terminology . . . some map upon which to rely. . . . Now, it is not a clear-cut map . . . but . . . it does have names and directions. . . ." He stood at a drawing board and wrote letters on the paper. The felt-tip marker squeaked rudely in the quiet room.

"The first is 'pain and suffering'; the second is 'disability'; the third is 'humiliation.' . . ." He began with pain. "Nobody can

guess . . . the pain of injury, as distinguished from the pain of
suffering. . . . She went through the surgical procedures, she was
in a daze . . . and in that first year 1974 she had true unmitigated
pain. . . . It will be your job," he said, looking across the ranks
of the jury, "to assess an economic value for that pain. . . . Let's
say," he continued, writing large red numbers on the board,
"thirty-five thousand dollars for all the pain . . . that occurred in
1974. . . ."

He went next to humiliation. "Scars, disfigurement . . . on
the body, the incontinence. . . . Would anybody say that it was
unreasonable that Anne Needham be paid ten thousand dollars for
that? . . ." As these numbers and sums went floating by on the
board and echoed in the crowded court, Anne Needham herself
seemed to be seriously trying to tune it all out. She looked everywhere in the room but the center of the argument, that unavoidable drawing board beginning to crawl with numbers. She
clenched her face and her fists and her body and just kept staring
around, as the categories broke her down into discrete slices of
some other life.

"She had," Charfoos was going on, "a suffering that is mental. . . . It is sometimes called depression. It is sometimes called
anxiety. And sometimes, in real life . . . it is called unhap-
piness. . . . Doesn't this young lady have a right to her unhap-
piness? Will she not be reminded every day of her life . . . if
every day she was nervous, and looked for a recurrence . . . her
suffering will be ongoing . . . and who could say we were wrong
if we assess that job a total of . . ." The marker squealed loudly
again: $20,000.

"I have a third category: disability. . . . The removal of the
children, the removal of the grandchildren, if anybody were to
say, 'Ms. Needham, you will be forced . . . to sit in a vacuous
box, foreclosed from all these activities, and that will be your job
for a year . . ." He wrote again: $40,000.

"We are not making her rich. . . ." He did some quick addition. "That is it. I am done." He wrote: $70,000. "But, the law
says . . . that she is entitled to damages from the time she got
hurt until now . . . and into the future of her natural life expect-
ancy. . . . I believe, fifty-two-point-eight years. . . . We are
faced with such a gap of time, it boggles the mind. . . ."

Decker broke in appropriately: "You've taken half an hour."

278

Charfoos continued, "How do I take that total of fifty-two-point-eight years? How long those damages?" He wrote some numbers on the board, with several zeroes: $3,000,000. "That is my recommendation. I do not ask you to go one dollar above that. Above that is punishment of the defendant . . . below that would not be appropriate . . . given her extensive life expectancy, future and past damages, and the injury that was done to her. . . ."

Phelan took over the lectern and placed himself in exactly the same position, his hands in exactly the same place, and began in a darker voice: ". . . My job today is to bring some reasonableness, some fairness, some common sense to your approach. . . . There has never been any question that this young person at a very young age was stricken with a serious disease. There has never been any question"—his tone subtly shifted—"that the disease was diagnosed, that it was treated by I think the most famous, brilliant doctors that we have in this country. . . . As far as I know . . . there has been no recurrence of this condition. It has now been over five and one-half years. . . . I pray God"—his face lit up with something like fervent desire—"that it will never, never, happen again!

"The operations," he admitted, "were painful, and I am sure mentally traumatic . . . but as Dr. Noller said to you . . . the operation was successful! The results were excellent! . . . I want you to understand," he said gravely, "that I approach this task here today with . . . reasonableness and fairness. . . . She has stated there were no problems with sexual intercourse . . . and she has herself testified that this urinary condition has gotten better. . . ."

There was a long moment left silent for the information to be absorbed. Phelan looked down at his pad as if wrapped in solemn reveries. Then he looked up with sincere eyes. "We have all had the opportunity here to see Anne for two weeks." Here he looked at Anne, who pointedly stared away. "I think she is a very attractive person; I think . . . as we all look at her we see a very attractive twenty-six-year-old person!" His tone and his glance challenged any one to differ from that obvious judgment.

"There is no way," he boomed, "that we or anyone can restore her ability to have children. Children, of course, are the cornerstone of this great country! . . . But," he addressed the jurors with an eager gleam, "there are other ways! . . . Adoption is always an alternative; helping with others to supplement this role. . . . That part of her life can maybe in some ways be fuller, more fulfilling, more rewarding, more satisfying. . . ."

He stepped up to the drawing board and pulled out his felt-tip marker. "I know it is always difficult to begin to talk about money . . . but that is what this lawsuit is all about. . . . Now I would like to talk to you about fairness and reasonability. . . . You are not to ignore common sense in this situation. . . .

"What the plaintiff has asked you to do here," he said indignantly, "is not to give her an income of seventy thousand dollars, but to give . . . what I find to be beyond anyone's reason, absolutely beyond fairness. . . . If one took this money and gave it to a bank, it would add up to four hundred thousand dollars every single year!" He shot the jury a quick look of pure incredulity. "I think this person deserves fair compensation," he protested. "I think this person deserves to be compensated . . . but unless I have checked every common sense . . . three million dollars is such an unreasonable and unfair sum that Mr. Charfoos didn't even mention it. . . . Incidentally," he quieted down considerably and confided in the jury, "I am not trying to negotiate. . . ."

He got down to business. "Let's say . . . that somehow pain and suffering was five thousand dollars a year. . . ." He scratched the number on the board and regarded it pensively. ". . . I am not . . . suggesting an annualized basis because I believe in the future! That this young person is going to go ahead, to form a meaningful relationship, to do something in her life to become a mother or a grandmother . . ." He began visibly to radiate hope. ". . . I don't think this is a person that is going to say that I am not going to help children . . . to adopt children, or help my sisters or my brothers, that this person is going to become involved. . . ."

The disturbing and distasteful fact occurred to Anne—as she tried not to listen to these orations, or, if she heard them pierce through her numb defenses, not to let them affect her unduly—that it was the enemy's job to paint her injuries, and therefore her life, in the rosiest, lightest colors, while it was her lawyer's duty to summon forth the darkest, the dimmest, the gloomiest version of her life and her damages, to compensate for their distortions, to suitably dramatize the terror of what she had been through.

Though she well understood this and had understood it all along, to be faced with wanting to believe the opposition argument while desperately wishing to reject hers made her uneasy and confused. She preferred not to deal with such ambiguities, to shut them from her mind. But somehow everything she had always wanted to avoid, to evade, to run away from had been given life through this trial, and like a demon let out of her worst, most distorted memories, all the fears and terrors that her future had indeed been ruined had come back to invade her peace. It was as if she would have to pay a premium price for seeking compensation: The powers that be would apparently demand her participation in this ritual humiliation before she could get her due. She hated dealing with both distortions, the paradox she was listening to . . .

"If I were to suggest to you," she could hear Phelan slyly saying, "that as reasonable and fair compensation three hundred fifty thousand dollars . . . Miss Needham could walk over to the First National Bank and put that money to work for her. . . . She would receive no less than thirty-five thousand dollars every single year so long as the First National Bank is present where it is now! . . . Thirty-five thousand dollars"—Phelan hardly needed to remind his listeners—"puts a person in an income bracket in the United States of America that is shared by very, very few. . . . Three million dollars," he said, waving his arms at the absurdity of it, "has nothing to do with reality! Nothing to do with fairness! . . ."

He settled back into dramatic solemnity. ". . . I do not want you to carry any impression," he intoned, "that I have attempted to diminish this young person's injuries. . . . I think what I have suggested is fair and reasonable and something that bears closely to reality. . . ." Phelan sat down.

Charfoos leapt up. "Pray God, he says, it will not occur again! . . ." He let silence hold for a moment. ". . . He says that her physical appearance appears to be good. . . . He is quite right in this case, but . . . the realities of her existence as compared to the magnet of her appearance . . ." His voice lowered from a baritone to a bass: "She has the misfortune of being on the outside good, and on the inside, sour, dead, empty!

"He says to her"—Charfoos' voice had sunk with indignation —"you can adopt children. I say to the defendant, let not the defendant . . . tell her what she should do . . . they are in no position to say. . . . They are not the ones to tell her." He paused, and drew breath. "The damages she has suffered are what they have done to her. Do not let them impose further on her by telling her how to lead her life, because of their wrong." Charfoos took his seat beside Anne.

Decker gave the jury some brief instructions before retiring. He warned again, "A corporate defendant is entitled to the same fair, unprejudiced treatment as an individual would receive from you under like circumstances. . . ." On the money question, he ordered, "You must not simply multiply the damages by the years expected, but rather take the cash value . . . you must be aware of what the money will earn over the period. . . ."

By 4:15 P.M., the jury was out.

Anne stood up and left the room. She wandered out into the corridor, where her mother and her sister Mary were standing by the window. The three women walked together down the corridor, and ended up standing at another window, staring down at the streets of Chicago twenty-seven floors below. Anne lit a cigarette. Her mother winked and smiled at her. Anne could feel herself breathing, and she thought, "I know they have to give me something." She didn't want to dwell on that question, "How much?" It had been hard enough hearing them arguing over the worth of her injuries, of what she had lost. But what else could they give but cash, she grimly thought. Somehow it seemed a trifle, unimportant. But then why was she shaking so?

She had held herself in for so long now, not just for these two weeks, but for the months before and the mistrials, and the weeks of preparation, that she knew it wouldn't be possible to relax right away. The tension had become habit forming, it had learned to inhabit her body long enough to feel almost comfortable there. Sometimes she didn't even feel it; until times like these, when it moved closer to the surface and made it impossible to be calm. But she looked calm, Mary Needham thought, watching Anne looking out the window.

Charfoos, Bleakely, and Sussman sat in a row in the vinyl seats across from the elevators. There wasn't much to discuss, just the wait, the pits. It was best to let that time not happen, to ignore its passing, to forget what it was about. The only question left was money. They had won the hard portion; now it boiled down to numbers.

The jury was out forty-five minutes. When the news came that the verdict was in, it was not read in open court. Charfoos and Phelan went together back into the judge's chambers, where the number would be revealed. Charfoos was back out in a few moments and whispered to Anne, "Eight hundred thousand." Anne felt a surge of relief rise in her, as suddenly Mary Needham senior and Mary Needham junior were jumping up and hugging her, and then Anne was crying on their shoulders, and her mom and Mary were crying too.

Then Anne turned, and there was Victor Needham in the hall, reaching out to give her a hug. And her sister Pam and her brother Nicholas had all been there waiting to get inside to celebrate. Next Anne hugged all her lawyers, one by one, and everyone was whispering their congratulations, because she had won. She had won: The thought was somewhere in every move that was made, it guided the members of the family and the members of the plaintiff's side into a cluster of jubilation. She had won, it was over. It was simple: It wasn't easy to accept.

Anne felt the attention being focused on her. She felt confident of that responsibility, to be at the center, without embarrassment or self-consciousness. She finally felt a sense of strength after so many years of powerlessness.

Now the crowd was breaking up. Richard Phelan was beside her congratulating her. She took his hand and accepted his congratulations, cool and civil, but some of that resentment did dissolve in the wash of happiness she felt. It was a funny feeling: For all the suspense and then the resolution, and the rushed confusion of the event, she had enough private space somewhere to feel happy. It was the inner place she had had to develop over the past five years.

Now it helped her to keep calm, to appear poised, to seem relaxed, as the flow of people swept by and around her, people she didn't know and had never met shaking her hand, offering their congratulations, saying, "I'm so happy for you." Happy for her! The moment was shared among this crowd of strangers, and there was something odd and satisfying about that, that the news was out and she was it: She was the event and the result of this process. It made her seem not an ordinary girl anymore.

She went along into the big steel elevator. She was packed in with a ton of people, all stuffed in together, but for the first time in a long time she didn't feel claustrophobic. She felt fine in that shifting mass, no need to fight for air, she hardly needed to breathe. The claustrophobia, the fear of losing air, had been partly a feeling of isolation; now the opposite seemed true. Everything was part of everything else, at least for that moment before it dissolved. For the moment though, she needed to keep her head, because she would be asked a million questions. They would all want to know, "What was it like?"

In the lobby, the television news crews were there. She stood between Charfoos and Bleakely in the hot glare of the mobile lights. A young female TV reporter approached holding out her microphone as if in tribute, a smile fixed across her face, her hair sprayed to a glossy, laminated hardness. "How did it feel?" "What was it like?" she heard the questions as if filtered through some dim electronic echo.

Anne felt strangely at ease. She stood by the elevators, not blinking from the lights, and spoke calmly to the circle of reporters and cameras: "There are a lot of girls out there with the same disease as me," she said. "This had to be done." More questions, from the back, people holding pads, and the knot of mikes being shoved at her. "Sure there were times when I wanted to pull out." Anne smiled and shrugged. "Lots of times . . ." The questions came in a sudden wave and grew to a chaotic flurry, then in only a minute or so, in the time presumably allotted to them on the evening news, the questions began to taper off, while the print people hovered around with pads.

Soon the news conference was over. The reporters were leaving. The lawyers too were on their way, fetching taxi cabs back to their hotels. Anne, after less than five minutes, was left standing with her family. All around, at five o'clock, the building was quickly emptying. Men in suits and women in skirts were rushing out of the elevators into the angular, black-marble lobby. The rush of people was different now, they each looked forward in their own direction, none of them glanced at her.

Now it was time to be Anne Needham, and go with the other Needhams. With them the celebration would last awhile. It was after five o'clock, and they would have to catch a train. They walked out of the Federal Building, into the harsh white plaza. The entire downtown was moving quickly toward the river and the park, to catch their own trains home.

21

Immediately after the trial, Anne took a two-week vacation in Hawaii to rest and recover from the strain. When she got back, the summer was over and she suffered something of a letdown. After all the excitement of the last few months she saw that little had changed. She had no job, she still lived with her mother, and she still had no real prospects but the one she had just been awarded.

She could conceivably be rich within a few years, so she decided to learn something about money. She signed up for some business courses at Prairie State College and she started reading the *Wall Street Journal*. It felt like another extended period of waiting, a bit too much like the waiting she had gone through before the first trial. Now she was waiting for another settlement, by the U.S. Court of Appeals for the Seventh Circuit.

She took a job with Amtrak as a reservations clerk. For a few months she commuted by train every morning to the Amtrak office in Chicago. A few months later, after more than a year back in Park Forest, she transferred to Amtrak in St. Louis with a young man she had met at her job. He went ahead and found a small house for them in a St. Louis suburb. In May they moved in together.

Anne came home for Christmas that year. It felt good being back with her family. Nicky was on leave from the Marines, Patrick and Victor Jr. came back from Carbondale where they owned a gas station together, Cathy and her husband were there with their new baby, Pamela and her husband were there with theirs, and Mary was there—she still lived at home. They had a crowd of people in for Christmas dinner, and the atmosphere was close and nice. Mary, Anne's mother, felt as if the family had finally come out from under a cloud.

Anne began the new year sure that her suit would be resolved within a few weeks, confident that the resolution would be in her favor. She knew White Labs had appealed the lower court decision on several grounds, and that her side in the appeal was being handled by an appellate firm in Chicago. She hadn't been following the procedure that closely, but she had seen a copy of the brief her lawyers had filed, and everything seemed perfectly in order. She started thinking a little, quite cautiously, about what she might do with the money. She talked with her sisters, half seriously, about going to New York for a week, putting up at some fancy hotel, and going shopping for clothes on Fifth Avenue.

At the end of January 1981, Anne found out she had lost her case on appeal. At first she didn't know what to think. She surprised herself by remaining calm. She really wasn't all that devastated; eventually her side would win, even if it took another year or so. Still, it was a considerable shock: She had tried to prepare herself for this eventuality, but she had never really believed it could happen.

After the original trial, the higher court had ordered the lower court to grant White a new trial. The decision to "reverse and remand" the Needham decision had been arrived at by three Federal judges. On September 9, 1980, the court of appeals had heard two oral arguments, one on behalf of White Labs, one on behalf of Anne Needham. White argued successfully that the trial judge had been mistaken in allowing the jury to decide if Dienestrol had been effective in preventing miscarriages.

The primary thrust of the plaintiff's brief had been to demonstrate that the Dienestrol ingested by Anne's mother had caused her cancer, and that the failure of White Laboratories to warn of the possible danger of cancer constituted negligence. But under a separate theory, the jury had been asked to decide whether the drug was effective in preventing miscarriage. The plaintiff's side maintained that if Dienestrol could be shown to have been totally unsuited for the purpose for which it was sold, it was a defective product. Under Illinois law, a defective product that harms a person causes the manufacturer to be held "strictly" liable for injuries caused by that product.

The Appeals Court ruled that Dienestrol was not defective under Illinois law. Judge Decker had "erroneously interpreted" the law, they decided, when he ruled in the district court that "an ineffective product is a defective product." To support that ruling, Decker had cited a case in which an impure drug serum had injured a woman who took it. The Appeals Court, in a highly literal interpretation of that precedent, ruled that "only a product which contains an adulterating impurity is defective." The higher court accepted White's argument that simply because Dienestrol was demonstrably ineffective, it wasn't necessarily defective.

Because the jury could conceivably have based their decision to find White Laboratories liable on the "inefficacy" theory and that theory alone, the Court of Appeals reversed their decision and ordered a new trial. Anne's lawyers' initial response to that ruling was to immediately file a petition for a rehearing before the entire United States Seventh Circuit, a body comprising more than a dozen Federal judges. The complex and at times circuitous reasoning employed by the Appeals Court to justify their decision seemed vulnerable on several counts.

On April 27, the Seventh Circuit denied the petition for a rehearing, and Anne's lawyers immediately began writing an appeal to the U. S. Supreme Court. If the Supreme Court refused to hear the appeal, then Anne would have little choice but to go back to the District Court for yet another trial.

Epilogue

As *Needham* v. *White Laboratories* languished in the Court of Appeals, several key decisions in other DES cases around the country significantly altered the shape of national DES litigation. In three separate decisions, high courts in several states upheld the controversial theory of enterprise liability and positively affirmed its relevance to the DES episode.

In December of 1979, the Michigan Court of Appeals ruled that 182 plaintiffs in the *Abel* and *Belz* suits in Detroit could go ahead with their case against 16 DES manufacturers. The case had previously been dismissed by Judge Thomas Roumell, who ruled that the plaintiffs' inability to identify specific manufacturers disqualified them from continuing their suit. In a two to one opinion by Judge Richard Maher, the higher court supported the concept of joint liability for all DES manufacturers: "Rather than deny the innocent plaintiff his recovery because he cannot prove which of two or more wrongdoers injured him, the court imposes joint liability on all wrongdoers."

In May of 1980, the California Supreme Court followed Michigan's lead by ruling that Judith Sindell, a DES daughter, could sue five DES manufacturers over the development of a malignant tumor in her bladder. The court affirmed the obligation of the legal system to adapt to changing times, in an opinion by Justice Stanley Mosk that echoed the Michigan decision: "The response of the courts can either be to adhere rigidly to prior doctrine, denying recovery to those injured by such products, or to fashion remedies to meet these changing needs." The California court accepted the concept that liability in such cases of "joint liability" should be apportioned among the defendants according to market share.

California has traditionally been viewed as an innovator in the area of product liability law. And the Sindell decision, which would influence dozens of trials throughout the country, represented an opening of the floodgates for plaintiffs injured by products which are virtually unidentifiable to the consumer. In an age of toxic chemicals, air and water pollution from multiple sources, acid rain, and dangerous drugs, joint liability theory promises that people injured by anonymous products should have some hope of just compensation.

Drug industry hopes of heading off the perils of joint liability were dashed, at least in California, when the U. S. Supreme Court declined to review the Sindell ruling. The Supreme Court decision, handed down in October of 1980, effectively allowed DES litigation to remain stratified along state lines. The high court's refusal to hear the Sindell case was seen as a refusal to intervene in areas of state law, rather than as an implicit endorsement of joint liability theory. But the Supreme Court retained the option of reviewing a similar case in the future.

Medical research continued as the legal battles dragged on. With initial fears over a virtual tidal wave of malignancies gradually subsiding, scientific interest began markedly to shift away from the cancerous toward the noncancerous DES daughter. With vaginal adenosis occuring in from 40 to 90 percent of DES daughters, the potential dangers of that affliction became the focus of a great deal of medical attention.

Adenosis of the vagina is a "benign aberration" that in time may develop into malignancy. Though suspicions of this possibility were originally common in the medical profession, from the beginning of the DES episode until 1979 no DES daughter under surveillance had been observed to progress from a condition of adenosis to clear-cell cancer. But in March of 1979 and again in March of 1981 case reports were published in the *American Journal of Obstetrics and Gynecology* which confirmed that adenosis could indeed turn into cancer. These reports underlined the necessity of frequent and complete examinations for all symptomatic DES daughters. "Although the incidence of vaginal adenocarcinoma has been noted to decrease after the peak age of 19 years," wrote Dr. Norma Veridiano and her colleagues in March of 1981, "patients with findings of vaginal adenosis should always be considered at high risk to develop this kind of cancer."

A widely publicized study in 1980, conducted at Boston's Beth Israel Hospital, found that some DES-related symptoms may in fact decrease or disappear in time. Evidence that the "cervical hood" and certain other benign abnormalities may diminish over a five-year period was hailed in some quarters as grounds for dismissing the DES "scare" altogether. Unfortunately, the statistics involving cancer risk remain unchanged. A widespread impression generated by this report that DES no longer poses a danger to exposed offspring is certainly a pleasant perception, but not an accurate one.

The most poignant aspect of recent DES research concerns the effects of DES exposure on the reproductive capacity of DES daughters. The original work on this problem was initiated by Dr. Raymond Kaufman and associates at the Baylor College of Medicine in Houston. In a study completed in 1977, numerous abnormalities of the cervix and uterus were detected in a representative sample of DES-exposed women. Out of nearly three hundred women examined, nearly two thirds were found to have abnormally shaped uteruses. And in that sample a far greater incidence of premature delivery and other complications of pregnancy were reported than in a control group not exposed to DES.

That modern medicine had inadvertently caused in the second generation of women accidents of pregnancy it had hoped to prevent in the first provides a tragic irony in the DES story. Dr. Kaufman's original findings were taken up by Dr. Arthur Herbst, now chairman of obstetrics and gynecology at the Pritzker School of Medicine at the University of Chicago, and by the National Cooperative Diethylstilbestrol Adenosis (DESAD) Project.

The DESAD study, conducted by Dr. Kenneth Noller at the Mayo Clinic and by researchers at Baylor College of Medicine, Massachusetts General Hospital, the Gunderson Clinic, and the University of Southern California, was published in the March 13, 1981, *New England Journal of Medicine*. The study compared 618 DES daughters to 618 unexposed women (155 of the control group were unexposed sisters of the exposed, and 463 were matched controls). The results showed an increased risk of ectopic pregnancy, stillbirth, premature birth, and miscarriage among the DES daughters.

Dr. Herbst's study was published in the February 1981 *Journal of Reproductive Medicine.* He found that "full-term live births" were far more common among unexposed women (85 percent) than among the exposed (47 percent). Nineteen of the 226 DES daughters examined by Herbst experienced primary infertility—an inability to achieve pregnancy after attempts over one year or more—while only four unexposed women had the same problem.

Though medical researchers are somewhat reluctant to make sweeping statements at this relatively early stage, Dr. Kaufman's preliminary findings do seem to have been borne out: Fetal DES exposure almost certainly has a marked adverse effect on pregnancy.

Meanwhile, another disturbing development pertains to the future of DES sons. Throughout the '70s, a Chicago researcher, Dr. Marluce Bibbo, had conducted a study of the effects of DES on males. In a preliminary report released in 1977, Dr. Bibbo and her associates reported numerous genital tract and semen abnormalities in a group of DES sons. Over 30 percent of the subjects examined were found to have various forms of genital lesions, particularly epididymal cysts, which afflict the sperm transport mechanism. Sperm analysis revealed both significantly low sperm counts in a fourth of the patients, and large quantities of defective sperm, which may produce mutations in the next generation.

The great majority of DES sons have not yet tried to have children, so the real effects of DES exposure on fertility and cancer incidence in males cannot yet be known. Bibbo and her colleagues concluded their report: "The present study indicates that transplacental effects of DES on the human male do occur. Administration of DES during pregnancy appears to be followed by the development . . . of structural and functional changes that may impair fertility. . . ."

By the force of her own will and character, Anne Needham succeeded in rising above her assigned status as victim to become something of a heroine. She forced herself to deal positively with a threat to her life which at first she knew nothing about. She saw herself initially as one of nature's victims. God had done this unspeakable thing to her. Life had dealt her a bad hand. But when Anne found out the real story of what had happened, she wanted to find out more. She resolved not to duck the issue; she pursued a confrontation for which very little in her previous life had prepared her.

But slowly Anne began to get angry. Her mother began to get angry. Anne and Mary gradually came to the realization that something positive could be done. As they began to get involved in the legal action, and they found out more of the facts in the case, their anger increased. But somehow the angrier they got, the better they felt about it. Anger was the means Anne employed to shift her role away from passivity toward activity.

She had considered herself the average American girl. She had been brought up without fear, or anger, or suffering. The world she grew up in was the world created by her mother's generation, that country of large families and neat lawns, of steady work and television, the world so aptly described by William H. Whyte in his best-selling study, *The Organization Man,* which used Park Forest as an example of the "new" American town. Anne might very well have stayed in Park Forest. She might have married, settled down, had children. She might have become a nurse, as she had once hoped, working in a maternity ward.

Anne wanted desperately to be the same after her ordeal, but she found out she couldn't go back. She moved for a while to a college town where other young people her age were casually rejecting the suburban ideal. Other young women, for a wide range of reasons, were electing to defer marriage and children. But unlike so many of her contemporaries of that time who didn't want to settle down and have children in towns like Park Forest, Anne had no real choice.

After winning her case, it seemed as if more than five years of victimization were finally over. More than a year later, when she found that her victory had been reversed, she didn't lose the sense of control and detachment she had developed over five years of fighting. She felt good about having put up the struggle. And she was sure she would eventually win. She was sure that her case marked a beginning and not an end, not only for her but for hundreds of other women like her all around the country. When she finally won, that would be the end to her fight, but only the beginning of theirs.

Index

298